D1525099

Monstrous Intimacies

PERVERSE MODERNITIES
A series edited by Judith Halberstam and Lisa Lowe

MONSTROUS INTIMACIES

Making Post-Slavery Subjects

CHRISTINA **SHARPE**

DUKE UNIVERSITY PRESS DURHAM & LONDON 2010

© 2010 Duke University Press
All rights reserved
Printed in the United States of America
on acid-free paper ∞
Designed by Jennifer Hill
Typeset in Arno Pro by Keystone Typesetting, Inc.

Library of Congress Cataloging-in-Publication Data
appear on the last printed page of this book.

The author gratefully acknowledges the assistance
and support from the Office of the Dean in the
School of Arts and Sciences, Tufts University.

In memory of my mother, Ida Wright Sharpe (d. 1998)

CONTENTS

ACKNOWLEDGMENTS

It has taken me what seems like an extraordinarily long time to bring this book to its end. Along the way there have been numerous people who have contributed to its completion in small and large ways. To all of them I offer thanks.

I owe a great deal to many people. Money from the Ford Foundation Postdoctoral Fellowship for Minority Scholars provided financial support and the time off that allowed me to rethink my project and the opportunity to travel to South Africa to attend a conference on truth and reconciliation and traumatic memory. Thanks also to the trustees of Tufts College for the generous support of the Tufts Junior Faculty Leave, and to Dean Leila Fawaz and Dean Susan Ernst for their enthusiastic and generous support in terms of additional money and time. Susan Ernst generously also provided the money to pay for the images that appear in the text.

I thank colleagues in the English Department at Tufts University, especially Elizabeth Ammons, Lee Edelman, Carol Flynn, Joseph Litvak, and Modhumita Roy. Special thanks go to Elizabeth Ammons and Lee Edelman, whose support of the book and of me helped ensure its completion. Lee Edelman in particular offered help and encouragement in immeasurable ways.

Thanks to students in several graduate seminars, particularly the students in Partially Visible: Race and Visual Culture, Home Is Where the Hatred Is, and Monstrous Intimacies, who, along with many undergraduates, contributed to my work in profound ways.

Thanks to Sophia Cantave for her early research assistance and her many insights and to Chiyo Crawford for organizing the art and permissions.

I am thankful to have been able to present at the following conferences and places some of the work of this book, in various stages, on the way to the chapters as they appear here: Slavery and Contemporary Art (Trier, Germany); DePaul University; the Women's Studies Committee Panel of the American Studies Association (Albuquerque); Sexuality Out of Place: Sexuality Studies Conference (Earlham College); Revisiting Slave Narratives Conference (Paul Valéry University, Montpellier, France); and the Dionne Brand Conference: No Language Is Neutral (Toronto). Special thanks to Amor Kohli and Anupama Arora for invitations to speak at DePaul University and Earlham College.

I also thank the following people for their generosity and encouragement: Maxine Sample, Sharon Holland, Paul Morrison, Ashraf Rushdy, Amritjit Singh, Kimberly Hébert, David Halperin, Judith Halberstam, Isaac Julien, Bill Mullen, Paula Lee, Tim Haslett, Deborah Horvitz, Charlene Gilbert, Kimberly Brown, and Jean Wu. Thanks to Ken Wissoker, Mandy Early, and Neal McTighe at Duke University Press, with special thanks to Ken for his patience, support, willingness to listen, and belief in the project. I would also like to thank the following people and places for their generous permission to use images: Fred Wilson, Pacewildenstein Gallery, and the Whitney Museum of American Art; Kara Walker and the SikkemaJenkins and Co. Gallery; Maria Murgia and the Bridgman Art Library International; The Robert Mapplethorpe Foundation and Art and Commerce; and the Museum of Fine Arts in Boston. Thanks as well to my brothers Christopher and Stephen Sharpe, and my niece Dianna McFadden for their love and support.

For his enormous, extraordinary generosity as a scholar I owe particular thanks to Ashraf Rushdy. For permission to use images from *The Attendant* (1992), many thanks to Isaac Julien.

To my three anonymous readers at Duke University Press, thank you for helping me make this a much stronger book. Their readings, particularly the comments of Reader 2, echoed others who read along the way and pushed me to occupy the center of my narrative.

I thank Hortense Spillers and Dionne Brand for each, in different ways, giving me a "grammar" and a "map."

A much earlier version of chapter 1 appeared in the collection *African American Performance and Theater History: A Critical Reader*, edited by David Krasner and Harry Elam (New York: Oxford University Press, 2001, 306–27). A revised version of that essay appears in *Revisiting Slave Narratives/Les avatars contemporains des récits d'esclaves*, edited by Judith Misrahi-Barak, and part of *Les Carnets du Cerpac 2* (Montpellier: Publications de Montpellier III, 2005, 159–76). As it appears in this book it has again been substantially revised and expanded. Chapter 1 appears here by permission of Oxford University Press. I am grateful to Judith Misrahi-Barak and *Les Carnets du Cerpac* at Oxford for granting me permission to reprint from these works. By permission of Duke University Press a section of the introduction is included in the forthcoming collection *No Language Is Neutral: Essays on Dionne Brand*, edited by Dina Georgis, Katherine McKittrick, and Rinaldo Walcott (Waterloo: Wilfrid Laurier University Press).

There are two readers who shaped this book in quite different ways and perhaps even more than they know. Kimberly Hébert's contributions went far beyond those of any ordinary research assistant. Conversations with her, her reading of my work, her alerting me to James Henry Hammond and "Man of All Work" (along with many other things which became central to the book), the questions that she asked, and her immense intellect challenged and pushed me to say head-on what I thought I was saying all along. I would have finished a book without her assistance, but it would not have been this book. Van Zimmerman read the book from the beginning, from before the beginning, as it was being written (and rewritten and rewritten), and his unflagging belief in what I had to say and how I had to say it and his intellectual and material support made possible its production. His careful reading and questioning, his belief in the importance of what I was trying to say, and his love and support sustained and challenged me in fundamental ways.

That said, this book's flaws and particular blindnesses are entirely my own.

Finally, I dedicate this book with love to my mother, Ida Wright Sharpe, who died too soon in 1998.

Making Monstrous Intimacies

Surviving Slavery, Bearing Freedom

The Blood-Stained Gate

> The door [of no return][1] signifies the historical moment which colours all moments in the Diaspora. It accounts for the ways we observe and are observed as people, whether it's through the lens of social injustice or the lens of human accomplishments. The door exists as an absence. . . . Where one stands in a society seems always related to this historical experience. Where one can be observed is relative to that history. All human effort seems to emanate from this door.—**DIONNE BRAND,** *A Map to the Door of No Return: Notes to Belonging*

> Several old logs and stumps imposed upon me and got themselves taken for wild beasts. I could see their legs, eyes and ears till I got close enough to them to see that the eyes were knots, washed white with rain, and the legs were broken limbs, and the ears, only ears owing from the point from which they were seen. *Thus early I learned the point of view from which a thing is viewed is of some importance.*—**FREDERICK DOUGLASS,** *My Bondage and My Freedom*

Within the first few pages of Frederick Douglass's *Narrative of the Life of Frederick Douglass, an American Slave, Written by Himself* (1845/2003b) there appears his powerful eyewitness account of the beating of his "own" Aunt Hester, his mother's sister, a scene that exemplifies what he elsewhere calls the means by which "the slave is [made] a subject, subjected by others; [while] the slaveholder is a subject but he is the author of his own subjection" (1855/2003a, 49).

Thinking together questions of subject/subjection, resistance, transmission, and slave, black, and free, a number of scholars have greatly increased
our understanding of this scene as one of at least aural and ocular witnessing. I think together these questions in order to explore the impact of this
scene on Douglass and the hold it continues to exert on the contemporary
reader and on narrative and social structures that continue to be produced
and reproduced into the present.[2] The possible deadening effects into the
present of the repetition of the spectacular brutality of Douglass's account
are so forcible that while Saidiya Hartman begins her groundbreaking
*Scenes of Subjection: Terror, Slavery, and Self-Making in Nineteenth-Century
America* with this terrible scene and Douglass's entrance through the
"blood-stained gate" into the slavery that it instantiates, she rejects reproducing in her text the text of this beating. She writes, "Rather than
inciting indignation, too often [such accounts] immure us to pain by
virtue of their familiarity" (1997, 3).[3] The anxiety that Hartman and others
articulate around repeating this scene inheres in the awful configurations
of power, desire, pleasure, and domination to be found not only in the
original scene, but also in its transmission, transformation, and renewal, to
which we in the present are equally inured. We know that the repetition of
such horror does not make the violence of everyday black subjection
undeniable because presented in its most spectacular form, does not
confirm or confer humanity on the suffering black body, but all too often
contributes to what Jesse Jackson calls—in the midst of the catastrophe of
and catastrophic response to Hurricane Katrina's devastating effects on
black people and communities in the U.S. Gulf Coast—"an amazing tolerance for black pain . . . [a] great tolerance for black suffering and black
marginalization."[4]

So I begin with Douglass and the "bloody [and blood] transaction"
(Douglass 1845/2003b, 46) that is Captain Anthony's sadistic, and unex-
ceptional in the world the slaveholders made, stripping, manacling, whipping, and presumably raping Aunt Hester.[5] It is one of the earliest scenes
in the written narratives of New World blacks that introduces and locates
the conditions of the production of a fundamental familiar violence, of
multiple subjections, the tolerance for and the necessity of them within
the spaces and the forms of intimacy that I am calling monstrous.[6] (This
scene of subjection also establishes the centrality of the gaze and questions of desire and representation.) Captain Anthony's making of a slave

and a slave master, a transaction intimate, familial, and sexual, is, at least, the beating/raping itself and the doubled (indeed trebled) "action of passing or making over a thing from one person, thing, or state to another; transference."[7] This familiar and intimate violence that Douglass places at the heart of slavery and his slave narrative emerges as the *proximity* of incest and amalgamation and recurs throughout my text as the proximity between "antagonism and identification" (J. Rose 1996, 111).[8]

In *Monstrous Intimacies: Making Post-Slavery Subjects* I read a series of visual and written texts, African and diasporic, from the nineteenth century to the twenty-first, that are concerned with such transactions—the violence, often sexual, by which one is "made a subject, subjected by others," and the other "is a subject but . . . the author of his own subjection" (Douglass 1855/2003a, 47)—that are often registered by conditions of violation, narrative, and other confinement, of produced and reproduced shame refused and/or transmitted from one generation to the next. Douglass's scenes of forcible sex and other violent subjections introduce the ongoing processes of subjectification during slavery and into post-slavery to which all postmodern subjects are made subject. These are subjections, I argue, that are most readable and locatable still through the horrors enacted on the black body after slavery and the official periods of emancipation and through further colonialism, imperialism, and the relative freedoms of segregation, desegregation, and independence, whether that body is in the Caribbean, the Americas, England, or post-independence Africa. That is, while all modern subjects are post-slavery subjects fully constituted by the discursive codes of slavery and post-slavery, post-slavery subjectivity is largely borne by and readable on the (New World) *black* subject.[9] Thinking about monstrous intimacies post-slavery means examining those subjectivities constituted from trans-atlantic slavery onward and connected, then as now, by the everyday mundane horrors that aren't acknowledged to be horrors. It means articulating a diasporic study that is attentive to but not dependent upon nations and nationalisms and that is linked, in different forms during slavery and into the present freedoms, by monstrous intimacies, defined as a set of known and unknown performances and inhabited horrors, desires and positions produced, reproduced, circulated, and transmitted, that are breathed in like air and often unacknowledged to be monstrous.

From those Africans forced to step over the threshold of the door of no return into the Middle Passage, to their dispersal in the diaspora and entry through the bloodstained gate, new forms of subjectivity are created not only for people of African descent in the diaspora but also for Africans, Europeans, and others. Extraordinary sites of domination and intimacy, slavery and the Middle Passage were ruptures with and a suspension of the known world that initiated enormous and ongoing psychic, temporal, and bodily breaches. *Monstrous Intimacies* is my attempt to account for the long psychic and material reach of those passages, their acknowledged and disavowed effects, their projection onto and erasure from particular bodies, and the reformulation, reproduction, and recirculation of their intimate spaces of trauma, violence, pleasure, shame, and containment. My intent is to examine and account for a series of repetitions of master narratives of violence and forced submission that are read or reinscribed as consent and affection: intimacies that involve shame and trauma and their transgenerational transmission. By doing so I seek to "provide [a] context for values and beliefs" (J. Rose 2007, 8) remembered, forgotten, disavowed, internalized, and imposed that articulate a black (and blackened) body struggling with similar aftermaths of traumas of slavery, colonialism, segregation and independence, and freedom—but with different signifiers. Those black and blackened bodies become the bearers (through violence, regulation, transmission, etc.) of the knowledge of certain subjection as well as the placeholders of freedom for those who would claim freedom as their rightful yield. Put another way, the everyday violences that black(ened) bodies are made to bear are markers for an exorbitant freedom to be free of the marks of a subjection in which we are all forced to participate.

In the remainder of this introduction I ground those monstrous intimacies during slavery and post-slavery in two circumstantial accounts of the incomplete movement from slavery to freedom. I pair the blood-stained gate from Frederick Douglass's *Narrative* with Essie Mae Washington-Williams's memoir *Dear Senator* (2005) in order to extend the ways we are immured in and inured to its force, to explore slavery's inherited and reproduced spaces of shame, confinement, intimacy, desire, violence, and terror and how we come to occupy and then to survive them post-slavery. I place the visual and written texts in *Monstrous Intimacies* in conversation with each other to clarify the use of blackness over time as well as the connections between representations and performances of blackness, the primal scenes of slavery, and the all too often unaccounted-for structures that propel us into the present and the future. Each text in this study takes up how freedom and slavery are performed and the desire to be human that emerges and is often erased from and contained by black bodies and narratives. Each of the pairings—Gayl Jones's *Corregidora* and the diaries of James Henry Hammond, Bessie Head's *Maru* and Saartje Baartman, Isaac Julien's *The Attendant* and British abolitionism's excesses, and Kara Walker and her critics—insists that the forces of violence that one found in slavery are located both outside and inside of the (black) subject of slavery. Each explores the monstrous internalization and perpetuation of that violence in various forms of power and desire among the formerly enslaved and those who claimed ownership over them. In each case, in each chapter, I argue that the complicated articulations of sex, violence, and use, the occupying or refusing to occupy the space of the other, are necessary to understanding power in relationships on the intimate level and in their larger historical expression.

I return now to Douglass's emphatic and repeated assertions that he will remember, that he "never shall forget" these scenes, his subsequent transformation of them, and the present desire and compulsion to dis-remember such monstrously intimate scenes altogether, and I repeat the scenes here as they are recorded first in the *Narrative* and then in *My Bondage and My Freedom* in the hopes of yielding something more. Douglass writes:

> [Master] was a cruel man, hardened by a long life of slaveholding. He would at times seem to take great pleasure in whipping a slave. I have often been awakened at the dawn of day by the most heart-rending shrieks of an own aunt of mine, who he used to tie up in a joist and whip upon her naked back till she was literally covered with blood. No words, no tears, no prayers from his gory victim seemed to move his iron heart from its bloody purpose. The louder she screamed, the harder he whipped; and where the blood ran faster, there he whipped longest. He would whip her to make her scream, and whip her to make her hush; and not until overcome by fatigue, would he cease to swing the blood-clotted cowskin. *I remember* the first time I ever witnessed this horrible exhibition. I was quite a child, but *I well remember it. I never shall forget it* whilst I remember any thing. It was the first of a long series of such outrages, of which I was doomed to be a witness and a participant. It struck me with awful force.

It was the blood-stained gate, the entrance to the hell of slavery, through which I was about to pass. It was a most terrible spectacle. I wish I could commit to paper the feelings with which I beheld it.

This occurrence took place very soon after I went to live with my old master, and under the following circumstances. Aunt Hester went out one night,—where or for what I do not know,—and happened to be absent when my master desired her presence. He had ordered her not to go out evenings, and warned her that she must never let him catch her in company with a young man who was paying attention to her, belonging to Colonel Lloyd. The young man's name was Ned Roberts, generally called Lloyd's Ned. Why master was so careful of her, may safely be left to conjecture. *She was a woman of noble form and of graceful proportions, having very few equals and fewer superiors, in personal appearance, among the colored or white women of our neighborhood.*

Aunt Hester had not only disobeyed his orders in going out, but had been found in company with Lloyd's Ned; which circumstance, I found, from what he said while he was whipping her was the chief offence. . . . "Now you d——d b——h, I'll learn you how to disobey my orders!" and after rolling up his sleeves he commenced to lay on the heavy cowskin, and soon the warm, red blood (amid heart-rending shrieks from her, and horrid oaths from him) came dripping to the floor. I was so terrified and horror-stricken at the sight, that I hid myself in a closet, and dared not venture out till long after the *bloody transaction* was over. I expected it would be my turn next. It was all new to me. I had never seen anything like it before. I had always lived with my grand-mother on the outskirts of the plantation, where she was put to raise the children of the younger women. I had therefore been, until now, out of the way of the bloody scenes that often occurred on the plantation. (Douglass 1845/2003b, 44–45; emphases mine)

What Douglass captures here is a quintessentially New World scene, a primal scene in which the slave child is forced to witness, see, hear, and, according to Douglass, feel a sight that approximates his mother's rape and his own monstrous conception and birth, his rebirth into a new subjectivity in which subjectification equals objectification.[10] As it appears in the *Narrative* the scene repeats and rearticulates the traumas of what Douglass declares in the first sentence but does not actually witness and cannot fix with a certain day, time, or year: "I was born" (1845/2003b, 41). Through constructing this scene and placing it in the first chapter of the text, a contemporary white audience is positioned from the outset to look at what they have not seen or have refused to see about the brutality of the internal slave trade, to look and see how a slave and a slave master (enslaved subjects and free subjects) are both made and born. Douglass positions his white readers to reckon with what he knows about the all-encompassing and routinized violence in slavery, positions them to see that they are witness to and participant in brutal scenes of conception and transformation. I position the reader to recognize in the blood-stained gate and the closet doorway through which Douglass looks and listens the first of several primal scenes, of many monstrous intimacies, conceptions, and births, to recognize white and black responses to being interpellated by sexually violent scenes of slavery and the exercise of various freedoms. When Douglass looks through the closet doorway into the kitchen he knows that despite his desire otherwise, there is no stopping his step over the threshold and passage through the blood-stained gate. First he was born. Then he was born into the significance of being born a slave, born into the symbolic universe of slavery. Made and unmade in the same moment.

In what follows I join the scene of Aunt Hester's beating from the *Narrative* of 1845 to the revised version that appears in *My Bondage and My Freedom* (1855/2003a) and then to Douglass's fight with the negro breaker Covey in order to think through Douglass's (and Aunt Hester's) incomplete transformation "into being" and the transformation of those scenes, of those narratives, into the present. In the ten years between the publication of the *Narrative* and *My Bondage and My Freedom* Douglass removes the reference to the blood-stained gate, changes Hester's name to Esther, gives her speech in addition to her "heart-rending" shrieks, and elaborates the closet from which he watches.

> Esther was courted by Ned Roberts, and he was as fine looking a young man, as she was a woman. . . . Esther was evidently much attached to Edward, and abhorred—as she had reason to do—the tyrannical and base behavior of old master. Edward was young, and fine looking, and he loved and courted her. . . .
>
> I was probably awakened by the shrieks and piteous cries of poor Esther. My sleeping place was on the floor of a little, rough closet, which opened into the kitchen; and through the cracks of its unplaned boards, I could distinctly see and hear what was going on, without being seen by old master. Esther's wrists

were firmly tied, and the twisted rope was fastened to a strong staple in a heavy wooden joist above, near the fireplace. Here she stood, on a bench, her arms tightly drawn over her breast. Her back and shoulders were bare to the waist. Behind her stood old master, with cowskin in hand, preparing his barbarous work with all manner of harsh, coarse, and tantalizing epithets. The screams of his victim were most piercing. He was cruelly deliberate, and protracted the torture, as one who was delighted with the scene. Again and again he drew the hateful whip through his hand, adjusting it with a view of dealing the most pain-giving blow. Poor Esther had never yet been severely whipped, and her shoulders were plump and tender. Each blow, vigorously laid on, brought screams as well as blood. "Have mercy; Oh! Have mercy," she cried; "I won't do so no more;" but her piercing cries seemed only to increase his fury. His answers to them are too coarse and blasphemous to be produced here. The whole scene, with all its attendants, was revolting and shocking, to the last degree; and when the motives of this brutal castigation are considered— language has no power to convey a just sense of its awful criminality. After laying on some thirty or forty stripes, old master untied his suffering victim, and let her get down. She could scarcely stand, when untied. *From my heart I pitied her,* and—child though I was—the *outrage kindled in me a feeling far from peaceful;* but *I was hushed, terrified, stunned, and could do nothing, and the fate of Esther might be mine next. The scene here described was often repeated in the case of poor Esther, and her life, as I knew it, was one of wretchedness.* (1855/2003a, 37– 38; emphases mine)

Douglass captures Captain Anthony's violence, his pleasure, and the everyday tyranny of Esther's (and his own) life in slavery in which any white person (man, woman, or child) has the right to demand anything of her (and him). By positioning H/Esther with Ned Roberts in the face of the master's prohibition and insisting that this particular misery continues for her, Douglass is directing readers to look and see a woman (not unlike themselves or their wife, daughter, sister) keeping open a space to "shed [her] slave identity in [her] own mind, if not in the eyes of the law" (by acting against the master's will and according to her own by meeting with Ned and being willing to pay the price of this stance) even while remaining within the institution of slavery (Bergner 2005, 23). Without access to Aunt H/Esther's story in her own words, I turn again to Douglass's representations of her and in particular to this extraordinarily rendered scene of ordinary brutality because it allows us to see that the space of violated intimacy in which Douglass positions H/Esther is within an institution where "every kitchen is a brothel,"[11] every black woman in the house or the quarters a potential worker in it, and where the terror of that "kitchen space" will be unremembered and come over time to be figured as a privileged space of blackness because of a spatial, and also perhaps visual, proximity to whiteness. In other words, this violation, this being, or being positioned to be, fucked over and across time is freighted with signifying access to a freedom narrative. The enslaved black woman in the house, in this instance Aunt H/Esther, often in a better material position than the black women in the field, is nonetheless positioned in the midst of the everyday intimate brutalities of white domestic domination, positioned within a psychic and material architectonics where there may be no escape from those brutalities but in the mind. Such spaces will, over time, become "site[s] of pain which will turn into site[s] of pleasure" (Brand 2001, 93).

Move forward ten years from the seven-year-old Douglass's terrified closeted watching "of the bloody scenes that often occurred on the plantation" to his first and final contest with the negro breaker Covey, and we encounter another primal scene; this one is also set explicitly within the context of the everyday terrors that Douglass experiences under Covey's equally jealous discipline (equal, that is, to Captain Anthony's careful attention to Aunt H/Esther).[12] The fight comes at the end of a six-month period of brutal treatment in which through "hard and long continued labor" and "flogging" Covey has succeeded in breaking Douglass and "transform[ing him] into a brute" (Douglass 1855/2003a, 123). Having determined, however, to stand "no longer" Covey's lash, Douglass experiences the fight as the pivotal transaction in his "shed[ding of] . . . the slave identity in his own mind, if not in the eyes of the law" (Bergner 2005, 23); its result is his "partial disenthrallment from the tyranny of Covey" (Douglass 1855/2003a, 131). It is another making and unmaking in the same moment. This story is of Douglass's becoming a man through a transformative act that would symbolically reverse his brutalizing passage through the blood-stained gate and rupture the state of things in slavery. In another narrative transformation, the image of the gate itself is excised from *My Bondage and My Freedom* and from *The Life and Times of Frederick Douglass.*

When Douglass renames Hester Esther (which means "something hidden" and is an anagram of Hester) in *My Bondage and My Freedom* it may be in part because Hester's resistance does not symbolically or otherwise end Captain Anthony's violation and there is no defensive posture that she can maintain that will repel his aggression and allow the narrative of transformative heroism to adhere to her body, just as it cannot fully adhere to Douglass's body. Despite what may have been Douglass's best intentions, what accrues to Hester's body in the narrative are violation, shame, and their repetition.

Another house slave, Harriet Jacobs, begins her H/Esther story, *Incidents in the Life of a Slave Girl, Written by Herself* (1861/1987), with "A Perilous Passage in the Slave Girl's Life," the point at which her text diverges from Douglass's because she cannot hide elsewhere her immanent sexual violation in a narrative which aims to reveal the hidden-in-plain-sight "monstrous features" of slavery.[13] This passage, Jacobs's own blood-stained gate, is her recognition that while she has in some measure and for some short time been protected there is no position that she can occupy openly that will stop this violation. In her narrative the master is incensed and aroused by her pleas, the mistress is another sexual tormentor, and the best that she can do is to choose Mr. Sands, a white man not her owner, to be the author of an already marked-out violation and the "father" of her children. In a further bid to place her children beyond her master's reach Jacobs, still protected and unprotected in her relationships with whites, stages her escape and comes to occupy a space of terror and proximity over her master's head, the dimensions of which are memorably marked as nine feet long, seven feet wide, and three feet high.

Douglass's narrative bind (which is also, at least, legal and textual) perhaps provides another clue to the signifying power of Hester's name change to Esther and to the continued utility of the Esther story in the present. By the time Douglass published *My Bondage and My Freedom* (and Jacobs *Incidents*) the story of the Jewish Queen Esther was providing enslaved and free African Americans with "a narrative core around which they could develop an heroic epic" (John Roberts, quoted in Nero 2003, 5) and had become central to black women's asserting the right to speak in public against slavery and in the interests of their people.[14]

Hidden (in plain sight) in the Esther narrative and in Douglass's positioning of H/Esther among blacks and whites as a figure of almost unparalleled beauty and virtue within the (sexually) violent, corrupting institution of slavery is the fact of the "bloody transaction" that is sex. Commemorated as a savior of the Jewish people, Esther is a racially passing woman whose proximity to power through the fact of sex secures the possibility and the right of survival for her people. It is the story of a woman's intervention in the fate of her people by being positioned to be fucked and thereby to get the king to act on behalf of the Jews. A story of resistance and a story of assimilation, Esther "teaches Jews strategies for living in Diaspora" (Zaeske 2000, 197).

In Hester's name change we might locate Douglass's register of a shift in the possibilities for black freedom and in his strategies and desires. In 1850, five years after the *Narrative* appeared and five years before the publication of *My Bondage and My Freedom*, the passage of the Fugitive Slave Act effectively extended slavery to the Canadian border and the Harvard professor and Swiss émigré Louis Agassiz commissioned the daguerreotypes of seven enslaved people, among them two sets of African-born fathers and their American-born daughters, all "pure" examples of the race.[15] The enslaved male and female subjects were stripped (their clothes pushed down or removed), posed standing and seated, and photographed from each side, the front, and the rear. Agassiz was one of the founders (or fathers) of the American school of ethnology; he was an abolitionist and a contributor to the emergent field of racial science, who believed in African inferiority and European superiority. Pro-slavery politicians embraced his polygenetic arguments that attempted to make manifest, measurable, and readable an essential black inferiority and black monstrosity, not the monstrosity of slavery and slavery's complicated black performances and not the violence of the law and the gaze.

The violence of the law and the gaze is very real to Douglass, whose own work and relative freedom were imperiled through the details he is compelled to reveal in his published *Narrative* because he failed to signify properly, visually or aurally, as a former slave for the whites who came to hear him speak. With the Fugitive Slave Act of 1850 slavery was legally extended into so-called free spaces, and the already constricted possibilities for black freedom in the North were made more insecure. But the Act and its enforcers did not staunch the flow of enslaved people seeking freedom, nor did its passage institute a wholly new practice; rather it formalized the mechanisms of the capture and return (and spurred new forms of resistance) of enslaved people that were already in place. Put another way, the Fugitive Slave Act was another step in criminalizing black freedom and the actions of those who insisted that (at least some of) the rights and privileges of freedom could accrue to the black body.[16] By the time Douglass wrote *My Bondage and My Freedom* a tenuous free space for black people in the North had further contracted and he was no longer content to "narrate wrongs" and not "denounc[e] them" (Douglass 1855/2003a, 266). Confronting new political and representational developments and realities, he had to resignify black, slave, and free, and his movement north, "a glorious resurrection, from the tomb of slavery, to the heaven of freedom" (Douglass 1845/2003b, 89), became "a resurrection from the dark and pestiferous tomb of slavery to the heaven of comparative freedom" (1855/2003a, 152). The signs Douglass saw along "the pathway from slavery to freedom" (1855/2003a, 109) were not "signs to somewhere free of the signs for the black body. [Because] of course by this time the black body had become so freighted with the excesses and needs of the New World culture that even somewhere free was not quite sufficient. The signs did not fall away" (Brand 2001, 46).

The signs remained, were renewed, and were made visible according to two very different eyewitness accounts: Douglass's account that would further the aims of abolition as well as citizenship for blacks and that of the daguerreotypes (the "mirror with a memory") commissioned by the abolitionist Agassiz that would be used to support slavery and to naturalize and justify the continued subjection of black people in and eventually out of slavery. Aunt H/Esther (as sympathetic sign, a space of white entry into the black body designed to produce an excess of empathy and then action) appears alongside Delia, Drana, and the five other ethnographic subjects on whom the (sexual) violence of the internal slave trade is not read because injury cannot be read on the unmiscegenated black body as injury. Recognizing the image's power to tell a visual narrative of black people's progress and to make black humanity visible to a white gaze, Douglass concluded that representational power cannot be entrusted to whites. His address in 1854, "The Claims of the Negro Ethnologically Considered," underscored this: "If, for instance," he said, "a phrenologist or naturalist undertakes to represent in portraits, the difference between the two races—the negro and the European—he will invariably present the highest type of the European, and the lowest type of the negro. . . . If the very best type of the European is always presented, I insist that justice, in all such works, demands that the very best type of the negro should be taken. The importance of this criticism may not be apparent to all;—to the black man it is very apparent" (quoted in Blessingame 1979, 510, 514).[17] If we join the images of the forcibly stripped and photographed Delia, Renty, Jack, Drana, Fassena, Alfred, and Jem to the image of the forcibly stripped and whipped Aunt H/Esther (and then, as we will see in the following section, to the images of Strom Thurmond, Carrie Butler, and Essie Mae Washington-Williams) we enter another narrative, in which "pain [is] being transformed into pleasure," in which readable progress is proximity to whiteness, and where both come to signify as a gift, as (positive) inheritance. If justice depends on the "point of view from which a thing is viewed" and on "the time and location we are in,"[18] and if justice is being recognized as human in a "white gaze" or in the gaze of those in power, then the injury slips from slavery (colonialism, segregation, lynching, ethnographic display, incarceration, etc.) to blackness (or being blackened) itself. How is such an injury addressed or redressed?

Almost 150 years after Douglass rewrote Hester as Esther, a woman positioned through sex and proximity to power to secure the right to a future, Essie Mae Washington-Williams, narrates the circumstances of her birth in 1925 to Carrie Butler and Strom Thurmond. I connect Washington-Williams's public announcement of her relationship to Thurmond and her memoir *Dear Senator* to Douglass's narrative and the process of rewriting and rescripting genealogy, to the displacement of shame, the weight of freedom borne by the black female body, and to the recirculation of these monstrous intimacies into the present across time, space, race, ethnicity, and nation. Washington-Williams is the inheritor of those forced and forceful intimacies outlined in Douglass's and Jacobs's narratives, the inheritor of those stories that they could and could not tell. As Douglass hides his subjection in Aunt H/Esther's story, so does Aunt H/Esther's story haunt Washington-Williams's. What is the nature of the haunting and what are some of our inheritances?

Post-Slavery: Haunted by Aunt H/Esther

> To be haunted is to be tied to social and historical effects.—**AVERY GORDON**,
> *Ghostly Matters: Haunting and the Sociological Imagination*

> How imprisoned we are in their ghosts.—**DIONNE BRAND**, *Inventory*

> Freedom is hard to bear.—**JAMES BALDWIN**, *The Fire Next Time*

In December 2003, almost six months after the death of Strom Thurmond, the Republican senator from South Carolina, former Dixiecrat, and longest-serving member of the upper house of Congress, Essie Mae Washington-Williams, seventy-eight years old and a retired schoolteacher, spoke out loud what had been privately acknowledged for sixty-two years by her and Thurmond, widely discussed by many others, but never publicly confirmed either by her or by the white bearers of the Thurmond name until after Thurmond's death.[19] Washington-Williams revealed what was called "the worst kept secret in South Carolina": that she was the long-speculated-about outside daughter of James Strom Thurmond, at the time of her birth a twenty-three-year-old schoolteacher still living in his parents' home, and a fifteen-year-old young black woman named Carrie Butler who worked for the Thurmonds as a housekeeper. "I have known this since 1941, when I was 16 years old," said Washington-Williams. "My father's name was James Strom Thurmond. . . . I am Essie Mae Washington-Williams, *and at last I am completely free.*"[20]

Washington-Williams stood at the gate of the twenty-first century poised to speak to the presentness of the awful intimate and monstrous configurations made evident in Douglass, Jacobs, Gayl Jones, Kara Walker, Isaac Julien, Carrie Mae Weems, and countless other visual, written, and oral texts. When she made her announcement, she and it were met with a variety of responses and questions and some resistance. There were the long-suppressed questions about her relationship to the late senator, her reasons for the long silence that ended only after his death, and the nature of the relationship between Thurmond and her mother. But given Carrie Butler's (and Thurmond's) age, race, class, and occupation, the time and place, as well as the late senator's much noted virility and penchant for aggressive womanizing, there was remarkably little emphasis on thinking through the context of Butler's relationship with Thurmond. Few questions were raised then and now about consent and how consent and choice actually would have functioned under the conditions of her employment.[21] I'd like to think those questions through alongside what we might understand to be the source and shape of Washington-Williams's newfound complete freedom.[22] Indeed, what could this really mean?

Russ Castronovo reminds us that despite the U.S. founders' desires and Noah Webster's best efforts in creating an *American Dictionary of the English Language* that would liberate the language of its colonial burden, the term *freedom* does not stand on its own, but is always freighted with being freed from something. *Freedom* means "not enslaved; not in a state of vassalage or dependence," "a state of exemption from the power of control . . . exemption from slavery" as well as "exemption or release from slavery or imprisonment; personal liberty; a letter of freedom: a document emancipating a slave" (Castronovo 2000, 113–14). The legal captivity of Africans and their descendants was central to the codification of rights and freedoms for those legally constituted as white and their legally white descendants. That is, freedoms for those people constituted as white were and are produced through an other's body legally and otherwise being made to wear unfreedom and to serve as a placeholder for access to the freedoms that are denied the black subject. Always constructed and conceived of in relation to those who wear unfreedom, when Washington-Williams declares her freedom complete, from what or whom and to what or whom is she freed? Is she freed retrospectively from the racial violence of "separate but equal" mandates, the violence of Thurmond's segregationist politics, the weight of being a black first? Freed from the pull of Carrie Butler's narrative and her fate of abandonment and death at age thirty-eight in a hospital poverty ward, freed in a way that functions much like Douglass's revisions of the *Narrative* that both connect him to and release him from Aunt H/Esther and diminish the force of the blood-stained gate? In her memoir, *Dear Senator: A Memoir by the Daughter of Strom Thurmond*, Washington-Williams recalls each of the ties that bind her mother to her and then lays claim to the freedom to claim Thurmond as father even if he never claimed her as daughter.[23]

The background. In 1925 the sixteen-year-old Carrie Butler gave birth to a daughter whom she could not afford to raise; as one reporter notes, the Butlers' poverty was "legendary."[24] She took the infant to live with her sister Mary and Mary's husband, John Washington, in Coatesville, Pennsylvania. Sixteen years later (having been reintroduced to her daughter three years prior in a visit in which Butler revealed that she, not Mary, was Essie Mae's real mother), Butler retrieved her daughter and took her to South Carolina for the funeral of one of the Butler sisters and then to the law offices of Thurmond and Thurmond, where she introduced her to her father, Strom Thurmond. Of this initial visit Washington-Williams writes:

> Finally, we arrived at a one-story white building that housed a law office. Thurmond and Thurmond, Attorneys at Law, the sign said. That was it. My new daddy was a driver for a big-shot lawyer. We went up the steps and knocked on the door. A black servant in a white coat opened the door. I wanted to throw my arms around him, but he just looked at me blankly. Then he showed us into a grand office, stocked floor to ceiling with law books and diplomas, where my mother and I were left to stand alone in silence. My heart was pounding so hard I feared it might be audible. A few moments passed, and then a fair, handsome man entered the room—a little nervously, I thought, as he tipped over a standing ashtray. *He wore a light blue suit and tie and looked every inch the lord of a plantation.* He gazed at my mother a long time, then stared at me even longer. Finally, his stone face broke into a smile. "You have a lovely young daughter," he said in a deep commanding voice.
>
> I was speechless.
>
> "Essie Mae," my mother said with a big smile of her own, "meet your father."
> (Washington-Williams and Stadiem 2005, 36; emphasis mine)

Raised in the North, away from a particular kind of interracial intimacy / proximity—arising out of plantation slavery, born of labor which continued through segregation and after in the relationships between whites and blacks—Washington-Williams is struck during this introduction by what she had never seen before and never imagined. In South Carolina she is struck and silenced by the grandness of the space and then again by Thurmond's "fairness,"[25] the evidence of his education, by what she characterizes as the "love" and familiarity that she witnesses between Thurmond and her mother, and finally by her mother naming him her father. (Despite her recollection of an attempted lynching in Coatesville in 1938 and other remembered and witnessed violence, she identifies the North as a space of less subjection.) Brought before him so that he might gaze upon Carrie's daughter without ever acknowledging that she is also his, Washington-Williams first recalls this encounter as a scene of subjection, like "an audience with an important man, a job interview, but not a reunion with a father" (23). Then she recalls it as an intimate meeting filled with longing and a love between her mother and Thurmond that dare not speak its name. This meeting with her mother, herself, and the man she will come to think of, though never address, as father concludes with a handshake, not a hug, and is followed the next day by his gift of two hundred dollars, sent to her through his sister. Over time a ritual exchange of money occurs that she comes to think of as a kind of payment for services rendered.[26] Over time as well her newfound desire to meet the man to be known as father is replaced by her desire for a *white* father through whose body she can lay claim to a shared American story, the plantation romance—the slave narrative's flipside—in which the "lord of the plantation," the slave master, a "gentleman and aristocrat," recognizes her as the legitimate daughter and future lady of the house.[27] In this representation of their meeting we encounter Washington-Williams's not unfamiliar claim to the freedom to be free of all but the romantic residue of slavery. It is a restaging of the entrance into the symbolic, a shift from the blood-stained gate of the kitchen family to the front door of the legal family.

Reading *Dear Senator* one becomes aware that Washington-Williams's representation of her coming of age in Coatesville in the 1930s and 1940s, her long relationship with Thurmond, and the social, political, geographical, and historical contexts in which this occurred are covering up a set of fears and desires.[28] It's clear that Thurmond and the specter of slavery haunt this family drama, but so does Carrie Butler, about whom, when first asked to describe their relationship, Washington-Williams can only say, "My mother had to work."[29] It is a description that seems, at least to me, to be an expression of profound and continued unfreedom within freedom. Why is neither Butler (who looks like a "fashion model" and has the "naturally aristocratic air of Katherine Hepburn") nor Butler's sister Mary, who raised Essie Mae and whom in the first half of the book she continues to address and think of as her mother, represented with even a single photo in the text? (Is this a marketing strategy consistent with the rococo flourishes that grace the bottom of every page and scream "romance"?) Photographs of a young Washington-Williams and Thurmond appear on the cover, but the only name in the title is Strom Thurmond's, not the mother's and not the name of the daughter, the author and putative autobiographical subject of the memoir.

We know that in North American slavery black women were regularly separated from their children, who were sold away or sent to other women on the plantation to be taken care of; child rearing interfered with the mother's work for the white family. The status of mother itself often was unsustainable or not allowed for the black woman within slavery, through desegregation, and after emancipation.[30] We know that during slavery the master (and other white men) raped and otherwise had sexual relations with the black women whom they held in captivity. We know too that sometimes these men had sexual relations with their own black daughters and sisters, who may have been recognized during slavery as blood but were usually disavowed now as then as kin. And while speculation about whether Thurmond engaged in those particular improper relations with his eldest daughter is not the issue here, I draw attention to both Washington-Williams's response and to this tangled consanguinity because Washington-Williams's *freedom* is not unlike her mother's *work* (whose work is not unlike Jacobs's and Aunt H/Esther's). That is, I imagine that in Washington-Williams's statement "My mother had to work" is the recognition that her freedoms, and Thurmond's too, are secured partially through her mother's having had to perform certain kinds of ideological and actual work. That she too will be made to perform certain kinds of work is what she hopes to avoid through recourse to a recognizable kinship relationship with Thurmond.

When Governor Thurmond, an active segregationist, arrived regularly at all-black South Carolina State College to visit a young black woman he was safe in the knowledge that were his white peers to find out, they would have recognized in these visits, just as the black community did, a wholly familiar scene. They would not have wondered if Thurmond's visits were to spend time with a daughter, and would have inferred and accepted that he was there to do what many white men in his position did: either see blood relations or have a sexual liaison with a young black woman. Both narratives were held in place by at least two open secrets: the silence about their relationship maintained by Washington-Williams and others for sixty-two years, long after there was what could be understood as a necessity to do so, and the unspoken monstrous intimacies (read, conditions and desires) that continue to propel this structure and permutations of it into the present and future. "That, after all, is the nature of such

secrets: they are not what cannot be known but what cannot be acknowledged" (Gates 1997, 190).

In an essay in 2005 on National Public Radio John McWhorter, a fellow
at the Manhattan Institute, suggested that those of us who continue to
focus on the effects of Washington-Williams's allegedly traumatic past
"dismiss an innocent grandmother of 13 as living a lie," dismiss her clear
statement that she has come forward because she is "seeking closure for
her and her progeny."[31] We must, he said, "process . . . [her] as a full human
being," and he questioned whether in doing so it is "really so urgent for us
to grapple with the relationship that created" her. To link the "clandestine,
coerced, interracial matings that Thurmond participated in" to choices
made and freedoms claimed now is, for McWhorter, to erase the spatial
and temporal distance traveled from there to here, then to now, to refuse
to understand that Washington-Williams's life was not defined by the
"Thurmond issue," and to reduce her and those whose family stories look
like hers to "cut-out[s] in the racism diorama."

In the midst of McWhorter's commentary on Washington-Williams he
introduces his own familiar family story. He tells listeners about his grandfather, who was "Caucasian in color" and "could easily have passed," and
whose own father was "a white shopkeeper who had a liaison with a black
woman who worked for him" and who "never acknowledged paternity."
McWhorter wants us to know that these circumstances (which I understand to be, at the very least, the structures that support a disavowed
paternity and a maternal relationship defined by labor) did not account
for the whole of his grandfather's life, which was filled with some success
and satisfaction despite "glum beginnings." In his familiar narration Mc-
Whorter grants the white man a fatherhood when "fatherhood is at best a
supreme cultural courtesy [as it] attenuates here on the one hand into a
monstrous accumulation of power on the other" (Spillers 2003c, 221) and
reduces the black (great grand)mother whose *maternity* (functional and
biological) is never in question to a cut-out figure of "a black woman who
worked for him" (McWhorter 2005). What interests me here is the very
ordinariness of this repetition, that this is so often the way that this story is
told.[32] McWhorter unspeaks horrors in spaces where those horrors often
are perceived to be sliding into (future) pleasures and therefore are not
seen to be horrific. And the violated black woman is subjected to yet

another violation. Put another way, McWhorter's narrative yields another wholly familiar alignment of work and freedom—as in "My mother had to work"—in which the contemporary black subject confers upon the white man a fatherhood that, more than the recognition of blood, is a one-sided imposition and retroactive ascription of maternal consent, freedom, and kinship onto a narrative where there may have been none. A common story then and now of violation—and of choices to labor made in spaces (real or imagined) of limited choice, of (in)humanity and the exercise of everyday tyranny—is reconfigured as freedom and laden with a desire for a kinship that is denied and disavowed. Using Jacqueline Rose's formulation, I argue that Washington-Williams has "burdened her desire for him [Thurmond] with the meaning of freedom" (Rose 2007, 1),[33] and a narrative of injustice and captive desires comes to be hidden in a kinship narrative of freedom or access to it. Such claiming reveals a contemporary monstrous intimacy, one that in the name of freedom makes it more difficult, if not largely impossible, to speak either the history that is "already seated in the chair in the empty room when one arrives" (Brand 2001, 25) or the contemporary conditions of ordinary brutality that compel one to want to occupy, either retrospectively or in the present, the space from which this inspiring story is the only story to be told.

In one of very few moments of resentment in her text Washington-Williams writes about a shift in the manner in which she receives money from Thurmond; over time the exchange no longer occurs at the end of their ritual meeting, but now consists of her flying to Atlanta and a brief meeting in the airport, where one of Thurmond's nephews gives her money. "I felt," she writes, "a little like a trained seal going after the money, but it was not easy raising four children on a teacher's salary" (2005, 192). Work and subjection are what connect the flight and feeling like a trained seal: the fact is that she too has to work (black and blackened subjects too have to work for various privileges) for this money in order to support her children before and after her husband's death, to maintain a relationship with Thurmond, and to further her children's careers.[34] There is also pleasure here, for the one doing the training but also for the one who has been trained and who in responding as expected gets a reward, through being positioned (willingly or unwillingly) to be so humiliated. In that connection between shame, desire, and reward appears the congruence between her mother's work and her own that is then undone by

Washington-Williams's recourse to a narrative of familial pride (as the opposite of shame), expressed as "If my father wanted to help, wasn't that what fathers do?" (192).[35]

Despite Thurmond's never publicly or even privately calling her his daughter, his politics, his racism, his dismissal of her mother, and his long silence about their relationship,[36] after his death Washington-Williams claims a positive kinship connection to him and to "Southern aristocracy." This claiming depends upon her not speaking the nature of their relationship, depends upon the rearrangement of the circumstances of her own and Butler's work in and out of the kitchen and on the forbearance of others. The claiming occurs through the transformation of her questioning of and anger about Thurmond's segregationist politics into her acceptance that the positions that he advocated and all that "hate talk" were "just politics" (Washington-Williams and Stadiem 2005, 25).[37] The sentiment that Thurmond's "hate talk" is "just politics" (that is to say, not indicative of how he really feels, but language in which speech and feeling are privileged and divorced from action) is articulated first by Butler and later repeated by Essie Mae until it becomes her own.[38] Gradually, within and across generations, a site of "pain [is transformed] into pleasure," and what was a strategic stifling of anger—a possible performance adopted as a strategy for navigating employment, rape, harassment, and other everyday racial violence and/or the exemption from it—slides into a familiar and familial silence in the face of the fear of being unowned, cast out.

Not unsurprisingly Washington-Williams wants to shut the gate on the scenes of her mother's subjection and her own and to install in their place the popular narrative of the neo–plantation romance of innocence and intimacy. (Who, after all, wants to be positioned to bear such memory?) When she writes, "My mother and father worked closely together in the kitchen, he was interested in vegetables and she was the cook, that was how their relationship began" (Washington-Williams and Stadiem 2005, 41), Thurmond's power, Butler's labor, and the everyday tyrannies of proximity in and out of the kitchen are replaced by a myth of *loving* instruction. What remains hidden in this figure of the black woman in the kitchen (the mammy-as-stereotype) and in this familiar narrative are the nature of Butler's labors, the kind of sexual violation in which all the white men in the family, young and old, have access to her body, and her role as the one who secures everyone in their place.[39]

So whether or not Carrie Butler loved and was loved by Strom Thurmond, she was not in the kitchen because of that love or an interest in vegetables; she was there because she had to work. She may well have loved Thurmond and he might have loved her. Or perhaps in order to be in a space over which she had little control she needed to believe that she was there for love. But, as Annette Gordon-Reed writes of Sally Hemings and Thomas Jefferson, "the romance is not saying that they may have loved one another. The romance is in thinking that it makes any difference if they did" (2008, 365). It is through both the fact of Butler's work inside the house and the (dis)placement of that black female body that labored (and perhaps created the only escape narrative possible, in her mind) that Washington-Williams can claim her "white lineage" as entitlement, as *birthright*, property, and a sign of full inclusion, to be passed down to her black children and grandchildren. Strom Thurmond's connections to the Butler women and theirs to him (and each other) are secured through a brutal and shameful history and present transmitted from generation to generation as a future promise. Washington-Williams's "complete freedom" lies in articulating these relationships not as coercion but as affection that will symbolically free her from continued (racial) subjection. Her freedom lies in her embrace of being rewritten as "biracial,"[40] in her reminder to those (black people) who mistakenly "tend to categorize her as black" and who think that the Confederacy and its flag "are old times in Dixie, that should be forgotten" that she is "every bit as white as she is black." Her freedom lies in her intention to be fully American—that is, recognized as not being fully black—and "to drink the nectar of both goblets" (Washington-Williams and Stadiem 2005, 223).[41] We might recognize in Washington-Williams's reminder a twenty-first-century struggle over what blackness looks like and an accompanying change in (narrative) strategies, desires, and demands (similar to that which occurred in the years between the publications of Douglass's first two narratives) in which the ability to pass into and pass on the signatory power of (future) whiteness appears as the only space of "complete freedom" that can be imagined. (If this is so, do those black and blackened people who can't or don't claim that proximity to whiteness (in this space) as positive inheritance become the sole visible bearers of the trauma of the survival of slavery and racism, sole signifiers of an as yet unerased proximity to the blood-stained gate?) Both Douglass's and Washington-Williams's representative narratives of subjection in slavery and freedom position us to see that in order to survive and map visible progress we may indeed have (or feel that we have) no choice but to erase the lack of agency, to turn violation into affection, to be silent about the sadomasochism of everyday black life, to hide the horror for future generations to uncover. In the end my reading of Washington-Williams's performance of freedom is meant to position contemporary readers and actors to see and feel anew the ways multiple intimacies (domestic, political, academic, social, familial, etc.) and the desire to be free require one to be witness to, participant in, and be silent about scenes of subjection that we rewrite as freedom.

The Chapters

In chapter 1, "Gayl Jones's *Corregidora* and Reading the 'Days That Were Pages of Hysteria,'" I use the work of Hortense Spillers and Saidiya Hartman to analyze Gayl Jones's neo–slave narrative *Corregidora* (1986/1975). It is a text, I argue, that expands our understanding of the complex effects of slavery and freedom in the Americas (Brazil and the United States) on the interior lives of the formerly enslaved and their descendants. Central to *Corregidora* are the ways that the traumas of survival and the necessity of remembering and bearing witness to past horrors (the sexual violence of slavery and then comparative freedom in Brazil experienced by Great Gram and Gram) that are not yet past are passed down through the generations and reanimated in the present. In contrast to the narrative of continued subjection hidden in Douglass's Esther story and the romantic story that Washington-Williams tells in *Dear Senator, Corregidora*, perhaps more than any other African American neo–slave narrative, focuses on the horror, on the raced sexual violences of slavery and freedom and the demands (and then the effects) of the formerly enslaved on their descendants to reproduce and to keep "as visible as the blood" (the blood-stained gate and subjection), in effect to reproduce the horrific experiences of violence experienced during slavery in order that they not be forgotten. In this chapter I return to the primal scenes of slavery introduced in the stories of Douglass and Washington-Williams (to what I call the *Corregidora* complex) in order to trace out the reconfigurations, the internalization, the reenactments of violent and familiar subjection into the present and their (violent) cessation; the monstrous intimacies are the original traumas and their subsequent repetitions, the ways that desires that are congruent with the law of the master are interpellated by the enslaved, remembered, and passed on to the generations as their own.

In chapter 2, "Bessie Head, Saartje Baartman, and *Maru*: Redemption, Subjectification, and the Problem of Liberation," I read *Maru* (1971) as Head's attempt to create a space from which to imagine real liberation. Like Gayl Jones, Bessie Head explores how one conceives of freedom in the midst of unfreedoms that may be national, geographical, legal/juridical, and/or discursive. Drawing on her own position as a "coloured" South African exiled both in South Africa and in the Bechuanaland Protectorate (which became Botswana after independence), her experience of apartheid and relatively more freedom in Botswana, as well as her self-imposed and externally imposed identification as "Masarwa," Head not only contends with the congruence between who is marked as the socially monstrous body but also with the problem of slavery continuing in the midst of African independence from colonial masters. Writing *Maru* three years after Botswana's independence Head has intimate knowledge of the myriad oppressions that fall outside of the most recognized racialized forms of the colonizer-colonized dyad and that remain unspoken and unaddressed. I position Margaret Cadmore Jr., the text's Masarwa protagonist, alongside the historical production of and the legal case around the freedom of the KhoiSan woman Saartje Baartman (1789–1815), who was displayed as the Hottentot Venus in England and France in the beginning of the nineteenth century and in death in the Musée de l'Homme until the last quarter of the twentieth century.

In chapter 3, "Isaac Julien's *The Attendant* and the Sadomasochism of Everyday Black Life," I return to questions of the politics of memorialization and narrativization, this time within the historical (slavery) museum's productions of history and subjectivity, in order to explore how black bodies become disciplined, resist being disciplined, and are recorded as undisciplined and how history and discursive relations are produced and maintained in relation to the politics and aesthetics of representing slavery and in relation to (black) representation itself. One can see this disciplining everywhere in *The Attendant*'s (1993) presentation of interracial scenes of s/m, its concern with the regulation of obscenity, with slavery, the culture wars, AIDS, blackness, queerness, and representation itself, as well as in Julien's depictions of the public and private lives of a black museum conservator and the eponymous museum attendant. Following the Attendant at work and in s/m scenes that merge with and diverge from his job and with and from the visual and historical narratives of chattel slavery offered in an antislavery museum and heritage site, Julien reveals the connection between contemporary labor, terrors, and desires, the labor and the excesses of chattel slavery, and power, sex, and identification. Julien's focus is on the sadism of slavery, the raced, sexed, desire-inflected power relations of s/m, and the sadomasochism of everyday life for the Attendant and the Conservator, whose work policing and conserving the museum makes visible at the same time their maintenance of the structures that subject them and are part of the routinizing of everyday violence in the name of new (national) narratives.

The monstrous intimacies involving the violent constitution of the post-slavery subjects that figure in the work of Jones, Head, and Julien erupt onto the black-and-white, flattened-out world of Kara Walker's slavery, yet not slavery, silhouettes. Walker mines slavery, the nineteenth-century form of the silhouette, visual and written slave narratives, the plantation romance, and post-slavery subjections to make visible the circulation of shame and confinement, black and white resistance to interpellation by the work, white disavowal of kinship, the presence and then the erasure of monstrosity, and the means by which post-slavery subjectivity is constituted. It is in this chapter, "Kara Walker's Monstrous Intimacies," that I bring together these crucial concerns of the book as I read a particular image that Walker refers to as the "Big Black Mammy of the Antebellum South Is the Embodiment of History" (a vignette in *The End of Uncle Tom and the Grand Allegorical Tableau of Eva in Heaven*). The figure of the mammy, however historically or culturally based she may be, comes to stand for or in the place of what one accepts as history and its effects. Beginning with an analysis of the historical production of the mammy, with all her various manifestations and ramifications, I lay bare a multitude of ways in which she shores up racial divides and intimate intra- and interracial familial dynamics, at the same time that she, in her place, secures all the other subjects in their positions in the social fabric. It is in this chapter that I turn to post-slavery and the white subject as I read between white viewers and critics reading Walker's work and their disavowal of it and some black viewers, readers, and critics reading and their approbation of Walker's work (and Walker herself). Partly because of these responses much of the controversy surrounding Walker's work has been staged publicly as a black intergenerational intraracial conflict, as a fight between the pre- and postintegration civil rights generations over black representational and political strategies.

I return now to McWhorter's commentary on what he believes to be retrograde readings of Washington-Williams and his choice of the diorama in order to link it to monstrous intimacies and the stereotype picture in our heads, the cyclorama, the silhouette in Kara Walker's work, the tableaux vivants in *The Attendant*, the stereotypes and images of Saartje Baartman and the performances of the Hottentot Venus, and the "Bushman diorama" in the South African Museum. I invoke these modes of representation and ways of seeing to alert us to the structures (visual, narrative, and otherwise) inherited and reproduced that guide how we fix the *eye* and *I*. In this introduction and in each chapter, in each space and time, I place the reader in the midst of monstrous intimacies in order that we may see and think anew about slavery and the access routes to freedom, the blood-stained gate, the closet and the kitchen, and the longing (to be human) created in the post-slavery subject in the spaces I call monstrous. Finally, I mean *Monstrous Intimacies* to intervene in and to position us to see and think anew what it means to be a (black) post-slavery subject positioned within everyday intimate brutalities who is said to have survived or to be surviving the past of slavery, that is not yet past, bearing something like freedom.

ONE

Gayl Jones's *Corregidora* and Reading
the "Days That Were Pages of Hysteria"

Slavery is the ghost in the machine of kinship.
—**SAIDIYA HARTMAN** quoted in Butler 2002,
"Is Kinship Always Already Heterosexual?"

When the pro-slavery Mississippi statesman Henry
Hughes wrote in *A Treatise on Sociology: Theoretical
and Practical* (1854) that "Hybridism is heinous. Im-
purity of races is against the law of nature. Mulattoes
are monsters. The law of nature is the law of God.
The same law which forbids consanguineous amalgamation forbids ethnical amalgamation. Both are
incestuous. *Amalgamation is incest*,"[1] he performed
an alchemical change whereby to break *the different*
taboos of either incest or amalgamation—of morality and nature, blood and ethnicity—was to break *the
same* law. Hughes was reinforcing an already accepted natural division of black from white, further
delineated in a system that he called warrenteeism[2]
(a precursor to *Plessy v. Ferguson*'s [1896] so-called
separate but equal mandate). His logic rested on the
prior articulation of a black and white crisis in race,
property, and labor relations in southern slavery in
the mid-nineteenth century.[3]

When a number of late-twentieth-century critics
read Hughes's curious statement and arrived at a
similar conclusion that "The taboo of too different
(amalgamation/miscegenation) *is interchangeable
with* the taboo of too similar (incest), since both

crimes rely on a pair of bodies which are mutually constitutive of each other's deviance, a pair of bodies in which each body is the signifier of the deviance of the other,"[4] it is because they read incest and amalgamation as reciprocal. As incest and amalgamation are paired in Hughes's polemic, however, their relation is not, or not only, one of reciprocity or of a metaphorical or rhetorical doubling. In Hughes's polemic the terms seem to have a relation in which *to contravene either taboo is to break exactly the same law*. That Hughes arrives at an equation in which *too different* is the same as *too similar* by a series of denials and displacements is incontestable. In the interest of reading this alignment psychoanalytically as well as historically, I suggest that "Amalgamation is incest," a phantasmatically powerful conjunction, also marks out a rhetorical space that might be recognized in the present as a marker of the juridical law, a "commemorative site of law . . . [which is] not simply textual, but . . . also involv[es] particular kinds of materialization of legal power" (Dayan 1999, 19).[5] That is, in Hughes's polemical alignment of amalgamation and incest we glimpse a midcentury semantic and legal reorganization of kin and property that occurred, and was concealed, under the sign of slavery.[6] Slavery provides both a time and space (real and fantastic) where to commit incest or amalgamation is to break *the same law* and the imminent rupture and onset of forgetting that break around which some cultural or national formation has taken hold. It is important to recognize that Hughes's conjunction and fusion of amalgamation and incest (each term fraught in itself) and their collapse into a singular understanding marks one nodal point around which subjectivity in the New World was reorganized and around which it cohered.

The Hughes quotation and the anxieties and shifts that it hints at initiate a theoretical context in which to begin my discussion of Gayl Jones's *Corregidora* (1975/1986) as a text in which the primal scenes of slavery emerge as those familial and legal entanglements that were central to the transformative enterprise of making some persons into kin and some into property. Thus the statement "Amalgamation is incest" and all that it assumes, disavows, makes equivalent, and differentiates is central to the formation of the modern American subject.[7] Let's return to the epigraph with which this chapter began and about which Judith Butler writes, "If, as Saidiya Hartman maintains, 'slavery is the ghost in the machine of kinship,' it is because African-American kinship has been at once the site of intense state surveillance and pathologization, which leads to the *double bind of being subject to normalizing pressures within the context of a continuing social and political delegitimation.* As a result, it is not possible to separate questions of kinship from property relations (and conceiving persons as property) and from the fictions of 'bloodline,' as well as the national and racial interests by which these lines are sustained" (2002, 15; emphasis mine). If "slavery is the ghost in the machine of kinship," it is in part because under slavery, system and sign, *lexico-legal acts of transubstantiation* occur in which blood *becomes* property (with all of the rights inherent in the use and enjoyment of property) in one direction and kin in another. With the force of the law and the gaze brought to bear on the institution of slavery, we witness what Hortense Spillers has called one of "the richest displays of the psychoanalytic dimensions of culture before the science of European psychoanalysis takes hold" (2003c, 223). Reading *Corregidora*'s exploration of profound intersubjective sexual violence (incest and amalgamation) within slavery and the family we see how (African American) kinship is lived and we get a clarification of an American slavery and post-slavery unconscious. Jones writes out something like a Corregidora complex; an Oedipus complex for the New World.[8]

Corregidora helps us think through how the naming of amalgamation as a taboo on the order of incest and *then their fusion* into one undifferentiated concept might work; how, in other words, this conjunction might function. What desires (national, individual, social, cultural) are simultaneously forbidden and compelled, produced and masked in this doubled taboo if we accept that "the 'prohibition of incest' must bear on a structure —a relation between subject and object—that is distinct from biological relations"?[9] What unspoken sociocultural relations distinct from but not exclusive of biological relations are both conceded and disavowed by the collapse of "Amalgamation is incest"?

Set in Kentucky in the mid-1940s to the late 1960s, *Corregidora* focuses on a blues singer named Ursa Corregidora, who is the fourth generation in a family of women with the same surname. This surname, the name of the Portuguese seaman and slaver who settled in Brazil on land and with slaves that he received from the Portuguese king, is part of what each woman retains and passes on to her daughter (who will also retain the name, and so on). A slave owner and "whoremonger," Corregidora (whose proper name we never learn) was the master of Ursa's great-grandmother

and the father of at least her grandmother and her mother.[10] After Brazilian emancipation in the beginning of the twentieth century, Great Gram
and a pregnant Gram leave Brazil in 1906 and settle in Kentucky after
living for a while in Louisiana. But the details of this move as well as the
complex interpersonal relationships (between and among the women, the
women and Corregidora, the women and other men) mostly inhere in the
phantasmatic family narratives or are largely absent from the text. It is
precisely those absences, those narrative breaks that power the novel.

The novel begins with one of those absences as Ursa introduces us to
an earlier self, who is twenty-five years old, married, and one month
pregnant. She recalls that it was April 1948 and she was leaving Happy's
Café after her final set when she and her husband, Mutt Thomas, had a
violent confrontation that ended when he pushed or threw her or she fell
down the stairs. (The ways that the incident is recollected throughout the
novel situate Ursa as pushed or thrown and also falling—desirous of a
means to end reproduction. The question of agency is complicated here,
and the unconscious plays the largest role in this text.) The fall down the
stairs results in hospitalization, a miscarriage, and then a hysterectomy for
Ursa. Very soon after she leaves the hospital she divorces Mutt and soon
after that she marries Tadpole McCormick, the owner of Happy's Café.
Ursa is an only child, the only daughter in a family in which there are only
daughters. Since birth she has been told by each of her foremothers that
her duty (her raison d'être) is to "make generations to bear witness to the
horrors of slavery" in order to keep "*it* as visible as the blood" (18, 72).[11]
The gaps in the narrative itself and in reproduction with which the text
begins, position Ursa from the outset as unable or unwilling to fulfill the
Corregidora women's demand to carry their history into the future. The
history of the women unfolds in passages that are at once Ursa's memory
of the family narrative and the family narratives being channeled through
her. As it unfolds we discover that Ursa is conflicted about fulfilling the
command "to make generations to bear witness" before the miscarriage
and hysterectomy and that the hysterectomy realizes a profoundly real
intrafamilial rupture that already has taken place even before Ursa's birth
and has been repressed.[12] At the same time that the plot follows Ursa's life,
Corregidora is also a collective narrative of those four generations of female descendants of chattel slavery. The text maps their unconscious
repetitions and their conscious, determined repetitions of "evidence to

hold up against [the enslavers]," which is driven by the destruction of historical documents ("the provisional government ordered the slavery archives burned in 1891"),[13] and it bears witness to an almost universal repression of the fact of slavery's extreme domestic violence.

As the last woman in a series of women who carry the Corregidora name, Ursa reconstructs and realizes a historical and familial narrative. A handed-down photograph that she possesses of "old man Corregidora," master/father/grandfather, stands as an object outside of her own body that she can point to as evidence of enslavement, emancipation, and her and her ancestors' survival of one or both. This photograph of their slave master/father that gains much of its value from some future understanding is weighted with a past that is not yet past and a connection to a past and future that are not yet visible. As Great Gram explains, "I stole it because I said whenever afterward when evil come I wanted something to point to and say, 'That's what evil look like'" (12).[14]

The photograph now in her possession, Ursa is the current Corregidora generation meant to bear and carry forward the memories of what Corregidora has done and been to her mother, grandmother, and great-grandmother, as well as a resemblance to and distance from him. Though she is not directly touched by him in the ways that Great Gram, Gram, and even Mama have been, Corregidora is nonetheless present for Ursa through the photograph, through the mothers' stories, their shared relationship to the law, reproduction, and justice, and through the reproduction of a series of desires and relationships in their own lives. Jointly the memories made flesh and the photograph work to make a particular experience of slavery real to the generations after Great Gram, and the time and the spaces of her enslavement are extended into the present. Not only does their embrace of "the potentially disabling proximity between antagonism and identification (taking the enemy's place, internally as well as externally, as the only way of ensuring his defeat)" (J. Rose 1996, 11) dictate the Corregidora women's lives, but slavery's laws have been incorporated into the daily instrumentality of the law post-slavery. By exploring the narrative of the history of the women as they are fucked and fathered by Corregidora and by looking into this patriarchy under slavery we can begin to articulate what is going on in Hughes's declaration "Amalgamation is incest" and to understand the Corregidora complex.

In *Corregidora* this fusion of the course of the narrative and the symbolic law occurs at the levels of form and content. Calling the slave narrative "a genre . . . and a truth of the American experience" in which there are "truths . . . that haven't already been told" (Rowell 1982, 42), Jones writes a neo–slave narrative in which she explores the power of the narrative (legal, familial, and social, to secure one's place in the nation, family, hierarchy) to inscribe and also to erase.[15] *Corregidora* allows us to explore how the family's demands on the subject to keep visible (but also keep repressed) horrific experiences of violence in slavery—in this case, the demands of the formerly enslaved on their descendants—become congruent with the law of the (slave) master. The "proximity between antagonism and identification" in the demands of and on the Corregidora mothers and daughters to keep visible and to reproduce evidence of slavery's horrific violence inhere in slavery's legal arrangements and the internalized logic of the slave master through which they were able to survive and through which they were originally wounded.

Generational "Genital Fantasies"

> How many generations had to bow to his genital fantasies?
> —GAYL JONES, *Corregidora*

In 1839 the New England-born South Carolina politician and slave owner James Henry Hammond purchased two enslaved people: eighteen-year-old Sally Johnson, a seamstress, and her one-year-old daughter, Louisa.[16] Married, a father, a plantation owner, and a vocal critic of miscegenation who believed in the absolute inferiority of the enslaved, Hammond nevertheless engaged in long-term sexual acts/relationships with both Sally and Louisa Johnson—immediately with Sally and with Louisa when she reached the age of twelve. In 1858, nineteen years after purchasing the Johnsons, now Senator Hammond delivered his famous "Cotton Is King" speech to the U.S. Senate, in which he declared the supremacy of the South, derided the North's rejection of chattel slavery, and called the North's embrace of white wage labor slavery by another name. In his staunch defense of slavery's proper order Hammond declared that unlike the North, the South was home to a "race inferior to her own, but eminently qualified in temper, in vigor, in docility, in capacity to stand the climate, to answer all her purposes" (quoted in Bleser 1988, vii).[17] He continued, "We use them for our purpose, and call them slaves. . . . Our slaves are black, of another and inferior race. The status in which we have placed them is an elevation. They are elevated from the condition in which God first created them, by being made our slaves. None of that race on the whole face of the globe can be compared with the slaves of the South. They are happy, content, unaspiring, and utterly incapable, from intellectual weakness, ever to give us any trouble by their aspirations. *Yours are white, of your own race; you are brothers of one blood.*"[18]

Two persons of that "inferior race" (not his "brothers of one blood") that Hammond used for his purpose and called slaves were the Johnson mother and daughter. The Johnsons left no written records of their own lives, and Hammond largely records only their status as property, the children he believed he fathered with them, those he maintained he did not, the disruptions these "relationships" (particularly with Louisa) caused in his marriage to Catherine Fitzsimons, and his sense of what would be "good and fair" to them.[19] According to Carol Bleser, the editor of Hammond's diaries, Hammond is "almost alone among the planter aristocracy [in actually documenting] his proclivity for sexually exploiting his female slaves" (1988, xvi). Known for this, for other sexual proclivities, and for a more generalized cruelty to enslaved people,[20] Hammond nevertheless transforms ownership, rape, sex, and other relations with Sally and Louisa Johnson into a narrative of benevolent paternalism. He confides in a letter to his eldest son, Harry, that in the event of his death, "Nor would I like that any but *my own blood* should own as Slaves *my own blood* or Louisa." Of freedom, specifically freedom in the northern states, he writes, "I cannot free these people and send them North. It would be cruelty to them."[21] Juxtaposing these two instances of "my own blood" (Harry and the Johnson children) and his reference to blood in his "Cotton Is King" speech, Hammond recasts the domination of Sally, Louisa, and their children in the following way: "Do not let Louisa or any of my children or possible children be slaves of Strangers. Slavery *in the family* will be their happiest earthly condition. Ever affectionately, J. H. H." (19; emphasis mine). This concealment of the violence of domination in the terms of affection is, as Saidiya Hartman contends, how the master narratives of seduction in enslavement are structured. "Seduction," she writes, "erects a family romance—in this case, the elaboration of a racial and sexual fantasy in which domination is transposed into the bonds of mutual affection, subjection idealized as the pathway to equality, and perfect subordination declared the means of ensuring great happiness and harmony" (1997, 89). When the one cast as seductress is white and kin, as we shall see, this particular legal and ethical alchemy cannot occur.

In 1843, four years after Hammond purchased the Johnsons, his family discovered that he had been engaged in a two-year-long incestuous relationship with his four teenage nieces. Again Hammond recorded in his journals (and his family preserved) events and thoughts that many others in his position did not:

> Here were four lovely creatures from the tender but precocious girl of 13 to the mature but fresh and blooming woman nearly 19, each contending for my love, claiming her greater share of it as due to her superior devotion to me, all of them rushing on every occasion to my arms and covering me with their kisses, lolling on my lap, pressing their bodies almost into mine, wreathing their limbs with mine, encountering warmly every portion of my frame, and permitting my hands to stray unchecked over every part of them and to rest without the slightest shrinking of it, in the most secret and sacred regions, and all this for a period of more than two years continuously. Is it in flesh and blood to withstand this? Nay are there many who would have the self-control to stop where I did? Am I not after all, entitled to some, the smallest portion of, credit for not going further? (Bleser 1988, 172–73)

The young women are his wife's relations, kin, although neither through his blood nor his right of property, and these are "transgressions that would be neither forgiven nor forgotten" (Bleser 1988, 22).[22] If it was not "in [Hammond's] flesh and blood to withstand" the temptations of those nieces which would surely have repercussions (for them and for him) if discovered, then one must imagine, at the very least, a similar license in relation to his slaves, who were his property to use.

The architectonics of slavery necessitated that despite Hammond's acknowledgment of *blood relations* (with Sally and Louisa Johnson) any acknowledgment of *kinship* between him and the enslaved (and between the enslaved) was, if not completely disavowed, at the very least made invisible through its subordination to relations of property.[23] This makes the acts that Hammond and his wife's family members engage in with one or both of the Johnsons recognizable only as amalgamation; no incest taboo is considered violated. The subordination of kinship relations to property relations throws the contravention of the incest prohibition into crisis at the very moment it might be articulated as such. But if the incest taboo is in crisis here because blood and property are severed from kin in the relations between the Johnsons, Hammond, and his extended family, the incest taboo is in crisis in relation to his nieces because with them, kinship and property extended in the other direction is what Hammond *cannot* disavow: "What is at issue [here] is the difference between the deployment of sexuality in the contexts of white kinship—the proprietorial relation of the patriarch to his wife and children, the making of legitimate heirs, and the transmission of property—and black captivity— the reproduction of property, the relations of mastery and subjection, and the regularity of sexual violence" (Hartman 1997, 84). It is precisely the sort of complex relations that Hammond draws attention to and disavows that the Corregidora women insist on reproducing (and repressing) in order to keep as "visible as the blood."

In Hammond's letter to his son he stresses, "Take care of [Louisa] and her children who are both of *your* blood if not of mine. . . . Do not let Louisa or any of my children or possible children be slaves of Strangers" (Bleser 1988, 19). Hammond's reference to Harry's blood and his own makes clear that he is the father of at least some of their children and that Harry himself, or other men from his mother's side of the family, are potential fathers of some of Louisa's children. Nonetheless in *Secret and Sacred* Bleser observes that while there are "certain ambiguities in this letter [they] . . . *need not be dwelt upon other than to note that Harry is probably not involved in fathering any of these children, but apparently members of his mother's family may be*. . . . The two main points to derive from this letter are first that it presents clear cut evidence for planter-slave sexual relationships and secondly it shows the attitude of at least one planter toward his resulting offspring" (19; emphasis mine).[24] It is, however, precisely to those "certain ambiguities," those consanguineous confusions, that we must turn. In doing so, the "familiarity" that Hammond confers and yet withholds in the letter ("both of *your* blood if not of mine") will bring us to points in addition to Bleser's from which we might begin further to unknot the complexity of relations of blood, kinship, property, and family that are central to slavery. This in turn leads us to focus on the very centrality of what Spillers calls "this enforced state of breach . . . [that avowedly] vestibular cultural formation where 'kinship' loses meaning, *since it can be invaded at any given and arbitrary moment by the property relations*" (2003c, 218).

Hammond's reference to Louisa's children being of Harry's blood, if not his own, both alerts us to the *proximity* of incest and amalgamation and also provides an example of the instrumentalization of sexuality in the making of the black family as property and the white family as kin. In this transferal of relations of blood as relations of power from father to son, regardless of who claims the *title* of father, patriarch, and perhaps master (father, son, wife's male family members), the *practice* of "making generations," of reproducing slaves as property (the exchange of money, kin into capital), was a "family affair" that cut across sex.[25] Hammond's letter to Harry offers one stunning example of that "enforced state of breach" and the license it confers to *kin* in "slavery in the family." In *Corregidora* we find another. Corregidora "didn't hardly use nothing but the womens," Great Gram recalls. "Naw, he wasn't the first that did it. There was plenty that did it. Make the women fuck and then take their money. And you know sometimes the mistresses was doing it too so they could have little pocket money that their husbands didn't know about. And getting their brothers and their brother's friends and other mens they know, you know, and then they make theyselves right smart money for their purse" (Jones 1975/1986, 23). Indeed in both instances we see some of the ways that "sexuality . . . appears . . . as an especially dense transfer point for relations of power: . . . not the most intractable element in power, but rather one of those endowed with the greatest instrumentality" (Foucault 1980, 103). This transfer is where genealogy is distinguished from pedigree, kin from blood.

Generational "Genital Fantasies": Part II

Hammond's story (and Louisa's and Sally Johnson's stories) is not only limited by what he chose to write about and how much he chose to disclose; it is also circumscribed by his position as a white male slave-owning patriarch. *Corregidora* allows us to think through generational genital fantasies from another position, from a perspective after the immediate effects of what is passed from the white father/master to the (black) slave/daughter and then from that daughter to her daughter. What, for example, might it mean that Great Gram and Gram remain with Corregidora after emancipation and that the Johnson women remain on the

Hammond plantation after Hammond's death and for decades after emancipation? "By the time of Hammond's death in 1864, Louisa and Sally each had four or five children, and since he kept the women and their children living apart from the other slaves, he may well have been the father of these children. After the war Louisa and Sally remained on the Hammond plantation, their presence accepted now by Hammond's widow, and as late as the 1880 census they were still in residence with their families" (Bleser 1988, n. 20).

Contrary to the ideology of the plantation romance (that enslaved people were happy and remained with the master and mistress out of loyalty and devotion), the formerly enslaved faced a present in which most other possible lives for them were rigorously foreclosed at all levels of society, in which their freedom was only nominal. So, however traumatic staying might be, it is no small wonder that numbers of the formerly enslaved were unable to leave. That is, notwithstanding legal emancipation, the very force of the law, trauma, sexual violence, the need or compulsion to work, and familial ties kept people bound to awful material and psychic configurations.

Great Gram repeats to Gram, to Mama, and then to Ursa (and they repeat to each other) the experiences of a sexual violence while enslaved by and living with Corregidora of the sort that we know to be largely obscured in texts, including those authored by the formerly enslaved, because of the dictates of the form and the work that those texts were produced to perform.[26] Some of Ursa's earliest memories are of Great Gram relating what are to her unbelievable stories of sex and violence: "*[Corregidora's] wife was a skinny stuck-up little woman he got from over in Lisbon and he had her brought over here. He wouldn't sleep with her, so for five years I was sleeping with her and him. That was when I was from about thirteen to about eighteen. . . . But they had me sleeping with both of them*" (Jones 1975/1986, 13). (This quotation appears after Ursa's second husband, Tadpole McCormick, tells her the following story about his grandparents: "My grandmother was white. . . . She was an orphan and they had her working out there in the fields along with the blacks and treated her like she was one. She was a little girl about nine, ten, 'leven. My granddaddy took her in and raised her and then when she got old enough he married her. She called him Papa. And when they were married, she still called him Papa" [13].) Master, father, papa, husband: Gram warns Ursa about the duration of these awful configurations when she says, "He fucked her and he fucked me. *He would've fucked you and your mama if ya'll been there* and he wasn't old and crooked up like he got. . . . He raised me and then when I got big enough he started fucking me. Seem like he raised me fucking me" (172–73; emphasis mine). Recall that Ursa says of Great Gram, "I thought of the girl who had to sleep with her master and mistress. *Her father, the master*" (67; emphasis mine).

Confronted with truths expunged from records and with truths not to be questioned but to be reproduced, the older Corregidora women even years later and in a different country compel each other and their daughters to repeat and to make visible their histories. "They burned all the documents but they didn't burn what they put in their minds. We got to burn out what they put in our minds, like you burn out a wound. Except we got to keep what we need to bear witness. That scar that's left to bear witness. We got to keep it as visible as our blood" (72). The history in question, however, is such that even in the event of written records one still is compelled to remember and repeat. We know that the written records from North American slavery do not halt the reconfiguration of slave law into Jim Crow law or the continued effects of trauma or the effects of its disavowal; the stories must still be told. The story that Great Gram tells of being forced to sleep with her master and mistress prompts the five-year-old Ursa to ask her, "You telling the truth . . . ?" Great Gram responds to the question with a slap and an order: "When I'm telling you something don't you ever ask if I'm lying. Because they didn't want to leave no evidence of what they done" (14).

The stories travel from Great Gram to Gram to Mama to Ursa: "In the old days he [Corregidora] was just buying up women. They'd have to raise up their dress so he could see what they had down there, and he feel all around down there, and then he feel their bellies to see if they had solid bellies" (173). Living out the materialized affective relations of slavery within freedom, their wombs anything but free, they raise daughters who carry the evidence forward, maintain the patriarch's name, continue to repeat the mothers' stories as their own, and act as the (current) evidence of those (past) crimes.[27] While the horror of being a chattel prostitute is what Great Gram lived and relived and the other Corregidora women make visible, they also relive the traumas, immobilizing in the way that historical and family traumas are, born of those monstrous intimacies and invested with something like desire. Ursa is charged not only with the telling but also with the living of the impossible instruction to stigmatize her body in ways that selectively mimic an unknown initiating trauma but *only* in the ways that *they* (the women) *need* to bear witness—to reinscribe the original inscription.

I turn briefly now to Brazilian slavery and to the year 1871 to underscore the signifying power of the womb as visible evidence, and I offer another historical reason why the Corregidora women insist on "keeping it as visible as the blood." In 1871 there were two significant challenges to Brazil's already faltering slave economy. The first challenge was the so-called Free Womb Law, which by emancipating the wombs of enslaved mothers freed their children, made illegal the sale of enslaved children under the age of eight away from their mothers, and ensured that slave owners provided for those children that they did not allow to go free at age eight until they reached the age of twenty-one. Martha Abreu writes, "At the bottom of the entire opposition movement [in opposition to the passage of the Free Womb Law], at stake was the future relationship between masters and slaves" (1996, 570). At stake was a legal claim that a slave master, like Corregidora, might have on the bodily and psychic life of future generations.

The second challenge was a related series of events that brought a number of cases before "a judge or judges of the court" on behalf of enslaved women who, "encouraged by police to come forward to tell their stories and to make audacious bids for freedom as part of a crackdown against procuring slaveowners" (Lauderdale Graham 1991, 669), sought this freedom on the grounds that their mistresses forced them into prostitution.[28] The passage of the Free Womb Law, the details of the prostitution cases in the courts, and the erasure of evidence by the destruction of the records of slavery combine in the fictional Great Gram's life and give signifying power to the birth of a free daughter who will bear evidence of slavery.[29] As Abreu writes, "A foreseeable line of argument against the 'Free Womb' was to complain of the failure to honour the rights of property established in the constitution" (1996, 571).

The law therefore created a new twist to familial relations already coerced, already violent, already intimate. Because control over future generations was now contestable, both enslaved women and slave masters were forced to shift tactics: "Slaves also tried to use the new laws, such as the free womb law, to obtain freedom for themselves and their children" (Abreu 1996, 571). Gram's birth in 1888—the actual year of emancipation and seventeen years after the passage of the Free Womb Law—means that she was *never* Corregidora's slave. (What do we do with this knowledge? Do we forget it in thinking about the text because it is not one of the repetitions that become fact through the very force of their repetition— even as we are made aware that those repetitions themselves are suspect within the logic of the text?)[30] The grandmothers do not account for the changed and changing circumstances of their lives or the differences between them, nor does their master narrative reflect the multiplicity of their stories. As Ursa says, they don't account for the lived life, only "the spoken one" (Jones 1975/1986, 108). And the "symbolic substitutions" for rape, incest, and other violence inherent in slavery are mapped onto the bodies of the formerly enslaved and their post-slavery generations and manifest as hysterical symptoms, as ways of making the body speak.[31] They pass on certain memories as a conscious ethical decision not to forget, to provide material evidence to counteract what has been destroyed. They also pass on memories unconsciously as hysterical symptoms.[32]

Further examination of how the Corregidora women bear witness necessitates paying attention to the names in the text. Great Gram and Gram are identified primarily and Gram exclusively through their relationships to their offspring and through their value to Corregidora.[33] Corregidora's favorite, Great Gram, is "a good little piece": "*My best. Dorita. Little gold piece*" (10). "Dorita" is a significant naming that largely is ignored. A diminutive of the last two syllables of his surname, Dorita provides several clues to Jones's articulation of the hysterical trauma at the center of slavery and hence, I argue, at the center of constructions of the modern subject. I read this naming as Jones's signifying on the slave master and father Corregidora and the father of psychoanalysis by recalling Freud's Dora.[34]

The surname Corregidora combines the Spanish *corregidor*, "magistrate and corrector," with the Portuguese *carregador*, "laden, to load or carry, to overdo." The Corregidora women carry forward on and in their bodies the evidence that the magistrate can read and that will not only provide the proof of their original trauma but will lead, in some future, to justice for them. They make generations to bear evidence as they seek redress for the excessive violence and injustices of the magistrate, that is to say, to make redress to the law itself. They produce generations in the absence of the written records to bear witness, to make their trauma visible to and readable by a symbolic Corregidora—or a Corregidora stand-in—that is both external and internal to them. In the text the Corregidora surname (and its diminutives Dorita and Correy) burdens the Corregidora women with the full weight of the law. As Mutt warns Ursa, reproduction could be the slave master's way of thinking. For the Corregidora women to reproduce is to reproduce (enough) Corregidora.

Corregidora begins with the violent encounter between Ursa and her first husband, Mutt Thomas, that results in her hysterectomy and a dramatic rupture with the Corregidora family commandment to bear female children, a break in the extension, in perpetuity, of Corregidora's genital fantasies. Even before the violence with Mutt that ends in her hysterectomy, Ursa realizes the dangers of such reproductions in her own life. She dreams, "My belly was swollen and restless, and I lay without moving, gave birth without struggle, without feeling. . . . I never saw what squatted between my knees. . . . But I felt the humming and beating of wings and claws in my thigh. And I felt a stiff penis inside me. 'Those who have fucked their daughters would not hesitate to fuck their own mothers.' Who are you? Who have I born? His hair was like white wings, and we were united at birth" (77). The dream sequence completes the Corregidora women's cycle of bearing witness by doubling back on itself. The dream is a revelation of the monstrous intimacy that powers the novel; it makes explicit the powers of horror that construct Ursa as (a black) post-slavery subject. In the dream old man Corregidora fucks Ursa and Ursa gives birth to him.

Entangled Desires

Whichever way you look at it, *we ain't them.*—**GAYL JONES**, *Corregidora*

Those men, raiding villages, leading coffles, throwing buckets of water, those examining limbs and teeth, those looking into eyes for rebellion, those are the captors who enter the captive's body. Already inhabiting them as extensions of themselves with a curious dissociation which gave them the ability to harm them as well. Slaves became extensions of slave owners—their arms, legs, the parts of them they wished to harness and use with none of the usual care of their own bodies. These captive bodies represent parts of their own bodies they wish to rationalize or make mechanical or inhuman so as to perform the tasks of exploitation of resources or acquisition of territory. These captive bodies then become the tools sent out to conquer the natural world. Of course they aren't merely tools but the projections of the sensibilities, consciousness, needs, desires, and fears of the captor.—DIONNE BRAND, *A Map to the Door of No Return: Notes to Belonging*

The projection of the slave owner's "sensibilities, conscious needs, desires, and fears" that Dionne Brand articulates necessarily has lasting effects. It is a projection, a violent introjection, and a possession the result of which can be seen in *Corregidora* in the ways that the captor's "sensibilities" and "desires" become part of the repertoire of experiences not only of the enslaved but also of their descendants. For Ursa Corregidora the past that she touches is not exactly or simply her past; it is both a past that she has lived through and one that has been transmitted to her, introjected into her, one that overtakes her. Sixty years and more after the end of Brazilian slavery the tools that the mothers insist would free them emerge from the genital fantasies that were not their own but that are now no longer only those of the slaveholders.

The first Corregidora daughter, born in the year of emancipation, Gram insists that she does not yet "know what [Great Gram] did. She never would tell me what she did. Up till today she still won't tell me what it was she did." But Gram repeats with the absolute certainty of one who cannot know otherwise (as if that knowing would kill *her*), "He would've killed her, though, if she hadn't gone" (172). Great Gram never does tell why she stays with Corregidora after emancipation or why she waits to leave, nor does she ever relate to her daughter what finally compels her to leave and leave Gram behind: "Mama [Great Gram] stayed there with him even after it ended, until she did something that made him wont to kill her, and then she run off and had to leave me. Then he was raising me and doing you know I said what he did" (79). In the place of an explicit explanation Gram repeats Great Gram's words: "Corregidora's whores was free too, but most of 'em Mama said he put down in the rut so deep, that that's bout all they could do now, though lot of 'em broke away from it too" (79). In other words, Gram might well know why Great Gram, herself one of Corregidora's whores, stayed even after "it" ended, if not why she left when she did.

Unowned but still living with the former master and tethered to awful relationships formed during slavery, what does Great Gram pass on to Gram, and what does she pass Gram on to? Born in 1888, the year of Brazilian emancipation, whatever Gram has witnessed between Great Gram and Corregidora, the story that Gram repeats to Ursa is one in which her mother is an agent who does something to Corregidora that made him want to kill her and caused her to leave her daughter behind. The effects of this undisclosed action necessitate Great Gram's abandonment of Gram and swift departure to preserve her own life. One central question that haunts this text is, What did Great Gram do?

I suggest another way to approach Great Gram's omission is by asking, What (more) has Corregidora done that Great Gram cannot bear? What if Corregidora's fucking Gram is not the consequence of Great Gram's departure but its cause? Indeed what if Corregidora has done with Great Gram and with Gram what James Henry Hammond did with Sally Johnson and then with twelve-year-old Louisa Johnson, an act that exceeds what Great Gram thinks of as licensed in freedom, an act that made Great Gram want to kill *him*? Perhaps what Great Gram cannot bear and can never avow is the intimate trauma of being the favorite, "Dorita," and having her own emancipated child fucked by her/their father. In echoes of the U.S. Supreme Court's decision in *Dred Scott v. Sanford,* perhaps she cannot bear that even in freedom there is nothing of hers that the white master cum father is bound to respect.

Great Gram tells a story about consequences, about an enslaved woman's refusal to submit to rape by the master. "There was a woman over on the next plantation," she says. "The master shipped her husband out of bed and got in the bed with her and just as he was getting ready to go in her she cut off his thing with a razor she had hid under the pillow and he bled to death, and then the next day they came and got her and her husband. They cut off her husband's penis and stuffed it in her mouth, and then they hanged her. . . . They made her watch and then they hanged her" (67). For Great Gram, "there were two alternatives, you either took one or you didn't" (67). And on Corregidora's plantation Great Gram has learned that it is dangerous for the enslaved to claim and defend familial and marital relations from the master. Asserting a self that is distinct from the master's desires for that self, certainly in the presence of the master or an agent of the master, often led to the kind of sexualized, spectacular violence that Great Gram reported happening on the neighboring plantation as well as on Corregidora's. As Great Gram says, "I guess that other plantation served as a warning, cause they might wont your pussy, but if you do anything to get back at them, it'll be your life they be wonting, and then they make even that some kind of a sex show, all them beatings and killings wasn't nothing but sex circuses" (125). After the woman's violent resistance to being fucked she is made to be witness to and participant in (and to watch them watching her) the castration and murder of her husband. In their details of seeing, being seen, being made to watch, these stories of Great Gram's clearly impart the operation of the gaze and the hypersexual investment in that gaze.

With this knowledge, in two moments of resistance (one before and one after abolition) Great Gram exercises both alternatives: to submit to sexual violence and live, and to resist and suffer the consequences. Before abolition Great Gram attempts to help a young enslaved man reach freedom. He has entrusted her, Corregidora's favorite, with his dream of running away to Palmares. Great Gram is afraid that he thinks she has betrayed him to Corregidora, and Corregidora is convinced that Great Gram and the young man are involved sexually. Unable to fight for the man's innocence or to convince Corregidora that he was not the object of her affections (nor was she the object of his), Great Gram attempts to buy the young man time to escape through her own body: "He [Corregidora] was up there fucking me while they was out chasing *him*. 'Don't let no black men mess with you, do you hear? I don't want nothing black fucking with my pussy.' I kept saying I wouldn't" (127). Doubly traumatized by this violence, Great Gram recounts, "[I] kept crying out, and ole Corregidora thinking it was because he was fucking so good I was crying. . . . And then somehow it got in my mind that each time he kept going down in me would be that boy's feet running. And then when he come, it meant they caught him" (128). For Great Gram, submitting to rape while the runaway is being chased and prolonging that rape to buy him time to escape are the twin articulations of a sexualized violence that reinforces the dangers of refusing the master's desires *and* the fleeting and illusory power in succumbing to them (e.g., by taking them on as her own). In the face of these dual traumas Great Gram remakes submission into a liberatory act; she transforms each of Corregidora's thrusts into another step toward freedom for the male runaway. As long as she submits to Corregidora she and someone else have a better chance of surviving. This too is the structure of the family romance ("the transposition of racial and sexual domination into affection") that seduction as a theory of power and affection attempts to conceal. This too prefigures the hopeless perpetuity of "making generations" in which the means of escape and submission are fused.

Acting as if or believing that there is some small power, however tenuous, that accrues to her position as the favorite concubine cum daughter ("her father the master"), favorite of all of Corregidora's women, Great Gram says, "Sometimes I would be a little bold with him, little bolder than the others, cause I know I was the piece he wonted the most" (126). Her ability to influence Corregidora's behavior is limited, and, aside from a little boldness, her resistance must be readable as submission by the master.[35] So whatever little "power" Great Gram exercised in this position, she remains unable to protect her daughter from Corregidora, the man who "did more fucking than the other mens did" (12). Thus despite the passage of the Free Womb Law and the end of chattel slavery each Corregidora woman finds her womb still in the service of the (former) master/father, and as such their desires and the price of their survival are caught up by Corregidora and his desires. Great Gram passes Gram on to the incestuous desires of Corregidora. And so on. Their desire itself is caught in his desire. It is as much from *this* transaction, this transfer of relations of power that the ritual of "making generations" emerges that is handed down from generation to generation. Struggling to be free of Corregidora, Great Gram produces evidence to attest to the fact of her former enslavement and to defeat Corregidora even as he is carried into the future.

"How much was love for Corregidora and how much was hate?" (131). Mama tells Ursa that her husband, Martin, Ursa's father, was the only one "bold enough" to ask Gram this vital question. Ursa has her own questions, and like Martin's they inquire into the construction of desire, into forms of betrayal and withholding between husbands and wives and between mothers and daughters. In an imagined dialogue with Mutt, Ursa explains that her mother is possessed by the injunction of Great Gram and Gram to make generations. She says, "[My mother] was closed up like a fist. It was her very own memory, not theirs, her very own real and terrible and lonely and dark memory. And I never saw her with a man because she wouldn't give them anything else. Nothing. . . . Still there was what they never spoke, Mutt, what even they wouldn't tell me. How all but one of them had the same lover? Did they begrudge her that? Was that their resentment? There was something, Mutt" (101, 103). Ursa is correct:

Mama, who neither pushes Martin away nor shares him with Gram and Great Gram, is "closed up like a fist," not like Great Gram's open palm that she reads as if "it held the words" she speaks to Ursa. We could say that Mama maintains the "correct" post-slavery set of taboos; she assumes the possibility of a kinship (exogamous relationships) that has not been available to Great Gram and Gram. The space of (purely racial) transubstantiation has closed, and its closing makes untenable the carrying forward of the injunction to "make generations." We see that Mama's story is both of that familial repetition and in excess of it.

In the intensity of the relationship between Corregidora and Great Gram it becomes clear that Great Gram's ritual of reproduction and her repetitions are placeholders for a trauma that cannot be got through, placeholders for what Great Gram and Gram withhold from each other and from Mama and Ursa, what they perhaps do not fully know, and what remains unspoken between them: "Experienced too soon, too unexpectedly to be fully known [the traumatic event] . . . is therefore not available to consciousness until it imposes itself again, repeatedly, in the nightmares and repetitive actions of the survivor" (Caruth 1996, 4). This thing experienced too soon reappears to Ursa as a nightmare on the night of her marriage to Tadpole McCormick. It appears in at least three different forms until she arrives at a song:

> While Mama be sleeping, the ole man he crawl into bed
> While Mama be sleeping, the ole man he crawl into bed
> When Mama have wake up, he shaking his nasty ole head
> Don't come here to my house, don't come here to my house I said
> Don't come here to my house, don't come here to my house I said
> Fore you get any this booty, you gon have to lay down dead
> Fore you get any this booty, you gon have to lay down dead (67)[36]

In this moment of repossession, repetition, and difference, Ursa gives voice to a blues song, "a new world song," a song that touches all of their lives. A song that gets at what's between the women and that offers a different response to the unasked question of what Corregidora did to Great Gram in the years after emancipation that was even more intolerable than what she endured during slavery. Having given birth to a child who inhabits a suddenly different yet strikingly similar world, after slavery's end Great Gram still cannot protect Gram from her father, whatever her status with him may be and despite the fact that he is no longer the master. She has no appeal to a taboo on either incest or amalgamation. Great Gram gives birth to a child who cannot bear witness to a slave world that no longer legally exists, but yet that child is forced to live the (after)life of slavery. As for Gram, she must further experience Great Gram's inability to protect her and Great Gram's subsequent abandonment of her to her father as betrayal. But in order to get the transmission Gram has to experience it, as Great Gram and Gram in turn expose Ursa's mother and Ursa to it, in a revenge of sorts for future generations. What, then, is the nature of these family transmissions that at every turn seem to threaten a redoubling of the primal scenes of slavery?

Hysteria

After her hysterectomy, each time Ursa reflects on desire, loss, and her inability to bear children she also wonders about her foremothers' lives and desires, the conditions under which each of them became sexually aware and the impact that awareness under such conditions had on each of them. Then she considers the collective impact on her own life. She is interested in not only the *what* of their repeated stories but also the *how*. How did Corregidora affect each woman individually, and how did he (and more than he, the internalization of a set of desires, power relations, and values identified as "Corregidora") affect the relationships among the women? Ursa thinks about the life of each of her female forbears and the effect that Corregidora has had on them in the past and into the present. She wonders not only *what* they experienced but also *how they felt* living through what they lived through and what was narrated to them. She thinks, "Mama could only know, but they could feel. They were with him. What did they feel?" (102).

> I thought of the girl who had to sleep with her master and mistress. Her father, the master. Her daughter's father. The father of her daughter's daughter. How many generations? *Days that were pages of hysteria. Their survival depended on suppressed hysteria.* She went out and got her daughter, womb swollen with the child of her own father. How many generations had to bow to his genital fantasies? . . . And you with the coffee-bean face, what were you? You were sacrificed. *They knew you only by the signs of your sex.* They touched you as if

you were magic. They ate your genitals. And you, Grandmama, the first mulatto daughter, when did you begin to feel yourself in your nostrils? And, Mama, when did you smell your body with your hands? (59; emphasis mine)

What would it mean for Ursa, the last of the Corregidora women, to refuse the hysterical response of being possessed by the ritualistic narrative that the women tell? Her questions, questions that she's not allowed to ask them, point to her attempt to capture the generations' experiences of sex, power, and what might advisedly be called an awakening of a sexual *self*, as *movement* from sacrifice and almost total consumption, to smelling one's self, to touching one's body. For Ursa a whole family history of desire and sexuality and the attendant monstrous intimacy of that history is condensed in the female sex, the genitals, the womb. She experiences a literal hysteria, four generations of hysteria. Ursa's presence in the world is a function of living under that hysteria: "Days that were pages of hysteria. Their survival depended on suppressed hysteria." The entire narrative of *Corregidora* comes down to the very thing that is the origin of the word *hysteria* itself. What Ursa wants here may indeed be the knowledge that what her mother holds onto is of the same stuff as that which she pushes away. In this lies a key to understanding the nature of blood as it is configured in her present. Ursa also wants to escape from that knowledge, to imagine a sexuality beyond Corregidora, a nonhysterical sexual awakening.

While hysteria is alluded to throughout the text, the word *hysteria* actually appears only three times, each time right after Ursa's hysterectomy. *Hysteria* is the word that Ursa uses in relation to her thwarted desires, and it is the word she uses when she talks to her neighbor Cat Lawson about Cat's sexual involvement with Jeffy, the fourteen-year-old neighbor girl Cat watches and whom Ursa awakes to find "feeling all on [her] up around [her] breasts" (39). The incident later resurfaces on Ursa's and Tadpole's wedding day, when an emotional Cat asks for Ursa's silence about her sexual involvement with Jeffy. By way of explaining her actions to Ursa, Cat relates her kitchen story of sexual trauma involving racism and unwanted sexual advances that she experienced while working in a "white woman's kitchen." After she recounts her story, Cat waits for a sympathetic response from Ursa that Ursa will not give her; instead Ursa asks, "You over your hysteria now?" (66).

Ursa's refusal of any sympathy for Cat is a traumatic and homophobic (and hence itself a hysterical) response, embedded (through the word *hysteria* itself) in the very same hysteria that Ursa has sacrificed her womb to be rid of. Ursa remembers that her great-grandmother was forced to sleep with the master/father and mistress from the age of thirteen to eighteen, that her grandmother was forced to sleep with Corregidora (her father) from a young age, and that her mother was pregnant with her at the age of seventeen or eighteen. In the space between Cat's revelation and any response from her, Ursa thinks of each one of these girlhoods that has been destroyed by sexual trauma. So in addition to undeniable homophobia, I read Ursa's refusal of a sympathetic response to Cat as her vehement response to overhearing Cat's sexual threat to Jeffy, a threat that would repeat on that girl the sort of traumas that have been enacted upon each of the (Corregidora) women and upon Cat herself. (That is, sixty-year-old Cat is fucking fourteen-year-old Jeffy, whom she is in the position of mothering. This for Ursa is unbearable. This too is repeated when Ursa finds Tadpole fucking fifteen-year-old Vivian and finds herself uttering the same threat to Vivian that Cat says to Jeffy.) Ursa's hysterical response, "You over your hysteria now?," is deeply grounded not only in a history she shares with Cat (and all the others in her life) but also in her accidental and intentional *ethical decision* not to repeat.

What Ursa experiences with Cat on a personal level she experiences on a much more symbolic level as well. The "days that were pages of hysteria" and the "suppressed hysteria" on which the Corregidora women's survival depended rely on an incommensurable logic: their continued belief in the law and its emancipatory potential (free womb, emancipation) and their knowledge that their wombs in slavery and after were not their own. In other words, they are in the position of believing in the power of the law to free them at the same time that they know that the law is precisely what has kept them enslaved. The law in all senses, oppressive and protective, appears in one name: Corregidora. Analogously they believe that they can produce freedom and then justice by reproducing slavery and witnessing. It is a strategy born of necessity, a logic that arises from the unbearable conditions of enslavement. But in its repetition it forces the women to reoccupy slavery's evacuated spaces in precisely the same way that Great Gram did. Put another way, when Mutt says that the women's emphasis on making generations could be the slave master's way of thinking, he is precisely right. To be caught in this unbearable situation, in the tension between the law as both emancipatory and enslaving force and the law's connection to the womb, compels the women to seize upon reproduction as *the* means of re-membering into the future. The mothers say, "When the ground and the sky open up to ask them that question that's going to be ask. They think it ain't going to be ask. They have the evidence and give the verdict too. They think they hid everything. But they have the evidence and give the verdict too," (41) revealing that they are marking themselves in a way that Corregidora can see. Re-creating the traumas on and in their bodies they believe that the symbolic "one for whom they bear witness" can see it (41). For example, Mama's statement to Ursa when Ursa lets a boy touch her, "If I could see it, I know you could feel it" (42), also reveals that Mama has come to know a gaze that works the other way around. If the women can feel it, that scar that they need to bear witness, then he, the one for whom they mark themselves, Corregidora or a Corregidora stand-in, some future phantasmatic magistrate or corrector, has to see it.

The suppressed hysteria in *Corregidora* involves a double repression: the repression of the traumatic event that becomes manifest through the symptom, and the repression of the symptom through which the trauma attempts to become visible. The text of *Corregidora* follows the "symbolic substitutions" for the traumas experienced by Great Gram, Gram, and the generations that follow. The fetishized and sacrificed Great Gram (and Gram as well) insists on the necessity of reproduction, insistently attempts to re-member sex and sexual violence. Each daughter's body replaces the papers that in the future would have been the proof that this (slavery, prostitution, ownership, incest) really took place.

Sitting in her lap, Ursa describes Great Gram's hands: "*[They] had lines all over them. It was as if the words were helping her, as if the words repeated again and again could be a substitute for memory, were somehow more than the memory. As if it were only the words that kept her anger. Once when she was talking, she started rubbing my thighs with her hands, and I could feel the sweat on my legs. Then she caught herself, and stopped, and held my waist again*" (11). While Great Gram recites the narrative of generational genital fantasies (sex with Corregidora and his wife) and examines the lines on her hands as if she is reading a text, the story that she tells is not one that is recorded in any written slave narrative, is not one usually recorded in any history.

In the midst of this remembering that would fill the void left by the destroyed evidence, Great Gram catches herself with sweat in her hands, a "something" in her hands that is in excess of the narrative that she tells and that is "transformed into bodily symptoms" (Parker 2001, 9). This something is the narrative of incest that emerges from the scene of her being forced to have sex with the master/father and mistress, a narrative that she must transmit knowing that she most likely will be met with disavowals and disbelief. In recounting the Corregidora narrative and passing it down to her great-granddaughter, Ursa (who is both the excessive product of the narrative and evidence for the narrative's truth in the eyes of some future justice), Great Gram discovers herself with sweaty palms, rubbing the thighs of a child, *her great-granddaughter*. In this scene Great Gram encounters through Ursa and her disbelief the post-slavery refusal to reckon with her story and her daughter's story, and she is forced to reckon with a post-slavery desire (working itself out on Ursa's body) that within the text itself only Martin will explicitly question. Whatever Great Gram feels in relation to Corregidora that gets read as desire is part of the nexus of reasons why she cannot/does not kill him off. The symptom is redoubled, and patriarchal incestuous violence is wed to violence and the desire of the master. The Corregidora women live with the near impossibility that this trauma could be resolved when it is so closely allied with what looks like desire for Corregidora, for recognition, and for the identity that is Corregidora's. Fearful of the same excess in her own life as that indicated by the memory of sweat from Great Gram's palms on her legs, Ursa is rarely able to feel sexual pleasure before the hysterectomy, and now unable either to feel pleasure or to have children. She says, "Afraid of what I'll come to. All that sweat in my hands. . . . *It bothers me that I can't feel anything*" (90). Ursa's fear of what she will "come to" expresses an anxiety about where her desire might flow and is a key to her discomfort with feeling clitoral pleasure and her disbelief, horror, and breakdown when she repeats to the fifteen-year-old Vivian the words with which Cat threatens Jeffy, words that Corregidora (and Great Gram) might have uttered: "I'll give you a fist to fuck" (87). Whatever *sexual* desire Ursa can no longer feel, neither desire itself nor her own urge to sexualized violence has been eradicated.

When Ursa wonders aloud to Tadpole if the hysterectomy has affected her voice, and hence her desire, Tadpole says, "[It] sounded like it had sweat in it. Like you were pulling everything out of yourself" (54). (The second time Ursa speaks this fear is the first time she speaks it to him. What she sees is that her desire is readable not only by Cat but also by Tadpole; in other words, her desire is still recognizable by a man.) Although Ursa attributes the difference in her voice to a physical and not a symbolic reason, she *expects* that the hysterectomy will register in some place other than the place where her womb was. She understands her overcoming of hysteria as at once literal and physical, but also symbolic. About to sing for the first time since her hysterectomy she tells Cat, "They didn't say anything about my throat. They didn't say it did anything to my throat" (44). While there is no empirical evidence that the hysterectomy physically affects her throat, the trauma does change the quality of her voice, which, according to Cat, now sounds, "a little strained. . . . like [she] been through something" (44). The desire that appears in words but also, as Ursa says about her songs, in something behind the words is audible. The sweat in her voice, like the sweat in her great-grandmother's hands in the moment that she starts to rub Ursa's thighs and then stops, indicates an absent presence in the way a symptom does. Might we not see the numerous instances of sweat in *Corregidora* as indications of some absent presence? Something forever lost? A sexuality that Corregidora has forever made impossible, that was always already impossible? The appearance of sweat in the text indicates desire and something more even when that something has been constituted under unbearable conditions. The hysterical symptom is the trace of an identity which, no matter how much it is denied, is more real than what we think "is."

For Juliet Mitchell it is "an alternative representation of a forbidden wish which has broken through from the unconscious, whence it was banished, into consciousness—but in an unrecognizable form" (quoted in Parker 2001, 9). For Ursa that forbidden desire involves her disavowed desire for Mutt (who for her is repeatedly linked to Corregidora), a desire that she fears will be evident in her voice. This disavowed or impossible desire for Mutt and the full pressure of her family hysteria on making generations all come together in her womb. The result is a miscarriage, a hysterectomy, and a change in Ursa's voice. For Great Gram and Gram (and less so for Mama and Ursa) the hysterical symptom may indicate as well the women's libidinous investment in Great Gram's relation to Corregidora, the position from which she derived some power. Part of what they reproduce is a series of relationships that are attempts to harness, for themselves, that very limited power that Great Gram had (or desired to have) in relation to Corregidora. It is a power exemplified in the story of Great Gram's trying to help her runaway male friend and a power that is maintained in relation to a forbidden black male partner (as well as, in Great Gram's case, her power in relation to the white wife who "couldn't do nothing").

The displacement of the women's individual stories and the foreclosing by a ritualized past of a space in which each one might claim desire compel Ursa to go back to visit her mother in the hope that Mama will share *her* own terrible *individual* story, a story that stands apart from the history of the Corregidora women. In the text the ritualized past appears like Ursa's repeated "I said nothing," as a placeholder, a cover story for a past that will not be contained. Ursa visits her mother to ask for the stories that she has heretofore refused to share. In the process of this telling, Mama corrects what Gram had told Ursa to prevent Ursa from asking her mother about her father, Martin. Possessed, she says, by her mother's and grandmother's stories, Mama recalls how her body prepared itself automatically, as if by itself, to have a child. Following by rote a compulsion to reproduce, Mama forswears volition and desire: "They'd tell me, they'd be telling me about making generations, but I wasn't out looking for no man. I never was out looking for no man" (112). In the midst of relating to Ursa the rote story of her conception, Mama stops, corrects herself midrepetition, and offers instead a tentative explanation: "But then I knew it was something my body wanted. Naw. It just seem like I keep telling myself that, and it's got to be something else. It's always something else, but it's easier if it's just that. It just always makes it easier" (116). Mama's repetition of the narrative that echoes her mother's and grandmother's desires is easier than the alternative of acknowledging her own desire and loss. The desire and loss that are always present when Ursa looks at her mother. "That's all I see," says Ursa, "desire and loneliness" (101).

I quote the following excerpt from *Corregidora* in order to further connect the generational genital fantasies to a hysterical symptom. Mama relates to Ursa that after she and Martin were married and living in the house with Great Gram and Gram, Martin became a witness to their ritualistic remembering. Mama begins, "With him there they figured they didn't have to tell me no more, but what they didn't realize was they was telling Martin too" (128–29).

Martin must've started through their room and there she [Gram] was, sitting on that bed in there powdering up under her breasts. I don't know if she seen him or not—this was your grandmama—but she just kept powdering and humming, and looking down at her breasts, and lifting them up and powdering under them, and there he was just standing in the door with his arms spread up over the door, and sweat showing through his shirt, just watching her. I don't know what kind of expression he had on his face. His lips were kind of smiling, but his eyes wasn't. He seen me and he just kept standing there. I was looking at Mama and then looking up at him, after he seen me the first time he just kept looking at her. She was acting like she didn't know we was there, but *I know she had to know.* He was just standing there hypnotized or something, I know she knew. She knew it, cause they both knew he wasn't getting what he wanted from me. . . . There she was just sitting there lifting up her breasts. I don't know when it was she decided she'd let him know she seen him, but then all a sudden she set the box of powder down and looked up. Her eyes got real hateful. "You black bastard, watching me. What you doing watching me, you black bastard?" . . . He started over there where she was, but I got between them. "Martin, don't." He just kept looking at me, like it was me he was hating, but it was her he was calling a half-white heifer. Her powder and him sweating all up under his arms, and me holding him. . . .

"Messing with my girl, you ain't had no right messing with my girl." (129–30)

It is in this narrative that the transgenerational trauma, the intimacy of family, and the interpersonal relations of the gaze, desire, and power all come together, and each person is aware that the other sees it. Mama moves within this recitation from recounting the uncertainty of the moment about Gram's knowing she and Martin are there to the certain knowledge that she does indeed know because of Gram's explicit rebuke of Martin. Mama knows that Gram taunts Martin, who knows intimately the way that desire works in the household; Mama says, "They [Gram and Martin] both knew he wasn't getting what he wanted from me" (130). Powdering under her breasts Gram explicitly evokes sexual desire and the gaze; she has internalized Corregidora's desires and identity along with her desire for revenge against him. Her saying "You black bastard watching me. What you doing watching me" repeats Corregidora's injunction against "his women" having relations with black men. Her statement, her entangled desires keep Corregidora and his desires alive. Any desire on the part of Mama or Ursa is caught in this gaze. Desire can only be monstrous.

Mama's story is one example of the ways that the women's bearing witness to slavery that was both directly experienced and indirectly experienced by them reproduces the space of enslavement post-enslavement, both among the women and with the people with whom they make a family. It illustrates the effects of transmitting these internalized generational genital fantasies. The horror of Great Gram's experiences, as well as her own, are reproduced by Gram and the slave master's injunction "Let nothing black touch you." Corregidora, who was dark like a "coal creek Indian," "wouldn't let [Great Gram] see him [the enslaved black man]": "He said he was too black for me. He liked his womens black but he didn't wont us with no black mens. It wasn't color cause he didn't even wont us with no light black mens, cause there was a man down there as light as he was, but he didn't even wont us with him, cause there was one girl he caught with him, and had her beat, and sold the man over to another plantation" (123–24). The injunction's repetition becomes evidence of the women's carrying forward Corregidora's desires as their own; it is evidence as well of Gram's attempt to bear the doubling of incest and amalgamation. What does "Incest is amalgamation" mean now? In the New World was incest always amalgamation?

Emptied of their original referential substance and preserved as a ritual, the injunction "Let nothing black touch you," first uttered by the jealous slave master to his "Dorita," is more than overpowering evidence of the absent presence of Corregidora, more than the effects of a whole set of familial power relations, and more than the internalized viewpoint of Corregidora. The memory of the horrors of enslavement and Corregidora's power over them is further internalized and reproduced through making generations and through the interactions of the women among themselves, incorporating as well the men with whom they would make a family. Ursa remembers that Mama would ask herself, "*How can it be [that] Corregidora . . . gave orders to whores, the father of his daughter and his daughter's daughter?*" Ursa continues, "*They'd tell theirs and then they'd look at her [Mama] to bear them witness. But what could she say? She could only tell me what they'd told her. How can it be? She was the only one who asked that question, though. For the others it was just something that was, something they had, and something they told. But when she talked it was like she was asking that question for them, and for herself too"* (102). Great Gram and Gram are held in place through their repetitions of their relations with Corregidora; they obey absolutely the compulsion, and they forbid each other and their daughters to ask the questions that might begin to alter the repetition.

What Great Gram and Gram want to pass on, preserve, and keep available in addition to history is the space from which Great Gram derived some power in enslavement. To do so they reproduce a series of relationships post-enslavement in the move from Brazil to North America, by which they attempt to harness the power Great Gram had in relation to Corregidora, in relation to the other enslaved and prostituted women, in relation to black men, in relation to white women such as Corregidora's wife, who "couldn't do a damn thing" (23), and that they have in relation to each other. They willfully carry forth the transgenerational racial hatred, sexual violence, and incestuous violation as a symbolic power that acknowledges and redoubles a legal continuum of the captivity of black bodies before and after slavery. They reproduce their attempts to repeat, to refuse, to cover over the shifts that have already taken place in the world and in their own understanding of what they are reproducing.

Better Than in the Beginning

Everything said in the beginning must be said better than in the beginning.
—**GAYL JONES**, *Corregidora*

The blues are not worth the dues [paid] in order to produce them, but they are a part of the condition of possibility of the end of such extortion.
—**FRED MOTEN**, "Black Mo'nin'"

The blues remembers everything the country forgot.
—**GIL SCOTT HERON**, *Bicentennial Blues*

Let us return to a beginning in order to say it (sing it) better in the blues. In the beginning is sexual trauma: trauma that Ursa lives through, trauma that precedes her birth, and trauma that is narrated to her often and often introjected indirectly, trauma she reproduces. The beginning preceded Ursa over several generations and it is imposed on her with violence. From the age of five Ursa repeatedly hears of Corregidora's violent sexual exploitation of her great-grandmother and grandmother, and she experiences firsthand predatory, invasive sexuality. From the beginning Ursa's encounters with sex are mediated through the stories that she overhears, the conflicts and sex acts to which she is a voyeur, and the sexual encounters and violence that her peers and foremothers talk about and attempt to enact on her.[37] These encounters, like Ursa's fall down the stairs at Happy's Café, are always situated at the nexus of the *I* and the *eye.* There is no break in the telling of the stories, no point at which the stories are not present, and no point at which the Corregidora women escape scopophilic violence.

When Ursa is five years old her mother sees her playing with a neighbor boy named Henry. Ursa remembers:

> He bet me I didn't know how to play doctor. I bet him I did. We'd made a seesaw by putting a board across a tree stump. I lay across the board on my belly, and he raised up my dress. Mama saw us. . . .
>
> She jerked me in the back door by the arm, and slammed the door.
>
> "Don't you know what that boy was doing? He was feeling up your asshole."
>
> "I couldn't feel it."
>
> "If I could see it, I know you could feel it."
>
> "Mama, I couldn't feel it."
>
> "Get on in here. Have people looking at you. What do you think, the neighbors ain't got eyes?" (42)

In this passage Mama's emphasis on the gaze overrides all other considerations of what Ursa might have felt or understood to have happened. In another play on vision, time, and perspective, this scene on the seesaw between Ursa and Henry that Mama witnesses is another instance where inside, outside, sex, and violence meet. It is as if this scene between Ursa and Henry acts out precisely what the mothers are afraid of: not just sex but also sex that can be witnessed, something beyond what Ursa can immediately perceive. After all, part of what distinguished Great Gram from the other enslaved prostitutes was that she was "cultivated" and had a "private room," whereas "some of the others there had to be three or four or five whores fucking in the same room" (124). The women maintain a class difference that is part of what they transmit through the generations. Their sense of class combined with their experience of race is also the source of the problem that they have with Ursa singing the blues in public.

Although they listen to the blues in private, Ursa sings about sex and desire in public places where men, black men, watch her. The women's disapproval of Ursa's career coincides with Mutt's disapproval ("I don't like those mens messing with you. . . . Mess with they eyes"). In the childhood seesaw scene, in spite of Ursa's protests that she didn't feel anything and that nothing happened, Mama insists, "If I could see it, I know you could feel it." On the surface Mama is stating the obvious and chiding the five-year-old Ursa for her denial, but Mama's comment effectively retrospectively encapsulates the logic of the Corregidora women's repetitions. First, Ursa is told to believe in a sexual violation that anyone can see but that she herself cannot experience. Second, the women re-create the traumas on and in their bodies because, in doing so, they (unconsciously) believe that the one for whom they bear witness must be able to see it. Thus Mama's statement that insists on what Ursa must feel, "If I could see it, I know you could feel it," also implies the reverse. If the women can feel it, that scar that they need to bear witness to, then he, the one for whom they make visible the mark in themselves, Corregidora or a Corregidora stand-in, can see it (and be subject to justice). The gaze of some (magisterial) other who could judge against Corregidora would also incorporate Corregidora's being compelled to see himself for what he is. It would amount to the Law confessing itself before itself. This, then, gets to the crux of their irresolvable resentment: Corregidora is never going to accept that what he did was a crime. The point of view that the women need to see and to have see itself (and which never will) is nonetheless part of them.

In the encounter that Ursa has with Cat in regard to Jeffy, Ursa is angry because Cat makes Jeffy aware of sexual violence too soon, a too soon awareness that Ursa has experienced in her own life. The questions that Ursa is unable to ask Cat are similar to the questions that she is unable to ask her foremothers: "What are you doing to the girl?. . . What about when it comes her time?" (65). What effects will Cat's actions and desires have on Jeffy's future? What Ursa reacts to between Cat and Jeffy is more than the fact of sex between two women (and the age and power differential); she also reacts to the possibility foreclosed in this exchange, to a series of foreclosures that, from her experience, carry into the future. Move forward from Ursa's earliest experiences of the stories of Corregidora and the scene on the seesaw and Mama's intervention to the adolescent Ursa hiding from

Henry in the house, to the twenty-five-year-old Ursa who still cannot feel anything. Her numbness in the scene with Henry is a hysterical symptom of a sexual trauma experienced long before. And what she seems to feel is contingent upon something someone else (some other eye or I) witnessed.

Ursa's hysterical symptoms are repeatedly manifested as aphasia and numbness, an inability to speak her desire ("I said nothing") and an inability to feel sexual pleasure ("I felt nothing"). Silence, transcribed in the text as the repeated "I said nothing," often stands in place of a response by Ursa to a direct question. In this space marked by the unspoken word are the blues, a blue(s) note. These silences at the level of *Corregidora*'s narrative structure inhere in what the text withholds (and thereby reveals) through ellipsis, flashback, ritualized dialogue, incomplete sentences, and Ursa's being described as having said nothing. For Jennifer Cognard-Black, "To write that there was silence erases the act of writing as a practice of revelation, sharing, communication; . . . to say nothing revokes meaning even as the words themselves appear to say something. . . . Ursa Corregidora . . . refuses to make reading easy for us" (2001, 41).[38] Cognard-Black is correct that Jones does not make reading easy, but the text of *Corregidora* invites an analysis of the process of reading. By indicating in the narrative *when* and *that* Ursa says nothing Jones records Ursa's withholding, which is an utterance in itself. "I said nothing" is a response that refuses linguistic signifiers. Again, if hysteria appears through the symptom, then suppressed hysteria involves also a repression of the structures through which the symptom becomes visible. The "I said nothing" is then a repetition with a difference, a textual placeholder for the blues note. Rather than a suppression of hysteria, the "I said nothing" marks the recognition of the reemergence of the symptom, marks the space of trauma, and marks what is refused a narrative structure. The very insistence with which the phrase "I said nothing" appears in the text, at times when Ursa wants to say something but does not, gestures to the insistent emergence of desire and the symptom as well as to Ursa's desire to withhold, to claim something for herself that is not a part of an already marked-out economy. Ursa's desire declares to the reader that there is something that she either cannot give or that she refuses to give or to give up.

Called on not only to be a witness to Great Gram's enslavement and the Corregidora women's survival but also to mark herself and reproduce horror on her body and into the next generation, Ursa acknowledges that after the hysterectomy she has a scar of her own. The evidence that she will hold up to bear witness to the horrors of slavery and its prolonged effects is *her* body, evidence she can feel. She bears a scar that is "worse when you touch it than when you look at it" (18). Ursa herself has to take on what the symbolic, phantasmatic Corregidora would have been made to feel. Unable to "make generations," Ursa says that that "part of [her] life's already marked out for [her]—the barren part" (6). Her body is indeed marked out; the boundaries and the limits of it are located. The Corregidora stories will stop with her, will not extend through reproduction into another generation. To mark out is also to obliterate or to cancel with a mark, and like the "I said nothing" in the text another articulation of repressed hysteria is marked out.

Hysteria and blood and property have come together in Ursa's body to point to what is hidden under the sign of slavery and the sign of freedom; the hysteria is the marker of the moment when amalgamation and incest in the New World were the same taboo and then that moment's repression. The womb was her mark, the signifier of the prescribed meaning of her life: to make generations to bear witness. This brings us back to the Corregidora complex, the constellation of desires in family relationships that include, in addition to patriarchy and incest, miscegenation and slavery. The hysteria in the text points to those things that still cannot be revealed. Though marked out, they remain hidden in the text, a mark of a double marking out that must be read.[39]

The hysterectomy that Ursa undergoes marks her permanently but also ends her particular narrative of marking, ends this story's transmission to the next generation. After the hysterectomy Ursa recognizes that she questions the necessity, the ethics of making memory in the same ways as her foremothers. Though she still feels subsumed by "what they had," she already questions the hegemony of their story: "But I am different now. . . . I have everything they had, except the generations. I can't make generations. And even if I still had my womb, even if that first baby had come— what would I have done then? Would I have kept it up? Would I have been like her, or them?" (60). Ursa now works on transforming into song the words Gram and Great Gram forced into her: "[She] sang it as they hummed it." As she says, "They squeezed Corregidora into me, and I sung back in return" (145). She reconfigures the need to witness that precipitated the demand for bodily reproduction into artistic production: "Let me give witness the only way I can. I'll make a fetus out of grounds of coffee to rub inside my eyes. When it's time to give witness I'll make a fetus out of grounds of coffee. I'll stain their hands" (54). They push Corregidora in and she forces him out. Coffee grounds (signifying on the coffee-bean woman Great Gram, Cat's sexual trauma, Mutt's work in coffee and tobacco, and the production connected to black bodies) figure in the text as a means of bearing witness that is not reproductive. Likewise it is through the blues, the form that "remembers everything the country forgot," that Ursa bears witness to slavery and desire in ways that signify for the descendants of North and South American slavery.[40]

During her recovery from the hysterectomy, while she stays in Tadpole's apartment, Ursa and Tadpole have the following exchange about Ursa's now impossible desire:

> "What do you want, Ursa?"
> I looked at him with a slight smile that left quickly. "What do you mean?"
> "What I said. What do you want?"
> I smiled again. "What all us Corregidora women want. Have been taught to want. To make generations." I stopped smiling.
> He looked at me. "What do you want, Ursa?"
> "More than yourself?"
> He raised me and kissed me very hard. (22)

Tadpole's insistent "What do you want, Ursa?" is precisely what Ursa cannot answer and what none of the Corregidora women can readily answer. It is in this context that Ursa expresses desire for someone else. When Tadpole asks her what she wants, the injunction to make generations, Corregidora, and the law emerge to make visible the structure of desire itself, the colonization of the individual through language.

A similar exchange is repeated on the final page of the text, this time between Ursa and Mutt, twenty-two years after their separation. Before their reunion we have, for the first time in the text, some idea of the interior of their relationship, when Jones provides a context in which there is jealousy over other men, as well as jealousy over the stories that Ursa holds and withholds. When Mutt "knocks his piece of shit" down the stairs he says it is the alternative to auctioning off Ursa, selling himself "a piece of ass." Twenty-two years later he reasons that his grandfather, who bought his grandmother out of enslavement only to have her "repossessed" because of a fabricated debt, would not approve of his auctioning off Ursa. He tells her, "It wasn't on account of you, it was on account of my great-grandaddy. Seeing as how he went through all that for his woman, he wouldn't have appreciated me selling you off" (160).

In another repetition of Mutt's jealousy, prior to his return his cousin Jimmy arrives at the Spider (the club where Ursa sings after she leaves Tadpole and Happy's) to hear Ursa sing. Drunk, as Mutt was twenty-two years earlier, Jimmy interrupts Ursa's singing with "You show your ass to these mens and then when they try to get on it, you say Uh-uh, uh-uh" (179). When Ursa learns that Mutt too is back in town and that he will sooner or later come to the Spider, she thinks, "I won't say I don't think of Mutt Thomas, because I do. . . . I don't know what I was feeling. A numbness." But as she continues she admits to feeling. "I was excited," she says, "yes, that's what I was" (180, 182).

The reunion that takes place between Mutt and Ursa occurs after Mutt reveals to her that he too has been overtaken by traumatic memories. He reminds Ursa of the story of his great-grandfather and great-grandmother, and this time he adds, "After they took her, when he went crazy he wouldn't eat nothing but onions and peppermint. Eat the onions so people wouldn't come around him, and then eat the peppermint so they would. I tried it but it didn't do nothing but make me sick" (183–84). As Ashraf Rushdy writes, "Mutt is no longer demanding of Ursa that she 'forget' the past, as he had earlier asked her to do, since he himself has attempted to act out an historical incident in order to determine what knowledge it could give him. His answer, therefore, is that the past needs to be recalled but not relived, at least not relived in the register in which Ursa has been reliving it" (2000, 280). Mutt and Ursa now each recognize the repetition of the past, and they realize that this kind of repetition makes one sick.

In the Drake Hotel after their reunion, when she is about to perform fellatio on Mutt, Ursa says, "It wasn't the same room, but the same place. The same feel of the place. I knew what he wanted. I wanted it too. We got out of our clothes. I got between his knees" (184). What is it that allows the articulation of this desire (for Mutt, for feeling, for the pleasure of giving pleasure) that Ursa has not spoken in words for twenty-two years? Is it that she has acknowledged, in receiving her mother's story and in telling Mama parts of her own, that the person to whom Mama attaches feelings of desire and who could possibly "remake [her mother's] world" is Martin, and for Ursa that person is Mutt?

Positioned between Mutt's knees Ursa admits that she both hates and desires Mutt. She remembers what has passed between them, the violence and her (and his) unfulfilled desires, and she does not "wait to be fucked." Instead she initiates fellatio, the thing that she would never do and the thing that Mutt would think that she would refuse him. In this sexual reunion in the same hotel but not the same room from twenty-two years before, they stage a reunion full of direct references to the past and yet distinct from that past, and Ursa, like Mama before her, becomes Great Gram and Gram. As always the sexual encounters in Ursa's present connect her to some sexual encounter either in her own or in her foremothers' pasts, and in this she repeats them, exceeds them, and reverses them. Ursa is clearly thinking about Great Gram and Corregidora and also about Mutt and herself and her mother and Martin. But unlike Mama and the grandmothers, as Ursa reflects on the past she thinks about the women's individual histories, the relationships among them, and their relationships with men. She is overcome by knowledge of Great Gram's actions, and she knows that in a "moment of excruciating pain and pleasure at the same time" it "must have been something sexual" (that she bit Corregidora's penis or threatened to) that Great Gram did to Corregidora. In the process of an unknowing reenactment Ursa says, "In a split second I knew what it was, in a split second of love and hate I knew what it was, and *I think he might have known too*" (184; emphasis mine). This knowledge is something that Ursa believes she and Mutt share.

Ursa recounts the scene with Mutt: "I held his ankles. It was like I didn't know how much was me and how much was Great Gram and Corregidora —like Mama when she had started talking like Great Gram. But was what Corregidora had done to *her*, to *them*, any worse than what Mutt has done to me, than what we had done to each other, than what Mama had done to Daddy, or what he had done to her in return, making her walk down the street looking like a whore?" (184). What Ursa knows when she twice tells Mutt "I could kill you" is that what has happened between Great Gram and Corregidora, between Corregidora and Gram, and for that matter between Mama and Martin and Ursa and Mutt is an intolerable intimate violence.

He came and I swallowed. He leaned back, pulling me up by the shoulders.

"I don't want a kind of woman that hurt you," he said.

"Then you don't want me."

"I don't want a kind of woman that hurt you."

"Then you don't want me."

"I don't want a kind of woman that hurt you."

"Then you don't want me."

He shook me till I fell against him crying. "I don't want a kind of man that'll hurt me neither," I said.

He held me tight. (185)

At the end of *Corregidora* a blues song returns us to the beginning of this hysterical text and to the beginning of the Corregidora women's hysteria. The movement in the text is from Great Gram, "Dorita," to Gram, who has no proper name (unmoored, her birth is the moment at which something could change but does not, as she remains a Corregidora), to Mama (Irene, nicknamed Correy), to Ursa Corregidora (which means "to bear witness in order to correct" and who is also called U.C., "you see"). The act of fellatio brings Ursa back to Great Gram and Corregidora and perhaps most significantly to Gram, the one who never knew.

Gram occupies a space in which there is a change. Her story might have been marked as different from Great Gram's; instead her story and the story of the vexed relationships between the women are largely subsumed under the reproduction of the Corregidora complex. Despite this insistent repetition, when Gram repeats Great Gram's narrative, her repetition refuses the certainty of Great Gram's story (of "who to hate" and "what evil look like"), and she adds feeling to rote memorization. In the midst of a repetition of what she survived when she was left alone with Corregidora (her father, the father of her daughter, her lover and her mother's) Gram tells Ursa, "It's hard to always remember what you were feeling when you ain't feeling it exactly that way no more" (79). "Perhaps," as Marianne Hirsch writes, "it is *only* in subsequent generations that trauma can be witnessed and worked through, by those who were not there to live it but who received its effects, belatedly, through the narratives, actions and symptoms of the previous generation" (2001, 12). In Ursa's life several generations of familial and personal repetitions are condensed. Ursa is snatched from the seesaw by her mother, held in place in Great Gram's lap, and snatched by her mother from the first place where she sings the blues; likewise Mutt attempts to remove her from the stage at Happy's.

Corregidora both begins and ends with a physical struggle between Mutt and Ursa in which his arms are around her. In the first instance, when they meet at the juncture of intimacy, violence, and control, Mutt grabs Ursa around the waist, from behind, and she "falls." In the second instance they meet twenty-two years later at the same juncture. This time, though, they acknowledge and refuse violence, and they both speak their "hate and desire. Two humps on the same camel" (102). Jones said, "I think what comes out in my work, in those particular novels [*Corregidora* and *Eva's Man*], is an emphasis on brutality. But I think that something else is also suggested in them . . . namely the alternative to brutality, which is tenderness. Although the main emphasis . . . is on the blues relationships or relationships involving brutality, there seems to be a growing understanding, working itself out especially in *Corregidora*, of what is required in order to be genuinely tender. . . . Perhaps brutality enables one to recognize what tenderness is" (quoted in Tate 1979, 147).

At the conclusion of *Corregidora* what comes to Ursa in the act of fellatio is how to *connect* her song (*"While Mama be sleeping, the ole man he crawl into bed"*) to her newly gained knowledge of what compelled Great Gram finally to break with Corregidora. In "a moment of pleasure and excruciating pain at the same time, a moment of broken skin but not sexlessness, a moment just before sexlessness, a moment that stops just before sexlessness, a moment that stops before it breaks the skin," Ursa arrives at an understanding of slavery, post-slavery, power, and familial relations, whose outward signs indicate another repetition of a master narrative of submission or affection (184). The monstrous intimacies are the original trauma and the subsequent repetitions. The form itself stretches out the difference, elaborates the movement from line to line. With each rhythmic elaboration of the breaks between and before actions (or lines) Jones attends to the contingency of power, pleasure, and desire. In *Corregidora* we are made to see that more complex elaborations of slavery "as the ghost in the machine of kinship" of post-slavery American subjectivity are long overdue and that the spaces for witnessing through particular kinds of disavowal, repetition, reoccupation, and reanimation are already long past.

TWO

Bessie Head, Saartje Baartman, and *Maru*

Redemption, Subjectification, and the Problem of Liberation

Before the white man became universally disliked for his mental outlook it was there. The white man found only too many people who looked *different*. That was all that outraged the receivers of his discrimination, that he applied the technique of the wild jiggling dance and the rattling tin cans to any one who was not a white man. And if the white man thought that Asians were a low filthy nation, Asians could still smile with relief—at least they were not Africans. And if the white man thought that Africans were a low, filthy nation, Africans in South Africa could still smile—at least they were not Bushmen. They all have their monsters. You just have to look different from them, the way the facial features of a Sudra or a Tamil do not resemble the facial features of a high caste Hindu, then seemingly anything can be said and done to you as your outer appearance reduces you to the status of a non-human being.

In Botswana they say: Zebras, Lions, Buffalo and Bushmen live in the Kalahari Desert. If you can catch a Zebra, you can walk up to it, forcefully open its mouth and examine its teeth. The Zebra is not supposed to mind because it is an animal. Scientists do the same to Bushmen and they are not supposed to mind, because there is no one they can still turn round to and say, "At least I am not a ——." Of all things that are said about oppressed people, the worst things are said and done to the Bushmen. Ask the scientists. Haven't they yet written a treatise on how Bushmen are an oddity of the human race, who are half the head of a man and half the body of a donkey? Because you don't go poking around into the organs of people unless they are animals or dead.

—**BESSIE HEAD,** *Maru*

There is a long, established, and diverse history dating back several centuries in Europe, southern Africa, and elsewhere of constructing "Bushman" perceived racial difference and sexual difference as radically other, and then positioning those Bushmen as people to and with whom anything can be done materially and discursively.[1] In much (white) South African writing the Bushman (KhoiSan), the mulatto, and the so-called coloured in apartheid's racial nomenclature were each, individually and at times interchangeably, figures of monstrosity, their presence an indicator of national disease, and their bodies useful materials for the nation's reconstructions of itself.[2] The practice of representing Bushmen as less than fully human continues in contemporary popular constructions of them (across geographical region and political spectrum) as still monstrous, as still a limit where the human becomes less than human, as still a space in which there is a mix of the human with something else.[3] In this chapter I examine Bessie Head's second novel, *Maru* (1971), and her depiction of a "Masarwa" woman in light of those histories as well as the history of representing Saartje Baartman and in light of Botswana's independence in 1966, what Modupe Olaogun identifies as Head's engagement with "slavery and enslavement, conceived of as the ultimate antithesis of independence and of the rights to personal liberty, . . . [her] sensitivity to a long view of the history of causes, or to an etiology that is simultaneously introspective and prospective" (2002, 172). I also examine *Maru* in relation to Head as a writer in exile from South Africa and in relation to the history of the KhoiSan woman Saartje Baartman, including the return in 2002 to democratic South Africa of most of her remains.[4] When we read Head's polemic in *Maru*—"They all have their monsters. . . . Of all things that are said about oppressed people, the worst things are said and done to the Bushmen. . . . *Haven't they yet* written a treatise on how Bushmen are an oddity of the human race, who are half the head of a man and half the body of a donkey?"—we see her concern with continuing unfreedom (1971, 11–12; emphasis mine).

Head, I will argue, is also particularly attentive to the history of apartheid's strategic naming and placement of a "coloured" race in South Africa and to the coloureds' own too willing occupation of that space of more privilege (than blacks). In a number of essays published between 1962 and 1965, Head writes about the shame and the contestations and contradictions faced by those who are produced by and inhabit the space of coloured. Constructed as an in-between category, coloureds were "defined by apartheid laws in a doubly *negative* manner as those who are both non-White and non-black African" (Western 1997, 9); as a general category they were South Africans simultaneously accorded certain juridical legal privileges relative to blacks but subject to some of the same restrictive prohibitions. In "An Unspeakable Crime" (1963), Head wonders why "coloureds are running over each to lend an ear to the government and its good boys" (1990, 8). She wants coloureds to stop siding with the oppressive state in exchange for partial status, to resist assisting the state's intrusion into their lives, to resist being "intentional supporters of the intolerable status quo" (8). Her writing in this period in South Africa and Botswana is fundamentally concerned with power, with apartheid's eugenicist ethnographic thrust, the limits imposed on ordinary life in South Africa, the imaginative constraints she cannot fully escape, and those injuries she has "never forgotten" despite leaving South Africa and "borrow[ing] the clothes of a country like Botswana" for the "purposes of [her] trade" as a writer (1989b, 143).

I analyze *Maru* and Head's depictions of *Maru*'s "Masarwa" (Bushman) character as part of a trenchant critique of ethnocentrism and racialism and as an exploration of the historical and ongoing subjugation of KhoiSan (Masarwa, coloured, and black) peoples in the midst of liberation. (Both critiques are from the point of view of one who is a victim of this system and yet within the structure of apartheid has certain privileges relative to others.) I then draw a heuristic analogy between Head's critique of racialism and the politics of exclusion in relation to the Masarwa Margaret Cadmore and the repeated presentations and representations of the early-nineteenth-century KhoiSan woman known as Saartje Baartman.[5] Baartman, whose life I detail later in the chapter, was brought from the Cape colony to England in 1810 and was exhibited in Europe as the "Hottentot Venus." The quotation from *Maru* with which I open this chapter connects the novel thematically to the life of Baartman, who was presented in Europe in life and in death as a scientific specimen. Proceeding from several textual and speculative points, I draw together a brief history of representations of Baartman, a reading of Head's biography, which I analyze in the context of reading *Maru*, and Head's documentation of indigenous forms of inherited bondage that continue in the midst of African liberation. I argue that questions of shame and the narratives that frame representations of Baartman's life and the (in)ability to read her resistance in them have an uncanny resonance with Head's life and work and with the ways that her life and work have been taken up by some of her biographers and critics. I read in *Maru* Head's attempt to create a space from which one might imagine imagining real liberation through suspending oppressive social relations as they are passed on, constituted, and reproduced in the present. Head's concern "with the trends that will evolve in Southern Africa, with independence" (Marquard 1978–79, 52–53) positions us at the beginning and end of *Maru* to join in the work of imagining, holding open, a space of freedom for and with those people who continue to live *psychic, actual,* and what Orlando Patterson has identified as *social* death in the midst of national liberation and other putative freedoms.

The plot of *Maru* is fairly simple. It follows a Masarwa woman who is orphaned as an infant by the death of her birth mother, and who subsequently is adopted, named after, and educated by a white woman named Margaret Cadmore, the wife of an English missionary living in Botswana. The novel focuses on the drama of the power of the hierarchizing gaze (scopophilic relations that involve science and history) to fix people in place as central to the text's exploration of young Margaret Cadmore's relationship to her adoptive mother, her experiences in secondary school and teachers college, and the relations and power struggles that ensue once she takes up a teaching position in a rural Tswana village. Margaret Cadmore Jr., a young Masarwa woman, grows up to exceed all sociocultural possibilities for one in her outcast position.[6] She is formally educated, becomes a primary school teacher, and then marries the eponymous Maru, a member of the Tswana elite and Dilepe village's would-be paramount chief. Most important, Margaret speaks what is unspeakable for someone in her social position. She says, "I am a Masarwa" and "But I am not ashamed of being a Masarwa," and in doing so she becomes the unconscious embodiment of the resistance to power (Head 1971, 24).[7] The Masarwa, Head tells us, are members of "a conquered tribe, the Basarwa or Bushmen [about whom] it is argued that they were the true owners of the land in some distant past, that they had been conquered by the more powerful Botswana tribes and from then onwards assumed the traditional role of slaves" (1990, 68–69). That the Tswana elite in *Maru* speak of owning Masarwa slaves as a matter of course clearly indicates that present as well as historical KhoiSan dispossession, enslavement, and display form part of the physical and cultural geography that Head encounters, that she is affected by, and that she writes directly in response to while living in Botswana. This is the geography within which Head constructs Margaret Cadmore Jr. as a woman with an uncanny double presence: a woman who appears both entirely within the production of the racialized society and as a dangerous excess with effects of her own. She embodies several strands of KhoiSan history (of which Baartman, and the uses to which she was and is put, is a defining figure), and she exceeds that history to the point of threatening it as she embodies it. The bulk of the novel is focused on Margaret Jr.'s signifying excess, the effects of oppression on her (and on the Masarwa), and her effects on power and the Tswana elites of Dilepe village.

When *Maru* was completed in 1969 Head had already lived for five years as a stateless person in Botswana. Three years after Botswana's independence and during another period of political struggle that saw the emergence of black power movements elsewhere in southern Africa and in the Diaspora, there were a growing number of independent states and independence movements on the continent, and Head had already experienced several disappointments. One disappointment was that restrictions on refugees were not eased: "[When] Botswana became independent in 1966, [it was] with a government that turned out to have an extremely hostile policy toward South African refugees. In 1966 they put us on a police roll, and from then to this day I have been reporting to the police every week" (1990, 27). In 1969 Head already knew that independence would result only in something *like* liberation. She already knew that the myriad oppressions that fell outside of the most recognized racialized forms of the colonizer-colonized dyad were in danger of remaining unspoken and unaddressed. She knew from her life and her research that the effects of those silences and humiliations and the shame that produced and reinforced them were ongoing and debilitating. She knew too that she was as susceptible to being the oppressor in her own turn as she was to being the oppressed, that "nothing prevented a communication between me and Botswana people and nothing prevented me from slipping into the skin of a Mosarwa person" (69). Given the brutal history of collecting "trophy heads" and the skin of murdered KhoiSan people, Head's "slipping into the skin" of a Masarwa has specific historical resonance. For Head, though, this getting inside the skin of the other (that is also the not disavowed self) was not to produce scientific evidence; it was in order to live the "affect of this engagement" (Bending 2002, 120).

Because Head experienced what did *not* change in Botswana's transition from protectorate to independent nation, her centering *Maru* on the figure of the Masarwa Margaret Cadmore Jr., a person in a *double* position (a privileged and a nonprivileged position), is one way that she asks the question posed by the presence of the KhoiSan: "What [does one] do with the in-between person" (who haunts nationalist, colonialist, and imperialist discourses and movements)? Through an in-between person in this double position, Head creates a redoubling, a woman who embodies the contradiction of the system but as an excess impossible for the social system.

Maru was written in response as well to lived exclusion and the socio-cultural anxiety about the place of the in-between, miscegenated person that Head and her son experienced in Botswana as African ethnocentrism and violence. In a letter to Randolph Vigne Head links this experience to the dismay that she feels about the black nationalism exemplified by Stokely Carmichael's Black Power speech at the Dialectics of Liberation Conference.[8] She writes, "This shout of rage of Mr Stokely Carmichael is a shout from the depths of the deep, true exultant power he is receiving from being the man down there. It's a kind of power that leaps up from the feet to the head in a drunken ecstasy. I feel Mr Stokely does not know this. He might fall down on his knees and glorify his enemy. I feel these things go on in the subconscious and we give them the wrong names" (Vigne 1991, 55).[9]

Concerned with what Head identifies and experiences as the pitfalls of a *certain kind* of exclusive pan-African black consciousness, I also read *Maru* as a prescient account of the dilemmas facing postapartheid South Africa and the construction of the new nation symbolized partly through the return and interment of Saartje Baartman's remains. In the nineteenth century "when many people looked at Baartmann, they saw not only racial and sexual alterity but also a personification of current debates about the right to liberty versus the right to property" (Magubane 2001, 827).[10] What current debates and everyday brutalities are made visible or masked in the representations of Baartman in the twentieth century and the twenty-first and in her return to South Africa in 2002? What is being shored up through the retroactive subjectification of Baartman and the reclamation of her from and for history, when that work is most often connected to a cultural and national(ist) project? In a project that I identify broadly as redemptive, what might be the effects of various communities claiming Baartman as an ancestor?[11] I want to problematize redemption, and I turn to Baartman not to somehow "redeem [her] beyond the discourse of racial alterity" but in the interest of thinking through why representations of, deployments of, and claims to her figure so centrally and powerfully in postapartheid constructions of South African national (racial) identity (Hobson 2005, 3). Looking at the symbolic work that Baartman is made to do in the present, what might Head's creation, just a few years after Botswana's independence, of an outcast Masarwa woman's encounters with power allow us to see now?

While many activists, scholars, and artists who write about Baartman are deeply interested in restorative justice for her (and as she stands in for KhoiSan, coloured, and black people) and are often interested in speculative history as well, I ask that we look more closely at the work that some of these projects do in terms of laying claim to a historically erased national (un)belonging. What would it mean for this work to be *for* Baartman? Is redemption possible? How does such redemption really work? How is it effective? Are projects of speculative history different from those that seek redemption? The distinguishing features of the better redemptive projects include considerations of the uses to which Baartman was put in the West and situate the display and dissection of her body firmly within a history of conquest, resistance, and racial science in southern Africa; redemption nevertheless imposes a particular totalizing narrative frame. In the end I argue that the work of redemption (and what must remain unspoken in such narratives) is no more *for* Baartman than are the other, more explicitly objectifying projects. As a political strategy, redemption, with its double emphasis on "deliverance from sin *and its consequences* [by the atonement of Jesus Christ, for example]"[12] (emphasis mine), replaces a real reckoning with history (state brutality, colonialism, slavery, apartheid, ethnocentrism, truth and reconciliation) and its consequences with a symbolic sacrifice; it demands that some atrocities remain unspoken and unspeakable. In contrast, the act of reclamation, the "calling or bringing back [something or someone] from wrong-doing" as an appeal "at law" or "protest" allows, at the very least, for the concept of in-

jury, the recognition that one was and is oppressed.[13] One can read the redemptive conferral of subjectivity to Baartman (and through her to coloured, black, KhoiSan people) itself as a retroactive and redeeming subjection analogous to objectification. That is, subjectification = objectification as Baartman once again is overwritten with multiple histories and used in the service of a number of national and political agendas that involve not the emergence of history but its repression. It is here that I locate *Maru*'s prescience (what is prospective about the text), specifically in the ways that it might position us to read the postapartheid redemption of Saartje Baartman by South African black, coloured, indigenous, and Afrikaner communities alike.

The final push for Baartman's return came with the first democratic South African government's petition to, and subsequent eight-year-long fight with, the French government for the return of her remains. The return, completed with Baartman's burial in the Gamtoos Valley in August 2002, was the ransom paid for the onset of forgetting particular traumas of imperialism, slavery, and apartheid and was no less freighted than Baartman's departure from the Cape and the display of her in life and in death almost two centuries earlier. For the newly democratic South Africa, the return and interment of her bodily remains were laden with the promise and the weight of national healing, were rallying points for multiple ethnic, racial, and political communities, and have been used to reposition inside those who were and are outside of the frame of the (now) dominant narrative.[14] There is, as Wicomb notes, "nation-building implicit in the matter of her return" and in the contestations around her ethnicity. Was she "Black, Khoi or 'coloured'" (1998, 93)?[15]

Beginning and ending with Margaret Cadmore Jr.'s removal from Dilepe village to a place a "thousand miles away," the text of *Maru* offers a narrative vision counter to contemporary efforts to re-place the coloured (and KhoiSan) population in (South African) history via Baartman as a form of redemption, a move that sometimes dehistoricizes but, one could argue, *always* works to deny past and present shame. Writing about postapartheid South Africa and Baartman, the South African novelist and critic Zoë Wicomb explores the "condition of [coloured] postcoloniality" in order to "consider the actual materiality of black bodies that bear the marked pigmentation of miscegenation and the way in which that relates to political culture" (1998, 93). She wonders what will be buried with and resurrected from Baartman's remains when "the origins of [miscegenation] which lie within a discourse of 'race,' concupiscence, and degeneracy continue to be bound up with shame, *a pervasive shame exploited in apartheid's strategy of the naming of a Coloured race, and recurring in the current attempts by coloureds to establish brownness as a pure category, which is to say a denial of shame*" (92; emphasis mine).[16] In line with Wicomb's exploration of shame, I read Margaret Cadmore Jr.'s being positioned on the outside in *Maru's* prolepsis as an alternative to the way that some South Africans would redeem Baartman (and themselves) from narratives of miscegenation, violence, and the shame of having been violated, by positioning her within yet in excess of those narratives by "establish[ing] brownness as a pure category, which is to say a denial of shame."

One also glimpses this desire to be rid of shame in the way that Baartman and the seventeenth-century Khoi woman Krotoä are linked in "the process of reclamation and redemption" (Irlam 2004, 700).[17] Briefly, Krotoä, converted to Christianity and baptized Eva, worked in the home of and acted as a translator for Jan van Riebeeck (first governor of the Cape of Good Hope) and was legally married to and had three children with the Danish surgeon Pieter van Meerhoff. After van Meerhoff's death "colonists took [Krotoä's] children away from her," (Scully 2005, e-journal) placed them in the care of a white Dutch colonist, and exiled her to Robben Island, where she died in 1674 in poverty and, reportedly, from the effects of alcohol abuse.[18] In this contemporary moment of nation building, placing Krotoä and Baartman in the frame as founding mothers switches the terms of a debate on origins, for the formerly coloured population, from shame (of miscegenation as well as inferiority) to legality and illegality (the illegality of the disinheritance). Through this shift Krotoä's mixed-descent descendants, for example, have access to whatever symbolic or actual capital comes of being born of a legal union.[19] But what of white South Africans? "How is it," asks Carli Coetzee, "that this woman, whose contribution to white South African identity (especially Afrikaner identity) has been disclaimed for nearly three centuries has come to be remembered by Afrikaners as 'our mother'?" (1998, 113). Through her children that were absorbed into whiteness, white South Africans (particularly Afrikaners) can lay claim to their indigeneity and then through that line to Baartman. In his *Letter from the President*, dated 6–10 May 2002, Thabo Mbeki writes of the negotiations for the return to

South Africa of Baartman's remains: "The struggle for the return of the remains of Saartjie Baartman to her motherland was a struggle to uproot the legacy of many centuries of unbridled humiliation. It was a struggle to restore to our people and the peoples of Africa their right to be human and to be treated by all as human beings."[20] Peter Marais, the Western Cape premier, noted, "The return of Saartje Baartman is going to give rise to the rediscovery of the pride of the Khoisan people."[21] Each of these claims might be read as redemptive. By what means do these largely symbolic acts, whether it is a return to Krotoä or the return of Baartman's remains to the land of her birth (of her original dispossession), become the process by which those people still not free in South Africa are liberated?[22]

It was 1964 when Head arrived in the British Bechuanaland Protectorate (1885–1966) on an exit permit from South Africa (an exit that allowed no physical return). With this move Head became one of the only South African writers in exile to remain in Africa.[23] With the exception of the posthumously published *The Cardinals, with Meditations and Short Stories* (1995), which is set in Cape Town, the rest of Head's work is set in rural Botswana. Because Botswana, as British Bechuanaland, had been administered largely from afar, it escaped much of southern Africa's violent history of settler colonialism—principally, according to Head, because of its inhospitable environment.[24] It is a land, she argues, "that was never conquered or dominated by foreign powers and so a bit of ancient Africa, in all its quiet and unassertive grandeur, has remained intact there" (1990, 66). This uninterrupted history that she calls "a bit of ancient Africa" made Botswana a place of imaginative possibility, a country in which she could "look back on a history that [was] not sick with the need to exploit and abuse people" (88). Once she was relocated there from South Africa, a place that "completely defeated [her] as a writer," and where, by contrast, "thieves had stolen the land . . . [and] all traces of true history have been obliterated," she wrote, "What was important to me about Botswana was that there was *a freer society* here. I was fortunate enough to trace those roots of freedom" (Head 1989a, 15; emphasis mine).

In Botswana, however, Head also traced the local "roots of racial hatred," insisting that despite "all [her] South African experience [while she] longed to write an enduring novel on the hideousness of racial prejudice," it was "the research that [she] did among Batswana people for *Maru* [that] gave [her] the greatest insights and advantages to work right at the roots of racial hatred" (1990, 68–69). She writes out these roots of hatred as "universal"; that is, "she comes[s] at the concept of universality . . . [by noting] on each separate occasion, the history which provokes it" (J. Rose 1996, 103). Recall the epigraph to this chapter: "Before the white man became universally disliked for his mental outlook it was there." She found that the Bechuanaland Protectorate's, and then Botswana's, *relative* freedoms resonated unexpectedly with her experience, critique, and refusal of the relative freedoms of being coloured in South Africa and resonated yet again with the tense relationship (particularly concerning the monitoring of South African refugees) between the neighbor states of South Africa and Botswana. These relative freedoms—born of her double positioning as coloured and then as exiled South African in Botswana, without citizenship anywhere—compelled Head's performance of a "peculiar shuttling movement" between geographical and (meta)physical states (1990, 67). In the interest of reading *Maru* and the scenes of its production, I extend Head's spatial metaphor of a "peculiar shuttling movement" to a spatiotemporal metaphor that connects her indictment of the social systems of the past and their appearance in the present to a possible future free from racial prejudice that she tries to imagine in the beginning of the text. This liberated future is the consequence of the story that follows it in the text. Head's designation of herself as a "dreamer" of real liberation in southern Africa is evident in her determination to challenge those oppressions that she sees, and that she and her son experience, in the midst of and after Botswana's transition to independence. Those dreams, writes Caroline Rooney, are "less personal fantasies than political and social visions that go beyond a given reality and maintain a certain oppositional idealism" (1992, 121). For Head this dreaming is a desire to work "right at the roots of [a] racial prejudice" that is universal and always particularly produced, and not merely one writer's "unconscious" *nationalist* conversation with homeland and adopted country.

With *Maru*'s publication Head became one of only a few Africans writing during the years of African independence in the late 1960s and early 1970s to break the long silence surrounding indigenous African slavery.[25] By taking on an often disavowed African past and present of slavery and ethnic and racial oppression intensified by European colonial racism, Head engages in an explicit, poetic critique of white supremacy, scientific racism, and African ethnocentrism and then focuses our attention on a series of power relations that also remind us "that the images of Bushmen dominant in the nineteenth century have continued to be felt with particular material consequence into the twentieth" (P. Coetzee 1999, 68).[26] For Head *Maru* would become one of those "strange novels that [she] had not anticipated writing," a novel that was produced out of a "terror of power and an examination of its stark horrors" (Head 1990, 77).

Once they were relocated in Botswana, Bessie and her son, Howard Head, found that they were seen both as "out-and-out outsider[s]" (Head 1977, 26) and as all too familiar (Bushman or Bojesman) and that they were subject to forms of oppression that Head had previously encountered in South Africa and attributed solely to whites. "The earmarking of Head as a pariah in Botswana," according to Rob Nixon, "brought together the perceptions of her as a 'tribeless half-caste,' as ethnically similar to the 'landless Basarwa,' and as a refugee. To compound matters, she bore the stigma of the single mother—a 'loose' woman, anchored neither through land nor marriage to the agrarian system of property that determined social value" (1998, 121). Given Head's symbolic identification as Bushman and Basarwa and as coloured, in addition to her status as a single mother, her experiences in Botswana again traumatically resonate with her earlier South African experiences. She reflects, "Botswana was a traumatic experience to me and I found the people, initially, extremely brutal and harsh, only in the sense that I had never encountered human ambition and greed before in a black form" (1990, 68). Prior to this experience she admits to knowing "the language of racial hatred [as] an evil exclusively practised by white people" (68–69). In response to this new knowledge and understanding of human ambition, greed, racial hatred, and the abuses of power with a black face, Head amends her critique of power qua white supremacy to include African ethnocentrism and indigenous slavery.

Put another way, Head once again recognizes "relative and contextualized social freedoms" (Lewis 2005), the simultaneity of oppressions, the slipperiness between oppressor and oppressed, and the necessity of engaging in both anticolonial struggle and struggles against ethnocentrisms that may not be a direct result of colonial imposition but nonetheless operate in similar ways and are additionally influenced, amplified, and complicated by it. Head insists on the specificity qua universality of the forms of oppression that she encounters in Botswana; here, again, I follow Jacqueline Rose, who says that such universals are always historically con-

tingent and historically produced.[27] Wary of all politics and political ide-
ologies, Head confesses, "The African experience of slavery, colonialism
and exploitation arouses feelings of intense anguish and there was a fear in
me that monsters would merely change roles, that black faces would
simply replace white faces of cruelty, hate and greed and that the people
would bleed forever" (1990, 77). In this novel, which has been dismissed in
the past for its supposed naïveté, Head takes on the workings of power;
one can read in *Maru* that it was "consciously in [Head's] mind that
African independence had to be defined in the broadest possible terms" (85;
emphasis mine).

Writing herself into the despised and abject body of the Masarwa
Margaret Cadmore Jr., a woman who comes to "*live* Masarwa as a rupture"
(Guldimann 2003, 56), is a gesture that Head means to be transformative
in the disruption of the insistent significations of Masarwa. This is, I think,
what Françoise Vergès describes with regard to the widely circulated
narrative that when Frantz Fanon arrived at the hospital in Blida-Joinville
he unchained the mental patients: "It does not matter whether [the] story
is true or not. Narratives which reconstruct the birth of a new era tend to
tell a story in which, in a corrupted or degraded situation, a man emerges
and with the power of his will and his humanistic concern, radically
transforms the situation. This *transformation is inaugurated by a gesture*, a
declaration, an unexpected act, *which ruptures the past and impresses upon
its witnesses the thought of a new beginning*" (1996, 48). Head creates in
Margaret Cadmore Jr. a subject who, in her insistent avowal of a socially
unacceptable position, makes such a gesture, a gesture that breaks open
the produced congruity between "looking like" and "being" and in doing
so momentarily ruptures the social order. This rupture, however, is not the
end for Head, who, in "imagining [in *Maru*] . . . the founding of future,
humane communities takes full cognizance of recalcitrance, obstruction,
and delay" (Gagiano 2000, 145). *Maru*'s work of resignification reflects
Head's keen understanding that there is not (and should not be through
disavowal) any outside to this body that has functioned transtemporally
and transculturally as a body of shame; reflects her feeling that "stripped
bare of every human right," the oppressed do not necessarily "really see
liberation on an immediate horizon"; and reflects her belief that the work
of the novelist is to "dream dreams a little ahead of the somewhat vicious
clamour of revolution and the horrible stench of evil social systems" (1990,

68, 28). In response to a national narrative in which "her people" have been included (in both state and nonstate narratives) principally as a body of shame, Head's work anticipates postapartheid redefinitions of nation and the attempted resolution of the question of coloured (Khoi) belonging. She creates Margaret Cadmore Jr. as an *individual* socially outside who is offered (and who subsequently refuses and is also at the same time denied) the choice of being inside. To be on the inside for Margaret Jr. would be to consent to enter the social hierarchy as coloured, with its relative advantages, to consent to relative power, to reify the hierarchical order, and to say, "At least I am not a Masarwa."

Misreading the Body as Evidence

In this section I want to make explicit the connections between the power of the hierarchizing gaze, Head's portrayal of Margaret Cadmore Jr., and representations of Head, her life, and the life of the woman known as Saartje Baartman.[28] Baartman, who comes to be known as the "Hottentot Venus," was born in 1789 in the lower Gamtoos River valley in the southeastern Cape. "Her father was in the habit of going with cattle from the interior to the cape and was killed in one of those Journeys by the 'Bosmen.' Her mother died twenty years ago—she had a Child by a Drummer at the Cape with whom she lived for about two years yet always being in the employ of Henrick Caesar; the child is since dead" (quoted in Strother 1999, 41).

Perhaps the most famous Bushman in the West because of the amount of writing about her after she left the Cape, Baartman was displayed in Europe (primarily in England and France but also in Ireland) at the beginning of the nineteenth century. The circumstances by which she came to England with Henrick Caesar, the brother of her former master/employer Peter Caesar, are not entirely clear, but it is certain that they arrived in 1810 and that soon after Henrick, who had entered into an agreement with Alexander Dunlop to display Baartman, exhibited her at Piccadilly. Subsequently the court case of 1810 generated publicity for Dunlop's and Caesar's exhibition, but as Yvette Abrahams notes, it was "apparently bad for business. Sara Bartman was removed from London and exhibited in the provinces until 1814 when she was taken to Paris" (1998, 220). Baron Georges Cuvier (considered the father of modern biology), along with other noted zoologists and physiologists from the Musée d'Histoire Naturelle, spent three days examining Baartman in 1815. After she died of a cold later that year (the effects of dire poverty and possibly alcohol abuse), Cuvier requested her body and dissected her, with particular attention to her buttocks and genitalia (which she had refused to reveal to him while she was alive). The findings were published in Frédéric Cuvier's and Geoffrey St.-Hilaire's *Histoire naturelle des mammifères*, in which study Baartman was the only human included. Her remains were removed to the Musée de l'Homme, where they would stay until their repatriation to South Africa in 2002. I turn now, however, to the brief time that the living Baartman was displayed in London. In an "arena of political contestation over the nature of colonization" (Wiss 1994, 12) Baartman figured prominently in the abolitionist movement in her capacity as the "Hottentot Venus."

In 1810, three years after the abolition of the Slave Trade Act and with an eye toward securing Baartman's repatriation to the Cape colony, Zachary Macaulay, Robert Wedderburn, and the African Institution petitioned the Court of King's Bench on account of the indecent nature of the exhibition, in which they suspected she was being kept as a slave.[29] After hearing and viewing evidence (including her testimony and a signed contract between Dunlop and Baartman dated 29 October 1810) the court concluded, "She came by her own consent to England and was promised half of the money for exhibiting her person—She agreed to come to England for a period of six years" (quoted in Strother 1999, 41). The court's decision would resolve the legal question of whether Baartman was chattel (someone else's legal property) or an entrepreneur with rights to herself as property, with "as good a right to exhibit herself as an Irish Giant or a Dwarf" (Qureshi 2004, 238). The outcome of the case meant that Baartman was to be understood as a subject able to consent freely, and resulted not in her liberation from a cruel master, the original aim of the lawsuit, but in her continued bondage understood thereafter in terms of freedom to "consent" and framed by a grammar of bodily "modesty." The entry into evidence of the contract between Baartman and Dunlop shifts the focus from one aspect of Baartman's bodily presence to another: from the cruel manner in which she is exploited by her master for his profit— "[He] holds up a *stick to her, like the wild beast keepers*, to intimidate her into obedience" (quoted in Strother 1999, 54)—to how her appearance is offensive to the decency of the paying (consenting) crowd, dressed as she is to "give the appearance of being undressed" (Strother 1999, 52). Abrahams reframes this evidence and reads this scene as one in which Baartman *provokes* Caesar into publicly performing violent acts. Abrahams argues that Baartman forces Caesar to perform for the audience *his and their coercion of her consent* (his coercion as the means to her consent within slavery; 2003, 18–20). Following Abrahams's lead, we should read Baartman's words and actions as they are recorded in the trial transcript, as well as in its silences, so that we might be able to see in them Baartman's *recognition of her oppression* and also her resistance in the form of her making her oppression visible to others.

Were Macaulay, Wedderburn, and the representatives of the African Institution to have won their case, Baartman was to have been repatriated, "liberated" to a Cape colony that was once again under British rule, where she would have been subjected, like all KhoiSan people, to the "special protection of the British government" and where Africans were still in bondage and would remain so through the 1834–38 period of emancipation.[30] Because the court case involving Baartman took place "in a period when the British were debating the prohibition of slavery . . . race took on a new significance when questions arose about the entitlement of non-enslaved blacks to partake of the fruits of liberty and citizenship" (Giddings 1992, 449). Are we to understand consent and freedom here to mean simply "At least she has more freedom than ——" (an alternate articulation of Head's "At least I am not a——")? Even as Baartman has the legal signifiers of a free subject conferred upon her by the outcome of the case, in fact she remains captive to her employer and becomes a kind of theoretical limit case that helps define the limits of freedom for the English subject. However the case could have been resolved, the freedom at issue was never Baartman's own. Had she not been viewed as a free citizen under contract in England, she would have been *set free* (redemption operating here in the sense of the "action of freeing a prisoner, captive, or slave by payment") on the Cape into a state of near slavery. By 1806 the British had reoccupied the Cape (received again from the Dutch, who occupied it again from 1803 to 1806), and "by 1809, British missionaries had won a highly publicized debate within the colony by assigning the Khoikhoi to the special protection of the British government" (Strother 1999, 22). This "special protection" required the KhoiSan to "register their 'fixed places of abode' so as to counteract 'vagrancy.' It also provided for the mandatory drawing up of contracts of service in the presence of officials. . . . Any European might detain a Khoi who could not produce a pass. . . . The proclamation also provide[d] for 'domestic' discipline" (Keegan 1997, 54).

Back in England, where the viewing crowd was encouraged to read Baartman's appearance in terms of beastliness (rather than as a display of the violence of the exhibition), one might instead see Baartman's staged resistance (Abrahams 2003, 17–18). The court transcript records:

> Deponents further severally say that during the time they were present the said female at one time appeared very morose and sullen and retired into the little recess off the stage and appeared unwilling to come out again when called by the Exhibitor and the Exhibitor felt it necessary on that occasion to let down a curtain which when drawn separates the stage and little recess from the other part of this room. . . . The Exhibitor after the curtain was let down looked behind it and shook his hand at her but without speaking and he soon after drew up the Curtain and again called her to public view and she came again forward upon the stage. (Quoted in Strother 1999, 45)

The representations of her, in which her subjectification equals objectification (and abjection), keep before the English public the violent process that is going on offstage in the Cape colony in the name of England.[31] Her resistance and the pressure on the exhibition get at the heart of the structure of all colonial and slave labor: the colonized and enslaved are considered to be human because they "consent" to labor, and yet they are also not quite human because they "consent" to it enough to survive within it. Not consenting to such subjectivity is an option that is not permitted and not to be acknowledged.

It is this double status of subjectification that most interests me. While there are countless instances in which people of "other" races are partially or even paradoxically subjectified (the "three-fifths compromise" in the U.S. Constitution is one example; the relative status of coloureds in apartheid South Africa another), the larger issue is that the interpellation of these subjects/objects is, at base, the interpellation of *the* subject. Baartman's 1810 court case was not about establishing her freedom so much as the freedom of English subjects to work. And it is precisely this condition of relative freedom within unfreedom (as one instance of double status) that Head herself occupies within South Africa's apartheid classifications and restrictions and again within Botswana's ethnic hierarchies and restrictions on refugees. Head's words in *Maru* (again from the epigraph to this chapter) connect Head herself and Margaret Cadmore Jr. and her dead birth mother to Baartman and larger colonial and national histories: "Of all things that are said about oppressed people, the worst things are said and done to the Bushmen. Ask the scientists. Haven't they yet written a treatise on how Bushmen are an oddity of the human race, who are half the head of a man and half the body of a donkey? Because you don't go poking around into the organs of people unless they are animals or dead" (Head 1971, 11). Looking more closely at Baartman, the KhoiSan, Head, and Margaret Cadmore Jr., I pay particular attention to several scenes involving Margaret Cadmore Sr. and Margaret Jr. and their relationship to social, cultural, and political formations that revolve around representation and the visual. Margaret Cadmore Sr.'s relationship to the orphaned Masarwa child is, on the one hand, not unlike Cuvier's zoological interest in Baartman and, on the other, not unlike the position of the court that declared Baartman a consenting subject. That is, Margaret Sr. brings to bear in her relation to Margaret Jr. the scientific, judicial, and abolitionist forces that had been brought to bear on Saartje Baartman: "As she put the child to bed that night in her own home, her face was aglow. She had a real, living object for her experiment. Who knew what wonder would be created?" (15).

It is important to note that many articles about Baartman enact a positioning of the subject analogous to the way articles about Head enact a positioning of her, and that articles on Head's work often include strikingly similar condensed accounts of the circumstances of her birth and/or an attempt to resolve her discrepant accounts of her own beginnings; like Saartje Baartman, Head is denied the ability to be resisting.[32] More pointedly it is because, as Desiree Lewis writes, "her life story highlights the taboos of 'miscegenation' and 'madness' [that] Bessie Head has been the subject of a great deal of voyeuristic absorption" (2005). The insistence on the extraordinariness of her origins takes on increased significance given the frequency with which people contravened the Immorality Act of 1927 (renewed in 1950, the Immorality Act is South Africa's codification of the prohibition against race mixing) and Head's claim to her own "ordinariness." Throughout Head's written accounts of herself she maintained a solidarity with black South Africans, enacting a political rejection of the apartheid nomenclature of "coloured" and the relative access that the category "coloured" would allow her to occupy in relation to blacks.[33] She said that she had lived the "back breaking life of all black South Africans," and she insisted that a life such as hers was common: "There must be many people like me in South Africa whose birth or beginnings are filled with calamity and disaster, the sort of person who is the skeleton in the cupboard or the dark and fearful secret swept under the carpet" (1990, 3). Likewise much contemporary writing about Baartman repeats a language of extraordinary physicality. Even writing that seeks to historicize and redeem her for/from history has some extended focus on her buttocks (which along with her genitalia are the primary site of her objectification) and makes liberal use of illustrations that document the ways she was scientized and memorialized. If, as others have argued before me, the recycling and remotivation of visual images and narratives of Baartman often participate (regardless of intention) in the generation of a certain prurient pleasure, then it is even more necessary to consider to what other ends the repeated deployment and production of both Head's and Baartman's bodies as *extraordinary* are put.

As one way to begin to probe this problem as it relates to Head, I quote her biographer Craig MacKenzie, in his introduction to his edited collection of Head's autobiographical writings that is posthumously published as *A Woman Alone:*

> [Head's] origins, to begin with, are ambiguous at best. Her early life is a blur of pain and uncertainty. Little is known about her marriage and the reasons for its breakdown. In fact it is only with her arrival in the literary world in the seventies and the relative stability that this created that her life begins to take on *familiar* contours. Even then most of the details have their source in the author herself, and independent corroboration of basic facts is hard to come by. *She proved to be an unreliable witness to her own life*, often contradicting herself in interviews, and the chief source of biographical data—her first three novels—present her life filtered through her rich but necessarily inventive literary imagination. (1990, ix; emphasis mine)

Despite MacKenzie's acknowledgment that "the task of mapping the life of an author like Bessie Head undoubtedly becomes an investigation into the enigma of human prejudice," his affirmation of Head's literary

imagination undermines the putative truth-value of her work as autobiographical at the same time as his portrayal of her autobiographical
unreliability undermines his admiration of her inventiveness (1990, ix).
The phrases "familiar contours" and "unreliable witness" subject Head
and her work to a disciplinary regime of authenticity that she consistently
rejects. That she does not provide MacKenzie with the biographical coordinates familiar to him that he desires to create a straightforward accounting of her life in no way makes Head an "unreliable witness to her own
life." Those coordinates would locate Head within a narrative, national
and familial, antithetical to Head's own experiences and representations of
family, nation, and nationalism.[34] In other words, the differing autobiographical details that Head provides have been used to circumvent reading
her work as bearing exceptional *witness* to the ordinary material and
psychic dimensions of her life and others' lives of oppression in South
Africa, Botswana, and elsewhere, in favor of reading *her* as both unreliable
and exceptional. An effect of this subjectification has been, until fairly
recently, diminished readings of her very reliable social testimony. Put
another way, the construction of her as deranged has delayed a full consideration of the enormity of her literary and political insights and interventions in the face of great obstacles that (most likely) included mental
illness in addition to racism, paternalism, ethnocentrism, poverty, isolation, and the problems of statelessness.[35]

Moving even further from the critical to the diagnostic is Susan Gardner's " 'Don't Ask for the True Story': A Memoir of Bessie Head" (published after Head's death). Gardner suspects that Head's familial narrative
"seemed almost too 'good,' in its horrible way, to be true," and she turns for
confirmation of that suspicion to a white male "Transkeian psychiatrist
and well-known biographer," whom she quotes as saying, "All of my Black
psychotics claim they have a white parent. Even family romance and
schizophrenia take a racial form in South Africa" (1986, 115, 122). Of course
Head's mother was white, and Gardner seems unaware that both she and
the psychiatrist speak in "the vocabulary of colonial psychiatry" (Vergès
1996, 53). Gardner and the Transkeian psychiatrist are correct that family
romance and schizophrenia do take a racial form, but not exclusively in
South Africa or in "Black psychotics." One might ask if it is the very
ordinariness of the black psychotics' claim to white parentage—a claim
that speaks to histories of racial and sexual terror and desire, not to

mention imposed hierarchies and relative freedoms and privileges for coloureds—that makes it a claim not only easy but necessary to dismiss.

Furthermore, when Gardner, from the perspective of a psychiatry that she admittedly distrusts ("I have," she writes, "never been anything but suspicious of psychiatric labels"), sees Head in the same way that that perspective sees "all . . . Black psychotics," does she not repeat the sort of posthumous treatment visited upon Baartman? Put another way, Gardner's perspective makes use of the same clinical gaze that is brought to bear on Baartman. Accepting this diagnosis of Head, Gardner fails to read Head's refusal of certain familial and national narratives as her resistance to the forces of power. (Gardner seems to think that if a certain inside narrative is open to Head, or to one in Head's position, it's madness not to access it.) To slip from reading Head's work as "about" madness to diagnosing her as mad and not disruptive—independent of the "madness" of her various societies—seems symptomatic of a still operative colonial psychiatry; it is to fail to "enter directly into [madness's] political and historical dimension" (J. Rose 1996, 107).[36] In that slippage is also the erasure of the multiple ways that oppressive social systems—apartheid, ethnocentrism, and slavery—drive people in all places in the power structure "mad." As Jacqueline Rose writes, "It is in relation to 'madness' that 'universality' shows its most dubious euro/ethnocentric colours, as it spreads its diagnostic certainty around the world" (100).

I read in Gardner's and MacKenzie's respective analyses of Head's "psychosis" and "unreliability" that she "never really knew who she was" and that "in the process of unravelling the strands of her anguished life story one encounters perhaps most of all, personal confusion," the same form of etiology as the nineteenth-century diagnosis of Baartman as steatopygous.[37] I refuse that biologizing of Baartman commonly summoned up in descriptions of her even by those writers who locate her display within a nexus of factors that includes scientific racism and who work to correct the syntax of illness and pathology that attaches to her. They, too, often end up repeating at least in part the very relations that they set out to analyze, for example, that Baartman "suffered to an unusual degree from steatopygia," that hers "were not ordinary buttocks but huge, spongy appendages that seemed to possess a life of their own so aggressively did they stand out from the body," and, worse yet, that "inevitably she became the butt of many asinine jokes."[38] Whatever their intentions, these reinscriptions of colonial diagnosis continue Baartman's pathologization, and through them we are reminded that "pathology is the place where history talks with its loudest most grating voice" (J. Rose 1996, 103).

My contention is simply that the continued reinscription of this aspect of Baartman's physical suffering in biologizing terms (if not exclusively in those terms) points to something about the incomplete work of liberation. The repetition of the diagnosis seems to indicate a suspension of the critical attention that is given, for example, to the sociohistorical contexts in which Baartman lived (in South Africa and in Europe), the uses to which she was put by science and race, and the abuses to which she was subjected and then found to have been free to consent to by the English courts. (For example, her body was forced to bear an additional burden because her presence entailed both a persistent reminder of and disavowal of England's role in southern Africa.)[39] I don't want to dispense with the question of Baartman's body; I want to resituate it in order to think about how she is being used now. What is the current descriptive embrace or disavowal of her *body*, in its materiality, shoring up? Returning to Head and the construction of her as mad, what disavowal is she made to perform? Jacqueline Rose is particularly insightful when she argues for repositioning and against dispensing with the *question* of madness when reading Head: "To try and read Head as a white reader [I would add, perhaps as *any* reader] is to find oneself jammed in on more than one side: by what I will call . . . the 'mau maus of the mind'—the risk of sliding into imperial diagnosis of the type that has rushed to read derangement where legible political protest was actually being expressed" (Rose and John Lonsdale, quoted in Rose 1996, 101).

In her allegorical, intensely psychological fiction Head holds up for scrutiny power relations (slavery, white supremacy, and ethnocentrism) that are insistently repressed and/or deliberately obscured. At the heart of her stories lies a broken injunction *against* telling and, quite often, a detailing of those lives and hereditary relationships (inherited and otherwise passed on, taken up) that are insistently buried, repressed, disavowed. Her "necessarily inventive literary imagination" in no way contradicts the social "truths" that she brings to light; rather than "prov[ing] [her] to be an unreliable witness to her own life," that inventiveness points, I think, to Head's investment in telling and then retelling stories about relationships that, marked as shameful, remain unspoken and largely unconscious

(1990, ix). I read Head as consciously circumventing fact and narrativity in her autobiography, fiction, and nonfiction for possibility, for the creative gesture.

Head's investment in the *creative force* of power compels her to write of power, of Africans often unspoken of and unexamined relationships to racism and slavery. Compels her to write and rewrite narratives of power's undoing through, for example, a wealthy white South African woman's illegal gesture of intimacy with a poor black South African man, or the relationship between a white woman and a black child, or the marriage of an outcast to a paramount chief. Gardner's and MacKenzie's posthumous submission of Head and her work to a biographical authenticity test (understood by the tenets of factual narrativity and colonial racist psychiatry) amounts to what Head would have called a hostile "take-over" (J. Rose 1996, 103). Here's Gardner: "It didn't surprise me that Bessie had apparently never tried to trace her [mother]. . . . It might simply not have occurred to her to write for something as mundane as a birth certificate, *although if there is anything ironically to be said in favour of South Africa's bureaucracy, it is that we are all identified and docketed—in other words, eminently traceable*" (1986, 122; emphasis mine). In the very mundanity of state power in its particular documentation of and intrusion into all aspects of black people's lives lies much of what cannot be said, ironically or not, in favor of South Africa's apartheid bureaucracy. That Gardner speaks favorably of this eminent traceability in relation to Head's failure (rather than her refusal) is eloquent of her willful and woeful misreading of the profound effects of that documentation on those who suffered them most immediately under apartheid, effects of power that inform the content of Head's books and the very contours of her life.[40] Irony of another kind emerges because Gardner does acknowledge the effects of this knowledge on herself, that she "lost track of [Head's mother, Bessie Amelia Emery], *for I could not bear anymore the revelations I was receiving*" (124; emphasis mine).

Further Misreadings

In 1996, six years before the return to South Africa of Baartman's bones and other body parts but in the midst of negotiations for their return and simultaneous with the Truth and Reconciliation Commission's hearings, the white South African art historian Pippa Skotnes guest-curated the exhibition Miscast: Negotiating Khoisan History and Material Culture at the formerly whites-only South African National Gallery (SANG) and (knowingly) stepped into a representational minefield.[41] For Skotnes, "despite the attendant problems of mounting yet another exhibit about the bushmen, it would only be possible to confront these stereotypes through the medium of display," in other words, through an attempt to rupture being and looking like, being and doing.[42] " 'Miscast,' " writes Annie Coombes, "was constructed as an experiential installation that focused on the complex ways in which vision and visibility produced their object historically" (2003, 231). Negotiating KhoiSan history through visual display (the production of historical objects in the realm of vision and visibility) at the SANG was Skotnes's explicit intervention to counter the popular Bushman dioramas of the nearby South African Museum and the presentation of history they embody, to open up institutional space for contested representations and to previously excluded communities (Skotnes 2001, 301–11). Explicitly framed in terms of "a critical engagement with the ways in which the Khoisan were pathologized, dispossessed, and all but eradicated through colonialism and apartheid," Skotnes's show uses visual materials and documents as an "exposition of the epistemological violence that provided the justification for such acts" and to mitigate Bushman loss (of evidence of slavery and murder, of history, stories, language, etc.; Coombes 2003, 230). She also tells a story about the ethnographers, the (negotiated) relationships that ensue between the ethnographers and their objects of study, and, to some extent, the relationship between the ethnographers and Skotnes herself.[43] But in its attempt to "forc[e] whites 'to confront European colonial violence and genocide' " it participates in the very reproduction of the KhoiSan as object even as "it rendered the previously forgotten history of colonialism visible, and in so doing called forth widely divergent responses from different communities" (Norval 2001, 197).

It is the reproduction of the KhoiSan as objects of history in the Miscast exhibition that Rustum Kozain objects to: "In no way," he writes, "is the exhibitor-photographer relationship even close to the exhibited-photographer one. In no way does the exhibitor as *exhibited* even approximate a subject position close to that of the exhibited Khoisan. . . . In *Miscast*, no such *gesture* obtains. The photographs of the exhibitors do not raise even an oblique challenge to the history of the relationship of power underlying representations of the Khoisan."[44] The representation and re-enactment of power relations that were particularly offensive to a number of museum guests were the body casts and the exhibition room in which visitors had to walk on images of KhoiSan people installed on the floor. That Kazain (as well as Abrahams and other Brown scholars and activists)[45] identifies in the show the absence of a challenge to historical power relationships in the presentation of KhoiSan bodies may be because Miscast is less about Bushmen (a knowledge of whom, Skotnes would argue, has been produced in relation to the arrangement of visual evidence) than about a series of material and discursive relationships, making visible the production of history in the visual realm and the process of subjectification. The negotiation of these relationships may necessarily involve a repetition that functions simultaneously at different levels, like the effect that walking on images of the bodies of KhoiSan people would have for their descendants compared to the effect on non-KhoiSan people who must be made to feel (or to live) this dispossession and its continuing effects. In that repetition is the trace of the very thing that would be lost in the framing of the question of KhoiSan presence differently: that KhoiSan subjectification is objectification.

One could argue that Head encountered her own set of difficulties in representing the KhoiSan twenty-five years earlier when she wrote *Maru*. Her repetition of the term *Masarwa* might seem to be a function of that despite her unequivocal statement, "Some time ago it might have been believed that words like 'kaffir' and 'nigger' defined a tribe. Or else how can a tribe of people be called Bushmen or Masarwa? Masarwa is the equivalent of 'nigger,' a term of contempt which means, obliquely, a low, filthy nation" (1971, 12). Her repetition of Masarwa—connected to a KhoiSan woman's refusal to let shame force her into a position of power, to the disruptive image that Margaret Jr. presents (being but not looking like a Masarwa), and to the image of her dead birth mother that she carries with her—is the means by which she hopes to disrupt Masarwa's significations.

"But I am not ashamed of being a Masarwa"

The various people in southern Africa known as the KhoiSan have been subjected to and have resisted for centuries disciplinary actions in the form of dispossession, murder, and enslavement. In the beginning of the nineteenth century, around the same time that Baartman's case was being heard in England, "The British governor was held to stand 'in nature of a guardian over the Hottentot nation . . . by reason of their general imbecile state.' . . . The dispossessed Khoikhoi assumed the juridical status of legal wards in need of discipline and protection" (Strother 1999, 22). Sometime in the mid-twentieth century, when *Maru*'s Mrs. Cadmore adopts the orphaned Masarwa girl and educates her in the mission school with the expressed purpose that "one day she will help her people," she continues in the tradition of the London Missionary Society and acts in loco parentis for the orphaned Masarwa daughter and, by extension, for the entire population. Mrs. Cadmore seeks to accomplish this through the daughter's at once accepting and exceeding Masarwa's significations.

That Mrs. Cadmore positions her adoptive daughter's birth mother as a goddess can be read as a repetition of both Head's personal history (her mother figured as a kind of goddess to her) and as an inversion of Saartje Baartman's punning designation by her enslaver/exhibitor as the "Hottentot Venus,"[46] a seeming oxymoron that is accompanied by a narrative that framed her as having "the kind of shape which is most admired among her countrymen." Z. S. Strother argues that this framing was a conscious shift in marketing that undertook to instruct audiences in a new way of seeing Baartman, one that enacted a shift from her prior exhibition as an anomaly (1999, 25). Head undertakes an analogous shift in *Maru* but to the inverse purpose. Margaret Sr. draws a picture of Margaret Jr.'s dead Masarwa mother and captions it "She looks like a goddess" in order that the visual signs that mark the mother as Masarwa (read: inferior) might be reframed so as to assert her stature as a goddess—the opposite of what that body would ordinarily mean to the Tswana population. The drawing in conjunction with the caption is meant to shift how people see a Masarwa and to rupture a particular way of ordering the world.

Turning to the beginning of Margaret Cadmore Jr.'s story in *Maru* and to the body of shame, it is the missionaries who are summoned "when no one wanted to bury a dead body . . .; not that [they] really liked to be involved with mankind, but they had been known to go into queer places because of their occupation. They would do that but they did not often like you to walk into their yard" (Head 1971, 12). Hence it is Mrs. Cadmore who is called to the hospital when the Batswana nurses refuse to prepare for burial the body of an untouchable Masarwa woman who was found dead in the bush. And it is she who "shrieks" at them, "Why the damn blasted hell haven't you washed the body for burial?" when she finds that the nurses have placed the dead woman on the floor of a "small back room where the slop pails were kept" (14).

A scientist and ethnographer at heart (functioning in the text to answer Head's repeated call to "ask the scientists"), Margaret Sr. is not one to "speculate on how any artistic observation of human suffering arouses infinite compassion" (14). Given to "logical reasoning," not compassion, she views the body and in an attempt to make things right she takes out her sketchbook and takes "revenge with a sketchpad and pencil" (13). Confronted with the dead woman and her living child (whom she adopts and to whom she gives her own name) she suddenly is opened to new knowledge of how the KhoiSan live and die in Botswana, and she cannot prevent this information from affecting her. She orders the nurses to prepare the woman's body for burial, and she takes revenge for their initial refusal (which means nothing to her), capturing "the expressions of disgust" on their faces in a sketch of them that she captions "These are not decent people" (14). Thus Mrs. Cadmore compels them to do what they had called her to do because they could not or would not in obedience to Tswana assumptions of superiority. While the nurses wash the dead woman's body, Mrs. Cadmore draws the portrait of the deceased woman. To that sketch she adds the text, "She looks like a Goddess." But she "took in too much" information; she saw "malnutrition" and "the hatred of the fortunate" for the less fortunate, indeed, "maybe she really saw human suffering, close up, for the first time, but it frightened her into adopting that part of the woman that was still alive—her child" (15).

Margaret Sr.'s drawing of the dead woman in relation to the nurses is an act of revenge against Tswana "inhumanity." (But it is an act that also distances the artist from the production of knowledge of KhoiSan inferiority.) Her sketch of the dead woman, I suggest, evokes the archived photographs of the late nineteenth century and early twentieth that sought to capture the KhoiSan in their literal and social death. (Margaret Sr. thinks, "I wonder where these people are buried? They don't seem to be at all a part of the life of this country" [13].) The unnamed Masarwa woman is identified in the drawing by those characteristics that sign her Masarwaness. She has, we read, the "same thin, Masarwa stick legs," an "ankle-length, loose shift dress which smelt strongly of urine and the smoke of outdoor fires," and "hard caloused feet that had never worn shoes" (12, 15). Such descriptions of the body of the birth mother repeat the syntax if not the sentiment of colonial representations of KhoiSan people, representations that often focused on their supposed "uncleanness" and "greasiness," their "painted faces," ragged clothing, and "smell of urine."[47] Like the photographs and other visual evidence that comprise ethnographic archives, the South African Museum's Bushman diorama and the work that Skotnes's Miscast exhibition would challenge, Mrs. Cadmore's sketch preserves a type that is (allegedly) disappearing at the same time that she intends to be instrumental in eradicating it through the erasure of the very signs of Masarwa-ness that she captures. Her sketch might, in some future time, be evidence simultaneously of the presence and the absence of those telltale signs of ethnicity (social status) and evidence of the distance between the KhoiSan mother and what she (Margaret Sr.) will produce of the daughter. Against a long and often brutal history of KhoiSan dispossession (continuing into the present) that is accompanied by shifting visual and textual representations of them, what possible meanings do we find in the drawing of a dead, impoverished Masarwa woman captioned "She looks like a Goddess"? What effects and affects is this drawing supposed to produce in the daughter who keeps it and in those others to whom she shows it?

The younger Margaret comes to know herself as Masarwa within the institutional spaces controlled by the missionaries—the church, the school, and the hospital—and yet in isolation from others of her racial and ethnic community.[48] The fact that this education "produced a brilliant student . . . [and] that the brilliance was based entirely on social isolation and a lack of communication with others, except through books, was too painful for the younger Margaret ever to mention" (19). The relationship between the two Margarets "was never one of a child and its mother. It was as though later she was a semi-servant in the house, yet at the same time treated as an equal, by being given the things servants don't usually get: kisses on the cheeks and toes at bedtime, long walks into the bush to observe the behavior through binoculars of birds, and lots of reading material" (16–17). The younger Margaret's knowledge of herself is structured in relation to this double positioning, an undefined difference, not quite daughter, not fully servant, something in between and also something in excess of existing social categories.

Offered some protection because her adoptive mother is the principal of the school who bestows on Margaret Jr. unembarrassed kisses, it was only gradually that she "became aware that something was wrong with her relationship to the world" (17). She was the child "who was slyly pinched under the seat, and next to whom no one wanted to sit" and whom the other children taunt with "Since when did a Bushy go to school?" and "You are just a Bushman." Raised as she is, she can have little idea of the significance of her own body in the larger community ("her relationship to the world") and "no weapons of words or personality" with which to respond to racist taunts. Her identification as but not with the Masarwa is forged through a series of traumatic encounters: through repeated occurrences of school violence and through her continual unwavering identification with the sketch of her mother, who died giving birth to her. She understands the words but wonders, "What did it [the racist comment] mean? When they said it with such anger? . . . What was a Bushman supposed to *do*?" Because she does not associate *being* a Bushman with *doing* any particular thing nor with inherent inferiority, as her persecutors do, Margaret Jr. wonders "what . . . it really mean[t] when another child walked up to her and looking so angry said: 'You are just a Bushman' " (17). She recognizes, however, that "in their minds [it] meant so much" (17). The mother's response to the observed mistreatment of her daughter and its consequent effects on her is to think, "1 can't understand beastliness because it would never occur to me to be beastly" and to say to the child, "They are wrong. You will have *to live* with your appearance the rest of your life. There *is nothing you can do* to change it" (18). Living, being, doing—all become wrapped up in her Masarwa *appearance*. For the daughter these words "never stopped the tin cans rattling, but it kept the victims of the tin cans sane. No one by shouting, screaming, or spitting could un-Bushman her" (18). In the end Margaret Sr. does not challenge the racial hierarchy, nor does she implicate herself in the discourses that give rise to and support its statements. And while she names and rejects the racism of the Tswana ("These are not decent people") she invests power in her own racial hierarchy that simply inverts the second and third terms: now white, Masarwa, Tswana.

Before Margaret Jr. graduates from the teachers' training college her adoptive mother retires to England without her, in order, it seems, to give her experiment a chance to work. In this, Mrs. Cadmore's penultimate appearance in the text, we are reminded of two primary colonial signifiers of Bushman bodily presence: odor and facial adornment.[49] Prior to leaving, Margaret Sr. travels to her daughter's college bearing some parting gifts and advice: "Don't wear lipstick. It won't suit you" and "Don't forget to shave regularly under your arms and apply this perfumed powder" (19). Full of "good sense and logical arguments," the mother passes on hygiene tips to the daughter; her warning that lipstick "won't suit" Margaret Jr. serves to remind us both of the work of the missionaries in the Bechuanaland Protectorate and of the history of European interest in the bodies of KhoiSan women. We can recognize in Margaret Sr.'s well-meaning advice to "shave regularly" a long-standing anxiety around the *undisciplined* KhoiSan body. When we connect this advice ("apply this perfumed power") to one of the only other glimpses of a Bushman that we have seen so far in the text—the image of Margaret's dead birth mother, with her "stick legs" and urine-soaked "shift dress"—we again see that it is precisely such supposed bodily indices of ethnicity (smell, clothing, voice, facial adornment) that the missionary Margaret Sr. intends her experiment to disrupt. It is after all Margaret Jr.'s appearance and her achievements that engender both her misrecognition by others as coloured and the racist taunts about her overstepping her place ("You are just a Bushman") that greet her presence.

The Bushman body in the framed and captioned sketch of her dead mother that Margaret Jr. carries with her also makes visible to her the deadly consequences of being and looking like a Masarwa. It acts as an interpretive frame for herself, for how to see a Masarwa, and yet again as a measure of the distance between the birth mother and her daughter. (The daughter is a woman whose "mind and heart were composed of a little bit of everything . . . hardly African or anything but something new and universal, a type of personality that would be unable to fit into a definition of something as narrow as tribe or race or nation" [16].) We might say that Margaret Jr.'s dead birth mother is placed within the frame so that the daughter might claim to grow up outside of it. Margaret Sr.'s decisive statements, such as the child "can't change her appearance," convince Margaret Jr. that her identification as a Bushman is grounded in the way she looks, in the way that she is perceived (not) to smell or (not) to behave in some undisciplined way. Margaret Sr.'s statements are determined as well by her efforts to force any change that occurs to be located in conjunction with how others *see* Margaret Jr.; she is invested in puncturing belief in the innate inferiority of the Masarwa.

The most disruptive thing about Margaret Jr. is her unabashed, unashamed declaration "I am a Masarwa," which shows that she assumes that there is a space between being and doing, between being and appearing that serves to disrupt being—an assumption ultimately devastating to the racial assumptions of the Batswana. While the other students in the Mission School never let her (or themselves or even her adoptive mother) forget "what she is," once Margaret Jr. leaves the mission for the teachers training college others see her relationship to the white woman and her education and dignity in such a way that they cannot even allow that she *looks* like a Masarwa and therefore she cannot *be* a Masarwa. Hence when Margaret insists on saying "I am a Masarwa," that statement prompts a visceral response and an accompanying perspectival shift because "the eye is a deceitful thing. . . . If a Masarwa combs his hair and wears modern dress he looks just like a Coloured. There is no difference" (52–53).

In Botswana, with no contact with those whom she can identify only in the abstract as "her people," and raised as she is to surpass boundaries of tribe and nation, Margaret Jr. continues to be an experiment and is now also an offering that Margaret Sr. makes to the Masarwa people. A would-be-nationalist who exceeds anything "as narrow as nation," Margaret Jr. is left behind to function as a *sign* of progress and as a kernel of disruption when Mrs. Cadmore returns to England. Her entry into and exit from Dilepe village as a new teacher reframe the national question "[What is to be done about] the problem of the Masarwa . . . the only millstone in the way of national progress?" (44). Back in England Margaret Sr. sends a postcard to her daughter to explain why she left: "I had to do it for the sake of your people. I did not want to leave you behind. [Signed] Margaret Cadmore" (20–21).

After graduation Margaret Jr. is assigned to the Leseding Primary School in Dilepe, a remote village that is the "stronghold of some of the most powerful and wealthy chiefs in the country, all of whom own innumerable Masarwa as slaves" (24). She arrives in the village in care of a truck driver who leaves her at the village café with Dikeledi, another primary school teacher who happens to be the sister of the eponymous Maru, Dilepe's next paramount chief. Although Dikeledi is immediately taken with Margaret— she is the first of her privileged and Western-educated peers to "put a good education to useful purpose"—she nevertheless is puzzled by what she regards as the disjunction between Margaret's Masarwa appearance, her English name, and her "near perfect" English accent (25). "In fact," in Dikeledi's view, "not one thing about her fitted another and she looked half like a Chinese and half like an African and half like god knows what" (23).[50] In a repetition of Margaret Jr.'s experiences in secondary school and college, Dikeledi mistakes her for coloured, that "variant of the word 'Bushman.' It was also a name they gave to the children of marriage between white and South African. Such children bore the complexion of members of the Bushman tribe." Dikeledi distractedly asks Margaret if "her father was a white man" (20, 24). (While in South Africa *Bushman* was a slur aimed at coloureds, in Dilepe *coloured* means someone of white and African parentage, as opposed to Masarwa or Bushman, though the Tswana considered both inferior. The school principal says, "Coloureds are just trash but at least she [Margaret Cadmore] could pass as one" [44].)[51]

In response to the question "Is your father a white man?"—the only correct answer to which can be "Yes. I am coloured," whether it is true or not—Margaret speaks what is constituted as the unspeakable.[52] She says, "No. Margaret Cadmore was the name of my teacher. She was a white woman from England. I am a Masarwa" (24). Surprised at this admission Dikeledi, the owner of numerous Masarwa slaves, tells Margaret that "no one need know" that she is a Masarwa because she will be mistaken for coloured. As Dikeledi says this aloud, she thinks, "Who had ever said, 'I am a Masarwa'? It sent thrills of fear down their spines. They all owned slaves" (44). Offered the chance to pass into the category of coloured, a choice for Margaret that Head scrupulously represents as a nonchoice, she says simply, "But I am not ashamed of being a Masarwa" (36).

Against the background of institutions run by the missionaries as the spaces within which Margaret Jr. has learned to identify as Masarwa, what does it mean that in the outside she claims the unclaimable? How does Margaret's claim to be a Masarwa function in relation to her misrecognition by those who, constructing themselves against their own conception of Masarwa, know what a Masarwa looks like and what it means to (not) be a Masarwa, but who nonetheless do not or cannot see Margaret as Masarwa? How does her claim function in a text in which the misrecognition it initiates is no simple mis-seeing but a profound sign of the success of

Margaret Sr.'s experiment ("environment everything; heredity nothing")
and her experiment's success beyond her intention? What does it mean to
occupy and to speak from this position of shame (the position from which
one cannot "still turn round to and say, 'At least I am not a ——' ") without
being shamed (Head 1971, 15)?

Dorothy Driver writes, "Margaret . . . is able to know herself as a
Masarwa not by positioning an 'other' but by placing an 'I' in its own
space. Not only are the subject and object of enunciation healthily split off
from each other (so that Margaret can look upon her own Masarwaness),
but the pride and independence with which the word I is spoken in turn
adjust the nature of the 'object,' the social image of Masarwaness" (1996,
47). Driver is correct about Margaret's response doing the work of placing
"that I in its own space," but to read "pride and independence" into
Margaret's assumption of Masarwa and therefore as evidence of identification is to misapprehend how she operates within the text. Her presence
seems to me to be precisely not her simply affirming a true identity but
confusing the coordinates of identity altogether. To read simple affirmation here is to ignore as well that there is in relation to Margaret Jr. a
nonuseful, nonrecuperable, political use that she is put to, one that is
largely symbolic. It is not to read her refusal to allow the oppressor to
redeem himself or herself through allowing her nominative freedom in
social death by coercing her never to speak of but to continue to live her
(once) inferior position in relation to them. (Coercion here means simply
the offer of the cessation of pain, to be left alone.) In light of this, Margaret's saying to Dikeledi (the benign slave owner), "I am a Masarwa" and
"But I am not ashamed of being a Masarwa" refuses, consciously or not, to
force another body to wear the shame that she is being allowed the
possibility of disavowing.

Pete, the principal of the Leseding Primary School, also at first assumes
that Margaret Jr. is coloured and on the heels of that assumption concludes that "he'd have something to talk about, such as that she must be
the first of *their* kind to teach in *their* schools. He'd also have to keep a
sharp eye on racialism. *Those* types were well known for thinking too
much about their white parent and not enough about their African side"
(39). (When has the outcast in Dilepe been inside teaching the children of
the elite? Like Margaret Sr. attributing the oppression of the KhoiSan

solely to the Tswana, Pete attributes racialism to the coloured.) However, after Pete asks Margaret if she is a coloured and she replies, "No. I am a Masarwa," he begins to think of her as an *it* and to plot to push her out of her position. "It's easy" to get rid of her, he thinks. "She's a woman." But exactly contrary to Pete's expectation that her position will be simple to undermine, her open claim to being Masarwa undermines *his* subject position and *his* position of authority, and her being protected by Dikeledi unnerves him altogether.

When Margaret Jr. first speaks to Dikeledi (in their initial encounter) from what is constructed culturally as *the* space of abjection, she withdraws from her purse the drawing of her birth mother and then tells Dikeledi, "My teacher made this sketch of my mother the day she died" (24).[53] Her confession elicits the following reconsideration and questions from Dikeledi: "You are right to tell anyone that you are a Masarwa. . . . Did a White woman write that? And about a Masarwa? 'She looks like a Goddess'?" (24–25). Returning to Baartman, that her "exhibitors felt the need to develop a how-to-read-the-exhibition poster points to a real anxiety on their part that perhaps the body did *not* speak for itself" (Strother 1999, 31). In *Maru* "the transparency of the image is questioned; the process of reading brings home the fact that what we see is ideologically mediated and that alternative intervention in the process of seeing can produce a new meaning for the Masarwa woman" (Wicomb 1996/1990, 54). And Margaret Sr. is linked to a colonial history in which "a common motif in the representation of bushmen is an odd tension between text and picture" (Landau 1996, 130). Finally, in Dikeledi's questions— "Did a White woman write that? And about a Masarwa? 'She looks like a Goddess'?"—we see that the rhetorical power of the image resides neither in the represented body nor in the sentence itself but rather in the signatory power behind the author of it. Is there perhaps something similar at work in relation to the Miscast exhibition? Is this, in other words, how resignification works?

The caption "She looks like a Goddess" should also bring the reader back to the scene of the initial creation of the drawing as the second of a pair, a complement to the sketch of the Batswana nurses that announces, "These are not decent people" (14). (The Miscast exhibition too is a complement to the Bushman diorama.) After their initial encounter Dikeledi takes Margaret to the Dilepe Tribal Administration so that Moleka (another member of the Tswana elite and also an owner of numerous Masarwa slaves) might secure housing for her. Like Dikeledi, Moleka instantly is smitten with the new teacher who "looks" like a coloured. Not yet aware that Margaret is a Masarwa, Moleka offers her the old library for accommodations, and he lends her (an untouchable) a bed from the Totem's (the elite's) supplies. It is the crossing of uncrossable borders and the kindness of elites otherwise constrained in their relations with those known as Masarwa that mark Margaret Jr.'s arrival in Dilepe village. It is a different set of encounters with her and the attempted consolidation of power in their wake that signal her exit.

Working at the Roots of Freedom

> It is not easy to escape mentally from a concrete situation, to refuse its ideology while continuing to live with its actual relationships.—**ALBERT MEMMI,** *The Colonizer and the Colonized*

> There is no third path and that is the one we are going to take.
> —**JACQUELINE ROSE,** *The Question of Zion*

Maru is divided into two parts, and within those parts are further subdivisions and several beginnings and endings. The prolepsis, for example, begins with black storm clouds on the horizon and ends with Maru rejecting harsh words, "walk[ing] in at the door and say[ing], softly: 'My sweetheart'" to Margaret. By offering us in Maru a character whose words are lived out in his actions, the text sets out on what could be a "third path," a vision on the horizon of a possible future and the work of founding a possible new era in the aftermath of a paramount chief's renunciations of power. The text begins, "The rains were so late that year. But throughout that hot, dry summer those black storm clouds clung in thick folds of brooding darkness along the low horizon. There seemed to be a secret in their activity, because each evening they broke the long, sullen silence of the day, and sent soft rumbles of thunder and flickering slicks of lightning across the empty sky. They were not promising rain. They were prisoners, pushed back, in trapped coils of boiling cloud" (5). The narrative then begins again, with a disquisition on the universality of prejudice.

Part II begins with Margaret Cadmore Jr. positioned in relation to a different, calmer landscape: "The rhythm of sunrise, the rhythm of sunset, filled her life. In the distance, a village proceeded with its own life but she knew not what it was. . . . She was not a part of it and belonged nowhere. In fact, so quiet and insignificant were her movements that the people of Dilepe *almost forgot* that there was such a thing as a Masarwa teacher" (93). Earlier in the text Dikeledi has taken "two slaves from her father's house and, without fuss or bother, paid them a regular monthly wage. They dressed well, ate well, and walked around the village with a quiet air of dignity" (25). The removal of these two men from slavery is not in any way disruptive: Dilepe village's power structures remain intact, the majority of the Masarwa remain enslaved, and these two former slaves go about the village "almost unnoticed." That Margaret Jr., whose entrance into Dilepe village is characterized by disruption, is almost forgotten and, like the two former slaves, is incorporated into the rhythm and flow of life in Dilepe, is a resolution that would be unsatisfactory for Head. In fact each new beginning in *Maru* (and there are several of them) demonstrates Head's profound understanding that there is *no place* for such a person as a free Masarwa within a society that equates Masarwa with slave. What would freedom for Margaret in Dilepe mean? What, in other words, does it mean for her to occupy and enjoy the position of a certain kind of relative freedom and status—through tolerance or forgetfulness or disavowal and displacement—that the majority of the other Masarwa do not enjoy, a position that in fact depends upon their not enjoying it?

What Head delivers is an analysis of power in relation to affect and its transmission. As the critic Annie Gagiano states, "Head's imagining [in *Maru*] of the founding of future, humane communities takes full cognizance of recalcitrance, obstruction, and delay. . . . [It is] a fully intended effect of the author's" (2000, 145). The uncertainty of the novel's many beginnings and endings is, I think, indicative of Head's unwillingness to proscribe what the future (Maru's, Margaret Jr.'s, Botswana's, South Africa's, African diasporic peoples') might look like after the giving up of power, except to acknowledge that it is a tenuous, volatile space, a space of unknowing, a space of possibility. Head also seems to be working out in *Maru* that the work of liberation from being the oppressed and from being the oppressor might in its initial stages look a lot like the old forms of oppression, might be in fact another form of the same old oppression, might remain the same old oppression. Contrast the end of the text that follows with the "black storm clouds not promising rain" of the beginning:

When people of the Masarwa tribe heard about Maru's marriage to one of their own, a door silently opened on the small, dark airless room in which their souls had been shut for a long time. The wind of freedom, which was blowing throughout the world for all people, turned and flowed into the room. As they breathed in the fresh, clear air their humanity awakened. They examined their condition. There was the fetid air, the excreta and the horror of being an oddity of the human race with half the head of a man and half the body of a donkey. They laughed in an embarrassed way scratching their heads. How had they fallen into this condition when, indeed, they were as human as everyone else was? They started to run out into the sunlight, then they turned and looked at the dark, small room. They said: "We are not going back there."

People like the Batswana, who did not know that the wind of freedom had also reached the people of the Masarwa tribe, were in for an unpleasant surprise because it would no longer be possible to treat Masarwa people in an inhuman way without getting killed yourself. (127)

The question of belonging remains unresolved, and full liberation has not occurred through "black faces replacing white faces [or other black faces] of cruelty and greed." For Head, liberation, real transformation will come about only through the rupture of established systems of power, through a commitment to "every new and unacceptable idea [being] put abruptly into practice, making no allowance for prejudice" (6). Taken together, Maru's and Margaret's renunciations of power and their avowals of humanity beyond ethnicity precipitate their exit from Dilepe and the awakening of the consciousness of the dispossessed Masarwa. Their actions constitute a rupture in the everyday in which the Masarwa would continue to be consigned to and resigned to the position of slaves.

"The Door of Dreams"

It is impossible to guess how the revolution will come one day in South Africa. But in a world where all ordinary people are insisting on their rights, it is inevitable.
—**BESSIE HEAD**, *Tales of Tenderness and Power*

Outside of South Africa, in the newly independent African nation of Botswana, wearing "borrowed clothes" and acting as a dreamer and story-teller, Head finds that she has a "not so pretty story to tell about the people who live there" as well as about those who live in that other unlivable space, South Africa.[54] Her story foregrounds indigenous slavery and what, in her words, Africans "liked . . . to think themselves incapable of [and that] is being exposed to oppression and prejudice. They always knew it was there but no oppressor likes to think of his oppression" (48).[55] While the central relationships in *Maru* are primarily about the acquisition or relinquishment of power, Head does not imagine the end of power through them, but creates a landscape in which there are moments of stillness: breaks, ruptures in power's (ab)uses. For if, as Head tells us, the continued misuse of power depends on the oppressor not recognizing the humanity of the oppressed, and if it is this continued misrecognition that allows for slavery and any number of other oppressions, then the profound intersubjectivity in this text works to make such misrecognitions difficult, if not impossible. Indeed most of part II (the final thirty-four pages of the text) focuses on the profoundly symbolic intersubjective relationships that exist beyond the *I*, beyond individual personality, beyond a subjectivity conferred by any independent ego. This intersubjectivity is explored largely through the figure of ready-made perfection that arrives in Dilepe village in the form of Margaret Jr., with whom each of the other three primary figures (Maru, Moleka, and Dikeledi) shares dreams and visions. In this section Head directs our attention away from Margaret's biography and body and their putative signing of Masarwaness (and others' reactions to her speaking from the place of abjection), which was the focus of part I, toward the playing-out of her disruptiveness and its effects on those around her.

In part I Margaret Cadmore Sr. is a colonist and missionary with social engineering ambitions through the proxy of Margaret Jr. In part II Maru is an imperialist with ambitions to become a "drastic revolutionary" and the man who desires a "puppet of goodness." Both characters, both social systems put Margaret Jr. to their own uses. Through her each character taps into something otherwise inaccessible to them (she is the means by which they really see "her people"). In this sense Margaret Jr. is not unlike the character Beloved in Toni Morrison's novel. Margaret's humanity, what, in Morrison's words, "Negroes believed could not be questioned" (1987, 198), is a point of access for each of the main characters' compromised humanity. The very mechanics of slavery alert us to the ways that slaves' humanness was always recognized, accounted for, disciplined, and circumscribed. Even as each of the primary characters in *Maru* reacts violently, involuntarily, and contradictorily to Margaret Jr.'s assertion that she is a Masarwa, they are transformed by their encounters with her. For Seth, Pete, and Molefa, who want to unseat Maru, her dismissal would be the means for them to ascend to power; for Moleka she is a conduit to feeling, the means by which he experiences an intimate soul connection; for Dikeledi this contact expands her already changing politics. Over the course of the year that Margaret spends in Dilepe "Dikeledi . . . became more pensive and silent towards the latter part of the year, while her friend Margaret grew in strength of purpose and personality" (112). Such descriptions indicate the flow of feeling and personality between them. Likewise in relation to Maru, Margaret was to become "another Dikeledi who alternated happiness with misery, finding herself tossed about this way and that on permanently restless seas" (115).

Also like Morrison's Beloved, Margaret's relations with Dikeledi, Maru, and Moleka are transfiguring for her. Most important, though, Maru plans that his marriage to Margaret and the public disgrace that will accompany it will enable him to break with his hereditary position, in which part of what he inherits and then must reproduce are a series of power relationships based on hereditary privilege and slavery. He finds in Margaret the "puppet of goodness and perfection [that he needed] to achieve the things he felt himself incapable of achieving. He could project the kind of creative ferment that could change a world, but he was not a living dynamo. She was" (70). In direct contrast to Margaret's desire to no longer be a social experiment, Maru tells Dikeledi, "Everything I have done has been an experience, an experiment. I just move on to more experience, more experiment. When she walked into the office this afternoon, I merely said: That's one more experience for me, but it shows all the signs of being a good one. A woman like that would ensure that I am never tempted to make a spectacle of myself" (70). Unable to be seen as an individual, Margaret remains representative of and the means by which Maru (like Margaret Sr.) sees "her people": "[Despite] being so highly individualistic himself, he dreaded working out any conclusions along those of tribe or race. . . . The conditions which surrounded [Maru] at the time forced him to think of her as a *symbol of her tribe and through her he sought to gain an understanding of the eventual liberation of an oppressed people*" (108; emphasis mine).

While we see everywhere Margaret Jr.'s profound effects on power and the way she disrupts those in positions of power, we read also in part II that she herself is "very violent and dominant but seemingly *unable* to project that hidden power" (71). We have evidence of her powerful projection after she is confronted by the students who have been coached by the principal to disrupt her class by shouting "Since when is a Bushy a teacher?" Margaret tells Dikeledi that she imagined she was strangling a little girl in the front row of her class. She explains her silence in the face of the children's outbursts: "I was surprised. . . . They used to do it to me when I was a child but I never felt angry. Before you came in, I thought I had a stick in my hands and was breaking their necks. . . . I thought I had killed a little girl in the front desk who was laughing because I clearly saw myself grab her and break her neck with a stick" (47). Dikeledi too sees an image of the little girl with the broken neck. That she shares Margaret's vision, witnesses this scene, is an effect of Margaret's visionary power, as well as an effect of Margaret's own vulnerability and resistance to power's excesses and the profound intersubjectivity of the characters. Ever aware of power, Head has written elsewhere, "Every oppressed man has this suppressed violence, as though silently waiting the time to set right the wrongs that afflict him" (1989b, 142). We can read here Margaret Jr.'s resistance to power, that it only seems that she is unable, instead of unwilling, to project her hidden power (there is evidence of her ability to project her power in her paintings, in her effects on other people, and elsewhere). That is, we can read Margaret Jr.'s failure to act out this violent fantasy of power as her *choice* to "avoid [acting out of] the sources of power" (Head, quoted in Brown 2003, 231).

Throughout this process, however, what no one witnesses is the effect of Margaret's own power on herself, the force inside her that makes her a point of access and excess for each of the others. When Margaret gets down to painting with all of the materials that Maru has sent her through Dikeledi, there is no one to witness that "most terrible discipline" of producing work that is in service to Maru's dreams and visions but also in excess of them. She does, after all, create at least one painting that Maru does not want, one that does not come from him, that is for Moleka and not for him. There was no witness, however, and "no word to explain the torture of those days [in which she paints thirty paintings], but out of it she had learned. *Something inside her was more powerful than her body could endure.* It had to be brought under control, put on a leash and then be allowed to live in a manageable form. She would never do work like that again" (102).

With no word and no witness for what Margaret has undergone in producing the paintings (and in being produced herself), do we see only her compliance, not also her resistance and their connection? The end of *Maru* that is the beginning, which (unsatisfactorily for many of Head's readers) leaves Margaret Jr. subject to Maru's personality and will, can be read as well as a marker of *unfreedom*. In the prolepsis we cannot read "liberation on the immediate horizon" because "we are an oppressed people [who] have been stripped bare of every human right. We do not know what it is like to have our ambitions aroused, nor do we really see liberation on an immediate horizon" (1990, 68), but we can at least read Head's and Margaret's recognition of unfreedom, their recognition of their and others' oppression and by whom. Writing in South Africa Head insisted, "The Coloured man knows he is oppressed and he knows his oppressor. He of all the oppressed groups in South Africa *knows his oppressor most because he is closer to him* [and shares in his power to an extent] and really understands the ruthless nature of his power" (1990, 11).

In the prolepsis Margaret is a participant in her own positioning on the outside of power, a move that is both a choice and a form of subjugation. In the prolepsis and at the end of the text (whose narratives are simultaneous, in the same time if not the same place) the reader is positioned with those Masarwa who remain in Dilepe village, emerging from their rooms with the "fetid air, the excreta and the horror of being an oddity of the human race," and we are one thousand miles away in a new landscape and in the doorway of the two rooms in which Margaret lives. In one room Margaret loves Maru completely; in the other room, which she can't remember, she dreams of Moleka and cries "deep, heart-rending sobs." Even though upon waking she has no explanation for her tears, no memory of this room or of her heartache, in this space is her desire to return to that moment of stillness in which she can be ordinary and be "important" to someone, be free of the significations of Masarwa, be human. Recorded in Margaret's painting and in the text of *Maru* is the oppressed's desire for human dignity and Head's vision of new nations with "new names for human dignity."

We are left in *Maru* at the literal end of the text with one Tswana "Dilepe diseased" prostitute's reassertion of Tswana superiority and the threat of violence to those who would continue to assert this superiority in the face of Masarwa getting a breath of "the wind of freedom": "People like the Batswana, who did not know that the wind of freedom had also reached the people of the Masarwa tribe, were in for an unpleasant surprise because it would no longer be possible to treat Masarwa people in an inhuman way without getting killed yourself" (127). The prolepsis offers no conclusions but marks possibility.

The story that Head tells "about the people of a free land . . . is not anything very polite, it seems," and it is one in which there is no ending, happy or otherwise (1990, 85). Beginning and ending with uncertainty, with struggles for liberation (social, political, spiritual, artistic, etc.) that are continuous and varied and with incomplete transformations, *Maru* is not a story of liberation achieved and the beginning of a bright new era. Margaret Cadmore Jr.'s body and her suffering are instrumental in the changes taking place in Dilepe at the end of the novel, and the nation qua Dilepe re-creates itself in relation to her body (and shame is displaced onto that problematically named "Dilepe diseased prostitute"); nevertheless her suffering is not fully redeemed, and the Masarwa who remain in bondage in Dilepe are not required to forget, to not speak their collective oppression. Head was determined to write about liberation's complicity with power and unfreedom when that liberation may be said to have occurred because "black faces replac[ed] white faces" or because "no scientist can ever again get a look at [Baartman's] body" (Abrahams 2003, 13–14).[56] For Head the continuing price of such incomplete liberation is too dear. Perhaps this is why her writing "haunts our present [in] the way it resonantly speaks, and speaks with a special force in relation to questions that must be asked about 'new worlds,' about individual and collective freedoms, and about the potential powers of writing" (Lewis 2005). Head evinces her concern with oppressive social and symbolic structures, with the ways that subjects are constructed in relation to them, and with the ways that these structures are internalized and exercised on others and on the self, what she refers to as the point at which we become evil. Bessie Head's "freedoms," as Desiree Lewis characterizes them, exist somewhere in the future as a "disruptive utopian vision [that] points towards what has not yet been named or disclosed." Though she was positioned by law and circumstance as one allowed access to certain relative freedoms, her rejection of this access in favor of liberation defined in terms as "broad as possible" turns our attention to the questions that must be asked about the desire that persists within the text, within newly independent Botswana, within the postemancipation United States, within democratic South Africa—in other words, post-slavery and postapartheid (the *post*-acknowledged to be legal, juridical, and incomplete)—to be positioned on the inside of newly constructed national narratives, a desire to be inside that demands what Head insists must be refused: the disavowal of oppression and the displacement onto other bodies of the shame of having been positioned outside.

Head's narrative, her dreams and storytelling, allow us to follow the trace left behind by one who was present at the birth of a new nation. We see in *Maru* the universal (and always particular) desire to be unmolested (that is, to simply be left alone as one who is *recognized as* what *is recognized* as human), a desire that Head knows necessitates that some other body bear the mark of monstrosity, be the stuff out of which the nation that re-creates oppression as freedom for some bodies (as, for example, separate development) discursively re-creates itself as free. This, finally, is what Margaret Cadmore Jr. and *Maru* might alert us to in the present: the dangers in the current embrace of Saartje Baartman as icon and the myriad ways that her redemption as incorporation has allowed continued injustice to be rewritten as freedom.

THREE

Isaac Julien's *The Attendant* and the Sadomasochism of Everyday Black Life

The Door of No Return—real and metaphoric as some places are, mythic to those of us scattered in the Americas today. To have one's being lodged in a metaphor is voluptuous intrigue; to inhabit a trope; to be a kind of fiction. To live in the Black diaspora is I think to live as a fiction—a creation of empires, and also self-creation. It is to be a being living inside and outside of herself. It is to apprehend the sign one makes yet to be unable to escape it except in radiant moments of ordinariness made like art. . . . The frame of the doorway is the only space of true existence. . . .

"Pray for a life without plot, a day without narrative." . . . To be without th[e] story of captivity, to dis-remember it, or to have this story forget me would be heavenly. But of course in that line too is the indifference, the supplication of prayer. Yet I want to think that perhaps there is also regeneration in its meaning.—**DIONNE BRAND,** *A Map to the Door of No Return: Notes to Belonging*

I begin this chapter with this rather long quotation from Brand's *A Map to the Door of No Return: Notes to Belonging* in order to situate my reading of Isaac Julien's film *The Attendant* (1993) in relation to narratives of slavery and the signification of the black body. The black British filmmaker Isaac Julien stages the framing and remembering of chattel slavery, the policing of space and desire, and the discursive production of histories and subjectivities in the highly regulated institutional space of the museum. In occupying the museum Julien attempts to disrupt the traditional hierarchical organization of museum space and its attempts to resolve relations between cultures and peoples in terms of positive and negative, presence and absence, high and low, art and artifact. Through the presentation of fantasies in *The Attendant*, fantasies that might seem to be the attendant's but that arise out of the hidden histories of the museum, its unarchived and very present depths, Julien reveals the disciplining of desire and history in the museum as he draws our attention to the museum's unconscious, its "kinky, haunted spaces" (Julien 2001). In doing so, he presents us with a new geography of relations that expands the possibilities of, for example, how chattel slavery is represented and remembered, that shifts how we look at and respond to those representations in our identification with and through them, that effects a change in what we presume to know and what we continue to disavow about freedom and about slavery and its continuing aftereffects on black and white people. In this chapter on *The Attendant* I am particularly concerned with African chattel slavery's continuing discursive relationship to the production of black (queer) bodies and relations; with the ways that ideas about consent and pleasure complicate those productions; with things that are not acknowledged; with what is *unseen*, not *permitted*, and that which we may possibly glimpse.[1]

In *Scenes of Subjection* Saidiya Hartman argues that the "crimes of slavery are not only witnessed but staged" and that the "constitution of blackness as an abject and degraded condition and the fascination with the other's enjoyment went hand in hand" (1997, 8). Antebellum slavery's multiple horrors and pleasures are staged at the whipping post, in enslaved people's forced performances of affect, like singing and "stepping-it-lively" on the coffle and on the auction block (17–23). Postbellum the crimes and pleasures of slavery persist, are reenacted and recirculated in national consciousness through the staging and interpretation of slavery and its excesses, in everyday relations of terror, in literary texts, visual arts, museum exhibitions, and memorials. While the attempts to monumentalize and memorialize slavery inform this chapter, my principal concern is with the imagining and making spectacular of slavery's horrors and an accompanying excess of pleasure that continues to be produced through identifications with and disavowals of blackness, by entering into and abandoning black (queer) bodies. In his conversation with the memorializing project of the Wilberforce House Museum, which calls itself "the world's first slavery museum," Isaac Julien connects contemporary labor, terrors, and desires to the labor and the excesses of chattel slavery, to power, sex, and identification. It is through these connections between daily life and libidinal excess that Julien explodes calcified modes of seeing and understanding. These connections are not, however, even collectively an end in themselves; rather they create an opening within which an as yet undetermined something else can emerge. That is, they might offer instances of what Irit Rogoff calls a place of being without, "not [a space] of being at a loss, of inhabiting a lack, of not having anything, but rather an *active, daily disassociation in the attempt to clear the ground for something else to emerge*" (2001, 34).

The Attendant is shot in the Wilberforce House in Hull and the Royal Academy in London, but the setting of the film is the Wilberforce House Museum, the home turned slavery museum that is a testament to the parliamentarian and abolitionist William Wilberforce and a monument to England's antislavery movement. François-Auguste Biard's famous antislavery painting *Slaves on the West Coast of Africa* (1833), which depicts France's involvement in the theft of and trade in enslaved Africans, has been installed there since 1840, two years after England's incremental abolition of slavery concluded (1834–38) and thirty-three years after the end of the British slave trade.[2] An archival institution, the Wilberforce House Museum constructs memory by mapping an ideologically specific history of progress, connection, and proximity, framing and articulating subjects and relationships through the arrangement of space and the production of aesthetics and aesthetic pleasure.[3] Part of what is being mapped in this space is Britain's "collective national consciousness about slavery . . . that [it] has a proud record to boast . . . [and that that] role may be contrasted with Napoleonic France's attempts to reintroduce slavery in the West Indies, particularly in Haiti" (Golbourne 2001, 127). When the Biard painting was installed in the Wilberforce House Museum it thereby served several purposes: it helped to establish the perspective that England was not the primary force in the Atlantic trade; it solidified the heroic stature of Wilberforce; it foregrounded France's continuing involvement in the trade after England made it illegal; and it diverted attention from "the brutal history through which Britain's global economic hegemony was consolidated" (Dawson 2001, unpaginated). It partially accomplished this symbolically through the presentation of black bodies. Constituting the opening shot of *The Attendant, Slaves on the West Coast of Africa* operates as a primary visual and affective reference for the film; it helps to establish from the outset Julien's attention to affect, his desire to intervene in "the neo-colonialist archive," and his desire to use film's "potential" to "mak[e] visible the psychic mechanisms at work which govern the racist phantasies, surveillance and stereotyping of non-white subjects in the West" (Julien 1997, online).

Julien's visual use of the slave trade scene of the classical antislavery painting immediately places *The Attendant* in direct and contestatory conversation with the politics of memorialization and with the historical museum's productions of history and subjectivity. Julien establishes that the (antislavery) museum's production of history not only includes images of slavery and earlier attempts to rewrite the history of slavery, often in less brutal terms, but it also foregrounds a *pleasure* in slavery and its representations that is hard to admit yet impossible to deny. The ambivalent pleasure in representation in the present informs not only Julien's work, but also the work of many black visual artists working in the "critical decade" of the 1980s and the early and mid-1990s. In particular it informs the art and films that take as their subject black (gay) men or the politics and aesthetics of black male subjectivity and representation, among them Fred Wilson's installation *Guarded View* (1991); Robert Mapplethorpe's, Rotimi Fani-Kayode's, and Lyle Ashton Harris's photographs of black men; and Marlon Riggs's groundbreaking film *Tongues Untied* (1989). Only eight minutes long and without dialogue, Julien's film has a number of subjects: the museum, a museum attendant and conservator, slavery, pageantry, fetishism, s/m, space, time, desire, mourning, and style itself, as well as the architectures of space, time, desire, and mourning. This list of the film's subjects, however, would privilege narrative over style and in doing so would say both too much about the work and not enough.

"Within the black repertoire, style—which mainstream cultural critics often believe to be the mere husk, the wrapping, the sugar coating on the pill—has become itself the subject of what is going on," Stuart Hall writes in "What Is This 'Black' in Black Popular Culture?" (1992, 27). *The Attendant* exemplifies the expansion of parameters that black British film underwent in the 1980s and 1990s. Julien was one of a group of filmmakers in this period who moved away from black film's (understandable) reliance on documentary realism to an experimental cinema that did not disavow political content but was concerned as well with style, with the apparatus and the politics of representation itself.[4] The emphasis on style in *The Attendant* is not simply, as some critics would have it, "[Julien's] putting his viewers to the test" through "erudite conceptualizations" (Weintraub 2003, 9). Rather *The Attendant's* style, its multiple looks—its appearance, the way that it employs the look, looking, and the gaze—is where I locate the basis of its power to disrupt established visual and cultural codes. In its visual extravagance—camp pageantry, tableaux vivants, opera house formality, and museum display—it refuses what Mieke Bal calls "the blinding effect of sameness in repetition" (Bal 1996, 205).[5] Style is *precisely* what "makes [*The Attendant's*] narrative so compelling . . . [in] its complex voyeuristic exchanges of looking and watching, mapping homoerotic desire with a digital blend of Cocteau and Genet, across landscapes of race and sado-masochism" (Bailey 1995, 62). Perhaps because its brevity deprives the viewer of a certain narrative pleasure and because its hyperstylized, uncanny stagings disrupt a *historicized* nexus of slavery, sex, desire, and power relations, our attention is turned away from "what one already knows" to "what one doesn't know (yet)" (Bal 1996, 205).

Desire is mapped out in *The Attendant* in its focus on four primary figures: the black male museum guard, whose job is to make the museum secure (the Attendant); the black female museum conservator, who maintains and restores the integrity of works of art in the museum (the Conservator); the white male visitor with whom the Attendant shares desiring looks and an s/m scene (the Visitor); and the black male figure who appears in and out of the tableaux that emerge cinematically from works on the walls of the museum and who is described in the credits as the Angel.[6] The sequence of shots that first establishes objects, relations, and their framing on display begins with the establishing shot of Biard's antislavery painting and is followed by a sequence that includes museum guests looking at the works; the Attendant standing guard and checking bags, reminiscing, cruising, and participating in an s/m scene with the Visitor; and shots of the Conservator at work. The action of the film takes place to a slowed-down soundtrack of Henry Purcell's *Dido and Aeneas*.[7] The film's loose plot works itself out through these scenes and in relation to two representations of chattel slavery: the Biard painting and the cross-section of the Brookes plan diorama located in the Wilberforce House Museum's basement, which Julien alludes to in his Tate Gallery talk but does not visually represent in the film.[8] Thus what is "below decks" and not represented in the film is a diorama of a ship with Africans in the Middle Passage; this diorama itself is a replica of the diorama that Wilberforce had made when he was fighting for abolition. Now, however, instead of paper figures pasted into the bottom of the model slave ship there are papier-mâché figures chained together in a heap. The ineffable is subject here to representation in order to produce and control an affective response and through that affective response produce an understanding of the horrors of the Middle Passage.

In *The Attendant* the multiple scenes of the horrors of chattel slavery that we see in the Biard painting (French sailors whipping enslaved Africans, leading a coffle, an African man held down while others look in his mouth, the branding of an enslaved woman, etc.) are transfigured and intercut with scenes of the Attendant and the Conservator at work. Two fantastic and colorful tableaux vivants of actors in gay interracial s/m scenes that mimic the Biard painting and the chained figures in the basement and an operatic performance by the Attendant, who appears in formal evening dress singing the part of Dido, Queen of Carthage, intercut in the black-and-white scene of the Attendant and Conservator at work in the museum. (Those papier-mâché figures in the basement that we do not see in the film nevertheless haunt the scene.) The thematic and stylistic concerns that we see in Biard's *Slaves*, his use of color particularly in capturing African complexions,[9] as well as his aestheticized depiction of scenes of cruelty, indifference, and desire endemic to the slave trade are replaced and restaged in Julien's film. We see this on the level of the gaze, in the relations between the Attendant and the Conservator and between the Attendant and the Visitor, in the visitors viewing the paintings in the museum in the film, and in the film viewer's look at the painting and the scenes of sadomasochism within the film itself.

The gaze is redoubled, forced back upon the viewer by way of Julien's hyperstylizations; as one looks at the s/m scenes one is compelled to reconsider the scenes of capture, torture, and complacency in the Biard painting. In the same fashion one is compelled to view the scenes of the Attendant and the Conservator at work through the lens of the Biard painting. Put another way, the uncanny juxtaposition of *Slaves on the West Coast of Africa*, s/m, and daily museum work shifts the look of slavery and the viewer's relationships to it from the past to the present, from the way the history of slavery is archived in the museum, narrativized in film, and presented in museological practices to the way it is worked out in everyday relations. For Kobena Mercer, "Isaac Julien's work suggests something interesting about his artistic relationship to the archival relations of the Western canon. When the use of 'style' cuts an opening into the closed codes of a culture, and an artist is said to touch upon a nerve, making a mark that alters habitual ways of seeing you could say that such practices involve a 'turn'" (2001, 8–9). Therein lies a source of the viewer's discomfort.

Julien consistently offers glimpses of the repressed, of the disavowed, and of the emergence of the uncanny. In particular his museum films, of which *The Attendant* is the first in a trilogy, make spectacular what the institution of the museum conceals with its authorized spectacle: "the uncanny [as] something [known and repressed] which [according to its desires] ought to have remained hidden but has come into the open" (Freud 2003, 148). Some of the challenges to seeing that this museum film poses may be found in its focus on the structural and ideological forces that produce the viewers through their own looking at history, that compel viewers to watch *and* to look away from, to acknowledge *and* to disavow, their particular positioning in and by presentations of official history.[10]

Turning the gaze to the repressed desires and libidinal investments that are installed in the museum's displays but not acknowledged to be there— juxtaposing, among other things, an archive of the history of slavery and the complications of abolition with interracial queer s/m tableaux vivants —is only part of what occurs in these eight minutes of film. Along with complex and often surprising articulations of desire and history, Julien casts the quotidian scene of institutional work as horror and pleasure, and then he ruptures those scenes with scenes of even more stylized spectacle. Such a breaking open of museum codes connects the largely invisible labor of the black museum attendant and museum conservator to the largely invisible structures that maintain *how* we see and, moreover, *who* sees objects and (historical) relations. Likewise Julien's focus on the work that goes on in the museum and the subjects who do that work makes us aware of its hidden "psychic and surveillance mechanisms," the complicated structures of power involved in its guarding and conservation, the policing and maintaining of authority by sustaining the integrity of the physical supports of official memory. The relationship of the Attendant and the Conservator to their alienated and alienating labor supports the museum itself. The tableaux vivants of the reconfigured Biard painting, the s/m scenes between the Attendant and the Visitor, and the scenes of the Conservator doing her work stage how bodies become disciplined, resist being disciplined, and are recorded as undisciplined and how history and discursive relations are produced and maintained. Positioned as guard and guardian of this site of remembrance, recollection, (re)presentation, and objectification, the Conservator and the Attendant are in an alienated, sometimes masterful, but also masochistic relationship to the institution of the museum and to the forces of law, morality, propriety, and history that coalesce there. We see in the figure of the Attendant himself the quasi-embodiment of the law and erotic fantasy, the embodiment of the sado-masochism of everyday black life.

That the Attendant's and the Conservator's relationship to the museum is in part masochistic (and that there is for each of them both pleasure and pain in being the bottom) becomes clear to the viewer when the work that they do is aligned with sexual and other disciplinary formations. We are called on to think through how and where one finds something like pleasure within these constraints. It is, I think, in that alignment of sexuality and disciplinarity that viewers first read the Attendant's and the Conservator's masochism *perversely* (that is, contrarily) solely through the lens of sexual desire (s/m and aural voyeurism) and not through the characters' submission to and maintenance of the heterotopic institution of the museum and the ideological and actual structures that continue to hold them in place. The Attendant and the Conservator *in their daily lives* perform "scenes of subjection." They are produced and produce themselves as subjects in relation to time, space, and place, in relation to the objects and images archived and presented in the museum, and in relation to their own labor that upholds the very structures that hold them captive to a historical narrative and its present implications. Sadomasochism appears here in the course of everyday life enduringly and almost invisibly "[in] the everyday routines of domination, which continue to characterize black life but are obscured by their everydayness" (Hartman 2002, 772). Julien challenges us to look at sadomasochism in *The Attendant* beyond where it becomes immediately visible, and once visible rendered perverse, as s/m in the Attendant's desire for the Visitor, through his willing occupation of a (sexual) space of abjection (slave, bottom).

Put another way, it is easiest to read the scenes of subjection that are staged in *The Attendant* as mere repetitions of sadistic scenes from the Biard painting. Such a gesture in the film would pathologize the Attendant and the Conservator, reinforcing and repeating certain disciplinary structures that circumscribe representational and actual possibilities for black subjects. It would position Julien as well, as not occupying both spaces but as having been fully disciplined by and having internalized and reproduced the colonialist-master archive. This is a point of view that refuses to understand that Julien is aware from the outset of the sadomasochism of everyday black life and that he very much wants to "contest the narrow plac[e] that one finds oneself in in a political culture where debates about 'black authenticity' reign" (Julien 1997). "Black authenticity" is dialectical —self-imposed and imposed from outside—and as likely to be compelled by dominant discourses as to be imposed intraracially and positioned as counter to dominant discourse and its assignment of subject positions. Julien makes no claim to an *essential* blackness whose enunciation "is . . . dependent upon an active avoidance of the psychic reality of black/white desire [and relations]" (2000a, 82). Rather he insists that we not look away from the myriad ways that we have been positioned to see (and be seen) in relation to slavery's archives.

Concerned as Julien is with the "sexual and racial violence that stems from the repressed desires of the other within ourselves," in *The Attendant* "fixed ideas about racial difference are brought into play by both black and white subjects in their everyday transactions, mediated in a sexual and racial identity which is internal to every subject and which is based on the consistent denial of the Other within ourselves" (Julien 2000a, 82). Julien stages "everyday transactions" (we hear in this phrase an echo of Douglass's "bloody transaction") with black and white (people and scenes) and queer scenes of desire, with other staged scenes of sanctioned looking (the cultural critics and art world insiders shown looking at the painting within the film) as a means to "interrogate the way in which [asymmetrical] power enters into looking at relations across the symbolic black/white divide of racial identity" (Bailey 1995, 60). Both the theater of s/m and the sadomasochism of everyday black life appear here as direct instances of the disavowed, the *black* unspeakable. We cannot dismiss s/m as or reduce it to a "white thing," renounce interracial sex or desire as "sleeping with the enemy," nor can we reduce interracial s/m or a general desire to submit, to be the sadomasochist, to a *simple* repetition of the historical sadism of slavery that is archived but yet disavowed in the Biard painting and in the Wilberforce House Museum. We also cannot dismiss forced submission and its everyday contemporary manifestations.[11] That is, we cannot continue to read slavery and slavery's effects as either unchanging or locatable only in the past or in forms that seem to replicate those of the peculiar institution (though they are to be found there as well). To the extent that in *The Attendant* a variety of desires become apparent through the actions of the Attendant, the Conservator, and the Visitor, they register as part of a constellation of desires and actions that constitute the ways that "identities are formed at the unstable point where the 'unspeakable' stories of [black] subjectivity meet the narratives of a history, a culture" (Hall and Sealy 2001, 34). These desires reveal what systematically is obscured in official histories and what might very well be disruptive to them.

As a repository for an official cultural history of antislavery, for the stories that a culture tells to itself and about itself, the Wilberforce House Museum registers slavery as prolonged and horrific and the abolitionist battle against it as heroic. One subject, however, about which it is largely reticent, despite the works assembled and displayed there, is the complex relationship among (anti)slavery, abolitionist struggle, and desire. Of the abolitionist who bears witness to slavery's scenes of torture and degradation Hartman asks, "Is the act of 'witnessing' a kind of looking no less entangled with the wielding of power and the extractions of enjoyment?" (1997, 22). Are we unable to recognize the production of desire and also of an appalled fascination with subjugation, captivity, and torture when looking at the subjects of the Biard painting (and the subjects in the slave ship diorama in the basement)? Desires are continually being constituted and produced in their (alleged) forswearing. What is forsworn in the Wilberforce House Museum's narrative of antislavery and mediated through visual representation returns in *The Attendant*'s spectacle as stylized scenes of subjection and desire; what returns in *The Attendant* is the repressed curatorial memory of an abolitionist fascination with subjugation that the architectonics of the Wilberforce House Museum and the hagiography of William Wilberforce would conceal. This return is not through Julien's staging a counternarrative of slavery that would claim a particular moral and historical truth. Rather this memory returns in the film's attention to the discursive production of the compulsion for white and black viewers to "play the slave a little bit" (Juliette Bowles 1997, 5), to occupy and then disavow the occupation of an abject, subjugated position.[12] While this compulsion is produced differently for different subjects *it is black bodies* that continue to be the port of entry or point of access into any number of physical, spiritual, or subjective states.

By the mid-nineteenth century in Europe and America the appearance of blacks in texts, artwork, and theater automatically signified the presence of some "excess" of feeling, and their presence was a placeholder for and a "vehicle [of] white enjoyment." I want to continue to argue that this entering into black bodies for enjoyment "in all of its sundry and unspeakable expressions" (Hartman 1997, 23), this "playing the slave a little bit," continues to be constitutive of subjectivity for all those African and Euro-American people whom I am calling post-slavery subjects and avows the post-slavery subject's performance of the violence of history, the violence of identification, subjectification, and the violence of erasure. This post-slavery subject includes those who already inhabit the black body as well as those whose inhabiting of it is fleeting. Julien's look at contemporary scenes of subjection acted out by the Attendant and the Conservator (their laboring in *this* time and space, their "everyday transactions") as well as in the tableaux and s/m scenes involving sexual subjection, mastery, and law reframes the playing around in blackness enacted in the Biard painting compelled in the viewer of it. We understand how identification is produced and managed for the white proto-abolitionist through the Biard painting's times and spaces of chattel slavery and through Julien's juxtapositions (Biard painting, s/m, work, slavery, etc.). We see that it is the identificatory compulsion produced in this space to "play the slave," to occupy that marked body, possess it, make it "dance, sing, [and] work." But what of its effect on the subjectivity of contemporary viewers? What do we see when we look at the painting, and how do we see it in relation to our own relationship to slavery and its representations? It continues to be a constitutive act for post-slavery subjects in the New World.[13]

"The black body," writes Dionne Brand, "is a space not simply owned by those who embody it, but constructed and occupied by other embodiments. Inhabiting it is a domestic hemispheric pastime, a transatlantic pastime, an international pastime. There is a playing around in it" (2001, 38). African and Euro-American post-slavery subjects live in and with the sociohistorical and political positions and contradictions that black bodies embody; we live with the knowledge that the time and space of slavery is simultaneously all too real, that it is past, and that it is all too present; we live within the "retroactive hauntedness of history" (Copjec, quoted in Cheng 2000, 14). Discursively produced in ways that signify enslavement and its excesses, black bodies are made to bear the burden of this signification (what James Baldwin calls the "burden of representation") in ways that white and other raced bodies do not; as they are "bodies occupied, emptied and occupied," and visibly marked in Euro-American contexts as the descendants of the Atlantic slave trade, they still have currency "as physically and psychically open space" (Brand 2001, 94).

Recognizing the coincidence of horror and pleasure, and in that recognition beginning to see and to frame the articulation of horror and pleasure differently, Julien places the Attendant in spaces of abjection, mastery, and enjoyment, in the role of the museum guard, the queen, the bottom, and also the master—a set of roles that refuses a (black) hetero- or homonormative masculinity. The Conservator is also placed in spaces of abjection and enjoyment in her roles as conservator in the museum, wife of the Attendant, operagoer, and dominatrix. Yet precisely how we identify the Conservator as abject and her desire as perverse is through the tight spaces where we find her and through her apparent ability to find pleasure within those spaces of containment. But it is in the Attendant's and the Conservator's staged submissions that one can see the repetition and reification of histories of slavery occurring not through the principal characters' sexual positioning (the point of view that would "pathologize interracial queer desire") but through their work, through the spaces that they occupy in upholding the museum's structures (Deitcher 2000, 18). (It is in the figure of the Conservator that the viewer can see another perspective of what haunts representations of slavery: the knowledge that depending on one's point of view, in slavery horror and pleasure were always aligned, that there is a point where pleasure slips into the horrific, and the fear for some that there may well be a point where the black (female) subject's horror slips into pleasure.)

With a historical image of slavery juxtaposed to s/m within a museum that stages an "acceptable" history of slavery, antislavery, and post-slavery, Julien's *The Attendant* works to rupture viewers' "structures of feeling" and belonging. I offer here in condensed versions three principal objections to the film that may be legitimate but are ultimately misreadings: first, that the alignment of s/m and slavery diminishes and trivializes the horrific centrality of the four-hundred-year-long history of slavery; second, that the alignment of s/m and slavery pathologizes interracial (queer) s/m by reading it "straight" through the lens of state violence; and third, that the juxtaposition of s/m and chattel slavery detracts and distracts from the urgent task of further understanding and theorizing, for example, interracial violence and its traumatic transgenerational transmission. Against these readings that would be important contestations to a simplistic alignment of s/m and slavery, but that would ultimately flatten out this film and ignore its complexity, Julien's juxtapositions of slavery, s/m, and desire rupture "structures of feeling," those "proper" affective responses to slavery, because through them he turns the viewer's attention back to the production of post-slavery subjectivity itself, to the ways that post-slavery subjects continue to occupy these abjected black bodies in their postures of submission and mastery and the ways that this occupation in the present is a source of (ambivalently experienced) pleasure. These juxtapositions also underscore a multitude of pleasures for the nonenslaved subject that already inhere in slavery from the outset. The stylistic estrangement in *The Attendant* of the traumas of slavery, the ways that this history is made strange and uncanny even as it remains familiar, opens up spaces that exceed established narratives and subjectivities in the movement from origins to performances to daily activity. In this rupture created within *The Attendant* we apprehend that the occupation of, the playing around in black bodies occurs not only through the spectacle of those "black bodies in pain [or pleasure] for public consumption" (Alexander 1995, 92) but also through "everyday transactions," through what I am calling the sadomasochism of everyday black life.

Scenes on and off the West Coast of Africa

Pray for a life without plot, a day without narrative.
I happened on this line by Derek Walcott in his book *The Bounty*. . . . It described perfectly my desire for relief from the persistent trope of colonialism. To be without this story of captivity, to dis-remember it, or to have this story forget me would be heavenly. But of course in that line too is the indifference, the supplication of prayer. Yet I want to think that perhaps there is also regeneration in its meaning.—**DIONNE BRAND,** *A Map to the Door of No Return: Notes to Belonging*

1 *Slaves on the West Coast of Africa*, ca. 1833. François-Auguste Biard.
Courtesy of The Bridgeman Art Library International.

François-Auguste Biard's antislavery painting *Slaves on the West Coast of Africa* consists of several tableaux that depict French sailors and merchants involved in the buying and selling of enslaved Africans, a French sailor branding an enslaved woman, black men whipping other black men and being whipped by white men, a French merchant with a book open before him, and another French sailor bartering with black men over a prone black body (figure 1). The eye is caught first by the contemplative French merchant with the tablet open before him. The gaze cuts diagonally across the deck scene and halts on this figure in the light, whose casual gaze then brings one reflectively back to the scene. To look on this merchant is to see a person, and by extension (through its installation in the Wilberforce House Museum) a nation, France, strangely unaffected by the horrible, but apparently habitual, scenes before him.

The merchant is part of the visual focus of Biard's composition, and his inclusion in the scene is the inclusion of the gaze of disavowal: the look of disavowed responsibility and concern that the painting is supposed to counter in its production of proto-abolitionists. Installing the painting in

1a Detail of *Slaves on the West Coast of Africa*, ca. 1833. François-Auguste Biard. Courtesy of The Bridgeman Art Library International.

the Wilberforce works effectively to confer on France (and not Britain) the responsibility for slavery; issues of the gaze and public reception are resolved by viewers resisting the focus of the composition and identifying elsewhere in the painting. Who, after all, wants to identify with, be identified with the disinterested gaze of the merchant who is unmoved by the scene?

The painting further illustrates "the cruelty and callousness of several types of slave traders and all the pains and humiliations suffered by the slaves" (Honour 1989, 149).[14] When Biard's contemporary, William Makepeace Thackeray, reviewed *Slaves on the West Coast of Africa* he moved the viewer through the painting to a different scene: the shackled enslaved woman who is being branded by one of the sailors (figure 1a). "Yonder," Thackeray writes, "is a poor woman kneeling before one of the Frenchmen. Her shoulder is fizzing under the hot iron with which he brands her; she is looking up, shuddering and wild, yet quite mild and patient: it breaks your heart to look at her. I never saw anything so exquisitely pathetic as that face. God bless you Monsieur Biard, for painting it!"

(quoted in Wood 2000, 44). The intended audience for the painting, those who are directed to this scene, are those people who have not witnessed or actively participated in these horrors, and Thackeray accords a great deal of affective, transformative power to the scene, in particular to the look on the face of the tortured enslaved woman, her suffering endurance.[15] Abolitionism will be advanced by viewers entering into this scene, by identification with this black woman, by imagining themselves in relation to her "shuddering and wild, yet mild and patient" look: the one who bears it, the one who does the branding, the one being branded, the one(s) watching. By entering into this mise-en-scène to play the master and to "play the slave a little bit," by entering into her body the viewer conjoins horror and pleasure and Biard's "master text yields to a strangely sadomasochistic subtext" (Mercer 2001, 10). Abutting the moral arguments for slavery's abolition are decidedly bodily pleasures. The circulation of this image and its mass consumption will "stir[s] the heart more than a hundred thousand tracts, reports, or sermons; it must convert every man who has seen it" (quoted in Wood 2000, 44). Entering that body is a religious experience.

"In response to the images of violated and abused slaves . . . circulated in the early nineteenth century, several commentators noted that while they were meant to inspire moral action, the drawings often owed their impact to other more dubious pleasures" (Dean 2003, 89). This is, I think, Marcus Wood's point when he writes that Thackeray "sets up a peculiar parallelism between [the Biard] painting and the British Parliament's remuneration of the Caribbean slave-owners upon the passing of the emancipation bill in 1833. Thackeray demands that this image be bought as England's just inheritance in its post-abolition phase; the nation should be rewarded with the purchase of pornography" (2000, 44). Abolitionists are made through desire, through identification, through entering into, occupying, and possessing (as extensions of their own bodies and desires) those captive bodies.

Such is the "Janus-faced affair," of "European modernity" that is "based on emancipatory claims and projects as well as on horrendous repression and exploitation" (Mercer 1997b, 15). Thackeray writes, "You . . . who have given twenty million to the freeing of this hapless people, give yet a couple of thousand more to the French painter and don't let his work go out of the country, now that it is here. Let it hang alongside the Hogarths in the

National Gallery; it is as good as the best of them" (quoted in Wood 2000, 44). Hanging in the Wilberforce House Museum the painting installs both antislavery and nationalist sentiments; it is Biard's painting, after all, and not J. M. W. Turner's *Slavers Throwing Overboard the Dead and Dying, Typhoon Coming On* (1840; figure 2), known as *The Slave Ship,* that is installed in the Wilberforce House, never mind that Turner's painting "commemorate[s] the Atlantic slave trade, and particularly English monopoly of this trade in the eighteenth century" (Wood 2000, 41).

Biard's *Slaves* and Turner's *The Slave Ship* were exhibited together at the Royal Academy in London in 1840 to coincide with the world antislavery conference. In England Biard's *Slaves* enjoyed a reception and popularity that *The Slave Ship* did not. Turner's painting was judged to be incomprehensible largely because of its alienating presentation of the Middle Passage and the slave trade in ways that made them unknowable and unconsumable. Additionally Turner's focus on the British slave trade set it on a "head on collision between [with] the official historical memory laid down by Clarkson and Wilberforce's hagiographers and espoused by a rising Victorian imperialist sensibility" (Wood 2000, 43). Biard's painting was described as "the visual equivalent of an abolitionist tract," while Turner's painting disrupted any easy formation of a proper affective relationship to the execrable trade (Honour 1989, 164).[16] The exception to this reception of Turner's painting is John Ruskin's response, in which he is as rapturous about *The Slave Ship* as Thackeray is about *Slaves.* Ruskin writes in his diary, "I write with the Slaver on my bed opposite me. My father brought it in this morning for a New Year's present. I feel very grateful; I hope I shall continue so. I certainly shall never want another oil of his" (quoted in Wood 2000, 59). While some critics of *The Slave Ship* saw only Turner's aesthetics, others saw only the subject of slavery; few saw both, but as Wood reminds us, "To forget aesthetics when looking at Turner is not to look at him at all" (60). The relationship between aesthetics and subject is of course dialectical and ideological.

"Imperialist slave iconography is appropriated and repositioned" in Julien's presentation and stylistic disruption of Biard's spectacular painting and its "master discourse of the 'race-relations' narrative" (Julien and Mercer 2000c, 64). But, as I argued earlier, appropriation is not what makes the film disruptive to dominant discourses, for one can see a similar appropriation and repositioning of slave iconography already occurring

2 *Slave Ship (Slavers Throwing Overboard the Dead and Dying, Typhoon Coming On)*, 1840.
Joseph Mallord William Turner, 1775–1851. Oil on canvas. 90.8 x 122.6 cm (35 3/4 x 48 1/4 in.).
Courtesy of Museum of Fine Arts, Boston and Henry Lillie Pierce Fund.

with the Biard painting's installation in the Wilberforce House Museum. That too is a rupture with history, one that displaces onto the French Britain's long involvement with slavery. One might incorrectly make a parallel argument that in the same way that a disavowal of British slavery and its excesses is installed in the museum with the Biard painting and its displacement of these horrors onto the French (in particular the merchant holding the book), so does a similar disavowal of slavery and its excesses occur in *The Attendant* through Julien's appropriation of "slave iconography" for an s/m scene. However, this particular anxiety of displacement is another reason that Julien's alignment of slavery and s/m disrupts "structures of feeling." When Julien suggests that "in this post colonial moment black queers should have the choice of acting out the roles of 'slaves' or 'masters' in the realm of desire and sexual fantasy" (Julien 2000a, 81) he is not attempting to install an alternative *history* of chattel slavery but to hold a space open, to imagine a gap in signification itself.

Toward repositioning slave iconography, in "Confessions of a Snow Queen," his critical commentary on *The Attendant*, Julien addresses the restrictions placed on black expressive possibility:

[It is] the popular "black," "straight" reading, that tries to use the signs of s/m (whips and chains) for a neocolonial racist/sexual practice [and attempts] to "fix" these images in time, perpetuating white power and domination. It is thus reductionist, a misreading of the "theatre of s/m" based on the politically correct notions of sexual practice from a world devoid of fantasy.

Could not the fetish slave-band in the film, mimicking the metal collars worn by black slaves—which, for some readers, enacts this colonial memory—be read as something else: *namely the unspeakable masochistic desire for sexual domination?* . . . Alternatively, could not the representation of interracial s/m be read as a practice of a racial and sexual dynamic which, in displaying the codes of a (Fanonian) master/slave dialectic, presents a transgressive simulacrum, one which both parodies and disrupts the codes of societal and racial power? (2000a, 81)

The whips and chains in slavery do look a lot like the whips and chains in s/m. Playing it straight, fixing those images and meanings in time is, perhaps, less a (black) world devoid of fantasy than one in which narrative, fantasy, and representation each has a cause-and-effect correlation to material reality.[17] The politics that Julien describes is one that, given the lack of sustained scholarly attention to transatlantic slavery, its effects, and the social investments that are related to it, would insist understandably but problematically on fixing in perpetuity *particular* and unchanging signs of white power and black submission. Attitudes of power and submission "cleave" and "cleave *to*" black bodies, "situated as [they are . . . as] sign[s] of particular cultural and political meanings in the Diaspora. [It is] . . . as if those leaping bodies, those prostrate bodies, those bodies made to dance and then to work, those bodies curdling under the singing of whips, those bodies remain curved in these attitudes" (Brand 2001, 35). Are we unable to imagine those bodies (and ourselves) outside of these attitudes, to imagine a "day without narrative" (42)? To be free, even momentarily, of the signs of these cultural and political meanings, to be in the space of the door that produced them, in the "nowhere at all," "the place of being without"? Julien refuses to leave those black bodies "fixed

[only] in the ether of history," perpetually and only assuming attitudes forced on them "from above" (Brand 2001, 35).

Exhuming Possibility

> I think necrophilia is at the heart of black filmmaking. Not in a literal sense but in a postmodern sense in which people are invoking figures, there is an act of feeding off the dead. . . . There is a kind of level of morbidity which I think people have to realize in the quest for identity. It is a morbid business.—**JOHN AKOMFRAH AND KASS BANNING,** "Feeding off the Dead: Necrophilia and the Black Imaginary: An Interview with John Akomfrah"

The Attendant walks past the Biard painting and its static two-dimensional scenes of domination and torture are transformed. Where there was a white slave trader examining the teeth of a restrained and prone black slave, now there is a contemporary interracial s/m scene comprised of two white masters and several black slaves who touch the face and chest of the prone black slave (identified in the credits as "the Angel"; figure 3). As the Attendant continues his walk through the gallery, he reaches the edge and turns away from another transfigured scene from the Biard painting, of four black men with a white man (the Visitor) at the center, holding a whip (figure 4). No call to ignore that "the legacy of slave imperialism persists, and [that] the world is haunted by its traumatic and ineradicable memory" (Julien 2000a, 80); on the contrary, this staging calls on viewers to look again as it complicates what it is that we think we know when we see this scene, and where we locate the persistence of slavery. The s/m tableau peopled with what appear to be white masters and black slaves brings us to Julien's engagement with the stereotype as the image that we are always already familiar with. In "True Confessions," Julien and Kobena Mercer tackled the persistent power of stereotypes and the stereotype's relationship to black aesthetic practices through their engagement with Robert Mapplethorpe's book of black male nudes, *Black Males* (published under the title *Black Book* in the United States), and their ambivalent position of "want[ing] to look" at the images of black men in the book and not always finding what they want to see (Julien and Mercer 2000c, 58). This desire to see, accompanied by the "recognition of not-seeing and the will to look again," is what Peggy Phelan describes as "the lure of the image repertoire. The double action confirms the distance between the gaze and the eye: the

3 & 4   *The Attendant,* 1993. Isaac Julien, director. Reprinted with permission of Isaac Julien.

eye ever hungry, ever restless, temporarily submits to the law of the gaze, the ocular perspective which frames the image, sees what is shown and discovers it to be 'lacking.' Not quite the thing one wants/needs/desires it to be" (1993, 34). When Julien looks for himself in *Black Males* he finds at first an archive of "the blacks" Mapplethorpe photographed and who "died so quickly." Echoing Fanon, one might say that in that moment Julien's "body was given back to [him] sprawled out, distorted, recolored, clad in mourning, in that white winter day" (Fanon 1967, 113). But because he desires to look again and in looking to see what he has *not yet seen,* in his own work I see Julien undertaking what Lyle Ashton Harris calls a "project of resuscitation—[of] giving life back to the black [male] body" (Bailey 1995, 63).[18] The Attendant continues his rounds, and (anti)slavery's ghosts are released from the Biard painting's framing narrative of philanthropy.

The Attendant

The first time we meet the Attendant he stands behind a table where he searches the bags of visitors as they enter the museum. He first looks into the bag of a visitor played by the writer Hanif Kureishi. He then casts a sustained look at the next person to approach his table, a white male visitor wearing a plaid baseball cap. As the Attendant looks at this man there is a cut to a scene in color with the Attendant in formal dress playing Dido, the Queen of Carthage, on an opera hall balcony, leaning toward the center stage that is occupied by the Angel. The Attendant sings "Remember me": "But ah! Forget my fate. Remember me. But ah! Forget my fate." The scene then fades back to the black and white of the museum, back to the visitor in the plaid cap who does not remember or does not acknowledge any connection to the Attendant, who perhaps does not even see him.[19] The Attendant's threnody, his call to remember past lives but not his fate, to recall "the epidemic living and the dead. Remember them, remember me" (Alexander 1994, 421), is sent to the film's audience as well as to the visitor in the plaid baseball cap.

Misrecognitions such as these are overdetermined; the museum's look and everyday viewing relations are structured through them. This particular misrecognition (or nonrecognition) recalls the invisibility of the museum guards staged in Fred Wilson's museum installation *Guarded View* (figure 5), an installation of four beheaded black male mannequins dressed in the guard uniforms of four New York museums. (I deliberately say "beheaded" rather than merely "headless" to underscore the violence of the erasure of the black museum guard within these spaces.)[20] Both Wilson's *Guarded View* and his later, site-specific work *Mining the Museum* (1992), which was created specifically for and in collaboration with the Maryland Historical Society, examine the blindnesses that structure the museum's look. In an interview published in the catalogue *Mining the Museum* Wilson relates that prior to the opening of the show he met with the docents, and then he excused himself, arranging to meet them later. When he returned to the museum he was wearing a guard's uniform, and he stationed himself in the room where he and the docents had agreed to meet. As the docents looked for Fred Wilson the artist they repeatedly walked past Fred Wilson the guard, because dressed in the guard's uniform he was invisible to them, able to walk among them unobserved and to

5   Fred Wilson b. 1954. *Guarded View*, 1991. Fred Wilson. Wood, paint, steel, and fabric. Dimensions variable. © Fred Wilson. Courtesy of Pacewildenstein, New York. Courtesy of Whitney Museum of American Art, New York; Gift of the Peter Norton Family Foundation 97.84a-d.

watch them as they did not observe him.[21] In an uncanny repetition, when *Guarded View* was placed at the entrance to the 1994 Whitney exhibition *Black Male* and across from a quotation from *Invisible Man* the installation itself was often not noticed, but the effect was transposed onto those black men who came to see the exhibit. While that installation remained largely unseen, like the black museum guards themselves, as one visitor remarked, "On slow days . . . any time a black man was standing still would constitute sufficient occasion to snap an instant tableau vivant. Potential dioramas were everywhere waiting to congeal" (Veneciano 1995, 12). In its failure to be seen the installation was doubly successful: it repeated the violence of the guard's erasure and of black men's incorporation into a prior museum narrative as ready ethnographic installations and tableaux vivants.

As the Attendant is checking bags, we see a museum guest positioned in front of the Biard painting as its single sustained viewer. That guest is Stuart Hall, one of the primary figures in British cultural studies over the past twenty-five years. For those viewers who are familiar with and recognize Hall, his cameo in the film explicitly places it in critical dialogue with British cultural studies. To those who recognize Hall, his appearance alludes to his argument in *New Ethnicities* that a real and sustained engagement with the shifts in representational practices in contemporary black

British cultural production would signal the "end of the innocent notion of the essential black subject" (Hall 1996, 165).[22] The author and screenwriter Hanif Kureishi (*My Beautiful Laundrette, The Buddha of Suburbia, The Mother*) also comes in contact with the Attendant and also does not engage the Attendant, nor does the Attendant engage him. But the terms of (dis)engagement are those prescribed by the museum, the museum's etiquette. Only the man in the plaid baseball cap receives the Attendant's probing look (an encounter remembered by the Attendant and forgotten or disavowed by the museum guest?), and he does not return it. In this moment we see the Attendant's seeing, a look (or a lack of one) on his part that is as much in relation to desire as it is to his role in the museum. The visitor played by Kureishi is not the recipient of the Attendant's look, although both the visitor played by him and the visitor in the plaid cap "apperceived the role of the [Attendant] without having to see him" (hooks 1996, 93).

bell hooks has this to say about the cameos of Stuart Hall and Hanif Kureishi: "Although Hall and Kureishi are not white they mingle as peers, as subjects in the same worlds. Like all the other visitors, they do not engage these workers. They are there as participants in the viewing relations dictated by the aesthetics of high culture" (1996, 92). Though hooks does not attend to the Attendant's desire in this formulation, the unreciprocated gaze and having jobs or roles in the museum that necessitate both visibility and invisibility would dictate that visitors not engage the workers. This is precisely an example of the sadomasochism of everyday life to which the Attendant, the museum Conservator, and the museumgoers submit with varying degrees of ease and with varying effects. The appearance in the film of Hall, Kureishi, and the other museum guests is but part of Julien's complex articulation of representation, power, desire, and viewing relations. In the same way that the Biard painting installs with it a history of European painting, so do Hall's and Kureishi's cameos locate *The Attendant* in relation to a body of black British cultural production. Julien's own feature film, *Young Soul Rebels* (1991), and Kureishi's screenplay for *My Beautiful Laundrette* (1985) come to mind as other cross-race, cross-class, and cross-identification gay romances.

The scene in the museum quickly resolves to closing time upon the entrance of the Visitor. The camera films the exterior of the museum as an extension of the Attendant's role as surveillance agent for the museum, and we follow the Visitor as he ascends the marble steps and enters the building to the sound of music. We move from inside the museum to outside and back again to establish the interpenetration of inside and outside, high and low, surveillance and voyeurism. Now inside the museum the Visitor stands before the Attendant's desk and hands over his bag for inspection. In a shot reverse shot, the Attendant examines the inside of the bag, looks at the Visitor, and the Visitor looks back; the look is held and returned, and they both smile. We see here an example of what Kaja Silverman describes in her analysis of *Looking for Langston* as "the shot reverse shot . . . [that] inscribes not so much a look and its object as two reciprocal looks" (1996, 110).[23] Small angels or cupids with bows and arrows appear in color within the black-and-white scene and encircle the heads of the Visitor and the Attendant, who each smile again as each casts a brief sideways glance at the miniature angel that encircles his own head (figures 6 and 7). The cruise and surveillance collapse into each other as the Attendant looks in the Visitor's bag and finds a whip, and then their hands meet in a caress on the whip handle as the Attendant takes the whip out of the bag for a closer look (figure 8). Jump-cut to an image of a gyrating gold lamé crotch flanked by the spiraling miniature angels or cupids who before were encircling the heads of the Attendant and the Visitor.[24]

The scene settles back to the Attendant at work and clearly eager for closing time. As his gold pocket watch ticks toward six o'clock, chimes sound, the museum visitors move on cue toward the exit, and the Visitor walks deliberately through the museum. Hall lingers in front of the Biard painting until the final chime sounds, then he turns from it and walks away. The ticking of the watch alludes to the ticking that announces Marlon Riggs's HIV-positive status in *Tongues Untied*, the first film that gave black gay men a public voice. This allusion also reminds us of *Tongues'* refrain, "Black men loving black men is *the* revolutionary act," a refrain that was, indeed is a necessary intervention in public constructions of desire and ideology but that nonetheless drowns out Riggs's unclaimed white partner —a painful denial that later comes back to haunt Riggs's work.[25] Barely suppressing what looks like glee the Attendant puts his watch away, follows Hall to the door, and firmly shuts it (figure 9). Moments before the Attendant closes the museum door for the evening the film cuts again to the same close-up of a gyrating gold lamé crotch. A reference to the

6-8   *The Attendant,* 1993. Isaac Julien, director. Reprinted with permission of Isaac Julien.

Nigerian-British photographer Rotimi Fani-Kayode's photograph *Golden Phallus,* this crotch draws attention to the phallic object (without the promise of accessibility) at the same time that it conceals it.[26] The gold lamé pants signal the desires of the Attendant that his uniform would conceal; they signal desire within confinement. The second cut to the gold

9 *The Attendant*, 1993. Isaac Julien, director. Reprinted with permission of Isaac Julien.

crotch makes it clear that the scenes in color indicate desire and the breaching of museum etiquette.

After he shuts the door the camera frames the Attendant's hands and midsection in a way that recalls Fred Wilson's decapitated museum guards and also another beheaded black man, Robert Mapplethorpe's "Man in Polyester Suit" (1980; figure 10). "In pictures like 'Man in a Polyester Suit,'" writes Kobena Mercer, "apart from the model's hands, it is the penis, and the penis alone that identifies him as a black man" (1997a, 244).[27] Recognizing Mercer's nod to Fanon ("One is no longer aware of the Negro, but only of a penis; the Negro is eclipsed. He is turned into a penis. He *is* a penis" (Fanon 1967, 170)—that "the model himself becomes the erotic paraphernalia, the very fetish of Mapplethorpe's camera," (Meyer 2001) and that this recognition is always overdetermined—it is still Mapplethorpe's "Man's" penis *and* hands and, perhaps, the suit itself, that alert viewers to his race.[28] Stuart Hall insists, "Yes. Mapplethorpe does fetishise, abstract, formalise, and appropriate the black body. But, on the other hand, we can see that Mapplethorpe is contesting the dominant representation of black masculinity in a lot of black photography—he lets loose his desire for the black male form which many black male photographers suppress" (Hall and Bailey 1992, 22). Indeed when Julien refers to some of his later works, *The Long Road to Mazatlan* (1999) and *Trussed* (1996), as "a Robert Mapplethorpe in motion," he acknowledges this and sets black men loose in the scene, in front of and behind the camera (Cruz 2000, viii); the black object is becoming the black subject. The Attendant is framed midsection, showing his torso, hands, and cheap polyester

10 "Man in Polyester Suit," 1980. © The Robert Mapplethorpe Foundation.
Courtesy of Art + Commerce.

museum guard suit, a particular black male uniform. But we do not see here a projection of what Mercer calls "white gay male desire"; precisely what we do not see is the Attendant's penis, that "one little thing, the black man's genitals," that is at the center of the Mapplethorpe photograph (Mercer 1997a, 244). What appears in the film is therefore a highly allusive and overdetermined rupturing of repressed narratives of black, gay, slave.

The signs that we are both to read this seriously and that we are not to read this straight are everywhere. Angels and cupids, gold lamé crotches, beads and medallions all indicate not only ruptures from the concealed spaces of desire, slavery, and history, but also some drift in the seriousness of the scenes. This is another point at which "unspeakable stories of subjectivity meet the narratives of a history" (Hall and Sealy 2001, 34). Loosed from the constraints of looking relations that would render the Attendant only another object in the museum and the painting free of libidinal desire, after visiting hours the museum resists being the peculiar institutional dead space of high culture as the Attendant and the Biard painting both come to life. The Attendant comes out from behind the table and moves toward the painting, and though we never see him look at it directly, the resuscitated actors in it look at him, and as they do so they make apparent that he and we are structured by the gaze of even sup- posedly inanimate objects. As the Attendant moves past the painting- become-tableau toward his after-hours encounter with the Visitor, the viewer is drawn into the gold picture frames (like the ones we will soon see the museum conservator preserving), where we find a libidinal narrative that is both present and repressed in the antislavery museum's narrative of morality and benevolence.[29] We experience this moment as a "piercing of the common place which creates a 'punctum'—a moment of surprise offset by the holding environment of the surrounding pictorial narrative" (Mer- cer 2001, 8). The actors in the Biard painting become resuscitated; they wear fetish gear; the Visitor appears in the second tableau in an attitude of mastery, one hand on the shoulder of a black man, the other hand holding a whip. The Attendant "comes out" in the phantasmatic spaces of the mu- seum, and his movement necessarily invokes the closet, publics and pri- vates, what is revealed and what is hidden, the licit and illicit. We see Julien creating what is to become a whole "body of work that enters into the phantasy spaces of the public sphere" (Mercer 2001, 8).

Scene One

Fantasy has, of course, never been simply a private affair.
—**ELIZABETH COWIE**, *Representing the Woman: Cinema and Psychoanalysis*

In 1990 in the United Kingdom fifteen gay men were arrested and later sentenced for consensual s/m play as the result of an undercover investiga- tion known as "Operation Spanner."[30] Eight of the fifteen men in the case known officially as *Regina v. Brown* were given "custodial sentences ranging up to four and a half years" (McClintock 1993, 105). Their activities all took place in private; none of the participants thought that he was doing anything illegal; no one went to the police, nor did any of them require medical attention after the fact.[31] The men videotaped their play, a fact central to their prosecution, and the court alleged that this videotaping was not, as the men maintained, for their own future use but for "recruitment" purposes.[32] So while these men engaged in private in what they believed to be consensual s/m, they were convicted on the majority decision of the court that in the interest of the public good an individual is unable to consent to violence. Therefore, although "homosexual practices conducted in private are legal in England," five of the defendants were charged under the Offences Against Persons Act of 1861 (Hanna 2000–2001, 264). In the decision Lord Templeman wrote, "Society is entitled and bound to protect itself against a cult of violence. Pleasure derived from the infliction of pain is an evil thing. Cruelty is uncivilised."[33] Lord Jauncey continues:

> This House must therefore consider the possibility that these activities are practiced by others who are not so controlled or responsible as the appellants are claimed to be. Without going into details of all the rather curious activities in which the appellants engaged it would appear to be good luck rather than good judgment which has prevented serious injury from occurring. *Wounds can easily become septic if not properly treated, the free flow of blood from a person who is* H.I.V. *positive or who has* AIDS *can infect another and an inflicter who is carried away by sexual excitement or by drink or drugs could easily inflict pain beyond the level to which the receiver has consented.* . . . When considering the public interest, potential for harm is just as relevant as actual harm. (Quoted in Hanna 2000–2001, 265; emphasis mine)

It is clear that "central to decoding Spanner [and what connects Spanner to arts funding and obscenity debates in the United States] is [the] statement that 'the public' is the 'victim' in the context of the case, and that this is problematic since the state 'admits that the public does not reside in any of the people who participate in the activity or the people who know about the activity' " (D. Bell and Valentine 1995, 310). Lord Jauncey's use of HIV and AIDS is another instance of the sadomasochism of everyday life and its corresponding repression.

This leaves the law in the position of the sadist while purporting to take into account a larger public good that would protect the public from sadism, while maintaining a disconnect between pleasure and pain and submission. In "Sex Is Not a Sport," Cheryl Hanna writes, "S/M involves not only the law of *sexual* consent, but also the law of *violent* consent" (2000–2001, 240); put more simply, this prerogative belongs only to the law itself. Where in this formulation is the masochist, other than the one who submits to the law? Though not the sole factor in the increased visibility of s/m, nevertheless this visibility is at least partially a response to the AIDS crisis. Even as *safer sex*, s/m is manifestly ignored by the justices in their emphasis on playing power straight and in the imposition of their own state discipline. In fact on the discursive ground of public good, their ruling potentially exponentially increases rather than limits the potential for harm. This distinction between public good and private harm and the effects of violence in these supposedly distinct realms is maintained by erasing the ways that in be(com)ing a subject one is called on continually to consent to violence.

Scene Two

The Attendant, who is the signifier of authority in this space, the local representative of the law, walks past the transfigured s/m tableau to the edge of the frame when the camera focuses on the second tableau, with the Visitor in the position of master, his hand on the shoulder of a black male slave. This image fades out and into a cut to the image of an eye in a marble bust that changes to marble as we watch. Then the camera pulls back to reveal the rest of the bust and a brown hand caressing (and doing what appears to be silencing) the white marble mouth. Cut back to the Visitor's black leather gloved hand as it caresses the handle of the whip that the Attendant now holds in his hands. Cut to the Conservator who is wearing white plastic gloves and carefully dusting a museum frame. She hears a noise, a whip cracking. She looks up, at something, and into the camera that the viewer cannot see. Back to the Attendant and the Visitor. The Visitor stands over the Attendant, whip in his hand frozen in midlash, and the Attendant, partially dressed in his uniform, lies on the floor in the foreground, grimaces, lifts up his head, and looks into the camera. Back to the Conservator who hears groaning coming from the other side of the wall. The repeated "Oh yeah, oh yeah" might be the moaning on the soundtrack of a pornographic film or the moaning of captive people in the slave ship re-creation. The Conservator stands with her hand and ear pressed to the wall, and the camera pans around until it is in front of her. Cut to the next scene, of the Attendant back in uniform, whip in his hand frozen in midlash, as he stands over the now prone Visitor, who lifts up his

11 & 12   *The Attendant*, 1993. Isaac Julien, director. Reprinted with permission of Isaac Julien.

head and looks at the camera (figure 11). Back again to the Conservator, who smiles, caresses the brush she was using to clean the frame, looks at something out of the frame, and then turns away from the camera and walks toward the doorway. In the shot of the Visitor whipping the prone Attendant, the Visitor is wearing fetish gear and the Attendant is still in his uniform shirt but without his hat and trousers. We hear a whip crack and we see the prone Attendant, jacket and hat off, trousers down, rise up slightly and look at the camera (figure 12). What is it we read on his face? Is it shame? Perhaps what Julien draws our attention to, what he has the viewer look at is the refusal of the shame, here of "sleeping with the enemy," of "wanting to play the slave," of desiring the position of the bottom as well as of the top, of being a snow queen. Cut to the Conservator listening on the other side of the wall, back to the Attendant and the Visitor. This time the Attendant is back in uniform and stands over the

Visitor with the whip frozen in a midair arc. We hear the whip crack, and the Visitor too raises himself up and looks ahead, into the camera. And what is his look?

On the other side of the wall from the Attendant and the Visitor, it is as if the Conservator is preparing the space for what she knows is to come, closing the eyes of the bust, silencing it. She hears something that is taking place outside of her field of vision, on the other side of the wall, or as if within the very walls of the museum itself. She stops dusting, places her gloved hands and her ear to the wall, and listens. A whip cracks; she pauses, waiting to hear more. The sounds that she then hears are both ambiguously the amorous sounds of a slowed-down gay porn tape (a whip cracking and the repetitive "Oh yeah. More") and the simulated moans of enslaved people in a ship's hold on a tape made by Wilberforce House Museum employees for the slave ship diorama housed in the basement.[34] ("A tape loop circulates a soundtrack—moans, coughs, and retching sounds, and the splashing of water repeating themselves over and over again" [Wood 2000, 295].)

What the Conservator hears (unearthly moaning or a slowed-down porn track) connects the exorbitant pain and pleasures produced in the staging of chattel slavery to s/m. It is through the Conservator's largely aural pleasure in what she hears and cannot see that the porn soundtrack collapses into the sounds of the Middle Passage, and that we are again invited to bridge space and time to perceive how the museum reconstructs history. The porn soundtrack merges with the slavery soundtrack and the museum workers' duties to attend, reconstruct, and conserve the horrors of the Middle Passage. As the low groaning "Oh yeahs" signify on the repeated sounds of "moans, retching, splashing" running on a loop in the slave ship diorama in the museum's basement, the soundtrack(s) alert us to the museum's repressed desires and to its intention to reach across a historical chasm to re-create the unrecoverable, the sounds of the Middle Passage, and to institute them.

Let us return to the Conservator with her ear to the wall overhearing the moans of pleasure and pain that are superimposed by the sound of the whip that cracks five times. An aural voyeur to the Attendant's fantasies, to the sounds on the other side of the wall, perhaps even within the wall, she is alert to the transgressions taking place outside of her view, beyond her reach. Intimately linked as the Conservator is with the museum itself, she

13   *The Attendant*, 1993. Isaac Julien, director. Reprinted with permission of Isaac Julien.

overhears what she does not see, just as the workers in the Wilberforce House Museum make present the sounds and scenes of that which is absent to them, that which is unrecoverable, what they cannot know. As the cracking of the whip comes to an end, the Conservator turns to look toward the camera, smiles, runs her hand along her brush, and moves toward the doorway. This gesture repeats one earlier in the film: the Conservator's caress of the brush repeats the Visitor's and the Attendant's caress of the whip. Her caress of the brush is another example of the fetishization of one of the scene's accoutrements, a fetishization of an instrument of work. Her caress, in other words, expresses both her authority and her subjection to the institutional conditions that construct subjective agency. As the Conservator moves toward the site of the Attendant's pleasure, as she enters the door frame, yet another frame within the film, she is stopped by a figure in the shadows, prevented from entering the physical space on the other side of the wall.

In each whipping scene the Visitor and the Attendant appear in front of two Tom of Finland drawings (figure 13). In admitting the Visitor, the Attendant, again representative of authority, lets into this space precisely what "for the public good" is to be kept outside of it. We might acknowledge Tom of Finland as another interloper in the antislavery museum. He who "measured the value of his work by his body's responses" famously said, "If I don't have an erection when I'm doing a drawing, I know it's no good."[35] This particular erotic response is one that the traditional museum would either want to exclude or contain and subdue, or sublimate to deny. The juxtaposition of the erotic Tom of Finland drawings, the two sets of

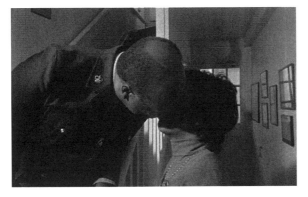

14   *The Attendant*, 1993. Isaac Julien, director. Reprinted with permission of Isaac Julien.

tableaux, and the Biard painting repeats the interpenetration of high and low established by the exterior shots of the museum; it repeats as well the displacement of authority.

After the scenes in which the Attendant and the Visitor have switched roles, when each has occupied the position of both master and slave, we see the Attendant descending a staircase, where the Conservator is waiting for him. This contained black-and-white space of the stairwell (which seems to be in a domestic space or at least in a more exclusive space) wherein he is on the stairs, the two of them separated by a banister, is opposed to the after-hours public and official museum spaces in which the fantasies are laid out. We see how confining this representational space of black heteronormativity is, how narrow the particular kinds of narrativity. And we see a space that signifies on Julien's reflections on what is un-archived, what is hidden in the museum (or behind the museum), and on the constraints of black representation. Their pact, the open secret that is her silence in recognition of his desire, is sealed with a kiss (figure 14). "We know that in the black community," writes bell hooks, "AIDS is on the increase. And part of the reason why is a matter of secrets and gendered roles that black people play into. They are oppressive" (hooks and Julien 1991, 177). Outside of the reconfigured Biard tableau vivant the only touch that is unmediated by gloves that occurs in the film is this chaste kiss between the Conservator and the Attendant. The forces of heteronor-mativity, AIDS, and mourning coalesce in this touch. Do we not perceive in the very looks of the Conservator, the Attendant, and the Visitor (their styles, who wears their body how, how they look and see, how we see them) their quite different and shifting relations to these forces and that they *are* all in relation to them?

Archiving Blackness

> Unhooked from land, custom, language, lineage, and clan/tribal arrangements, modern "race," joins the repertoire of fetish names bolstered by legislative strategy, public policy, and the entire apparatus of the courts and police force.
> —HORTENSE SPILLERS, "All the Things You Could Be by Now"

> To be a "good" people, to be "respectable" and "worthy citizens," we've had to combat absurd phantasmagoric stereotypes about our sexuality, our lusts, our loves, to the extent that we disavow our own sensuality to each other.
> —NTOZAKE SHANGE, *Erotique Noir/Black Erotica*

Published in the United States at the height of a new round of morality and censorship debates, *Erotique Noire/Black Erotica* (Decosta-Willis, Martin, and Bell 1992) is perhaps the first collection of its kind, a collection of erotic writing by, about, and for black people, with a foreword written by Ntozake Shange, who also, not coincidentally, wrote the foreword to Robert Mapplethorpe's *Black Book*. In that foreword to the Mapplethorpe book, Shange writes about the homoeroticism of the images and claims the black men in the photographs for herself, as "together she and Mapplethorpe look through the book for images of former lovers" (Gaines 1992, 29). Shange writes, "I love photographs. I even wrote a play called *A Photograph: Lovers-in-Motion*; a love story, a brutal love story, a war of sex and aesthetics. So when I was offered the opportunity to write something/anything about Robert Mapplethorpe's work, I was terribly enthusiastic. Black men, black and white prints of said black men, overshadow other obsessions" (Shange 1986, n.p.).

I quote Shange here in order to position her scopic obsessions alongside Mapplethorpe's and in relation to her own desire for complicated explorations of "sex and aesthetics." This desire for complicated explorations would lead to Shange's being accused by some African American critics of "calculated complicity with white racists" (Murray 1997b, 13). Timothy Murray suggests that what is "fascinating about the imaginary search for former lovers shared by Shange and Mapplethorpe is how its unrighteous fantasy, its mixed specters of race and sexuality, unsettles the safety of any one commonplace" (14). Shange later rewrites this once shared fantasy precisely in the terms of safety, when, six years later, with all the force of a traumatic return, she rethinks her position in relation to black people, sex, and aesthetics, as if to disavow her enthusiastic preface to Mapplethorpe's *Black Book*. She writes in her preface to *Black Erotica*, "*Here in these stories and poems we are not myths and stereotypes, art forms or sex objects.* We are simply folks at intimate play; our fierce rhythms of desire, *the exotic unencumbered by the 'other,'* close and hot" (1992, xx; emphasis mine). With Shange's essay to frame the text and with contents drawn from love letters, gay and lesbian erotica, poetry, and essays, *Black Erotica*'s editors undertake an archivization of a black sexual community that is "unencumbered by the 'other.' " Shange's foreword makes manifest the repression of what Julien refers to as the desires of and for the other within oneself. In *The Attendant* Julien takes on what Shange and the *Black Erotica* editors would repress and disavow: there is no erotic (and certainly no exotic) without the other. It is a statement that would be true historically as well as psychoanalytically: one cannot cleanse one's fantasies of the other, of slavery, of the gaze, and there is no fantasy without the other.

Making their selections for the book, *Black Erotica*'s editors rely on seven criteria that no one piece must fit, though ideally all of them should. They are in agreement that the submitted pieces should be "well written," "effective," and "original"; present "sex as a beautiful, joyous, and powerful experience"; and "not demean or diminish people by using stereotypes and caricatures to disrespect other people or persons of different sexual orientations" (Willis, Martin, and Bell 1992, xxxiii). Their preface and introduction touch upon their responses to a variety of erotic submissions that are exclusively literary, but they agree that s/m falls outside of their collective definition of the erotic; in fact they declare, "[s/m] turns the three of us off."[36] In *The Attendant* it clearly turns on not only the Attendant and the Visitor but also the Conservator, who overhears the scenes between them. To this editorial admission the editors of *Black Erotica* add the following: "Although many sensitive and sexual people practice SM because they enjoy the heightened feelings and rush of adrenaline that come with the sexual frisson of fear, we exercised editorial license in rejecting stories of violent sex" (xxxiii–iv). For the editors s/m, fear, frisson, and violent sex are part of a headlong rush of descriptions without definition. They know s/m when they see it; much like Justice Stewart, who famously said that he could not define hard-core pornography but that he knows it when he sees it, Decosta-Willis, Martin, and Bell never define *it* other than to locate it (simplistically) as violent sex. There is, I submit, a difference between the staged scenes and accoutrements of consensual s/m and the sadomasochism that is evident in countless documents of slavery and in contemporary everyday life.[37] Characterizing the people as sensitive and the stories that they receive as sad, *Black Erotica*'s editors introduce s/m only summarily to disrespect and dismiss work that explicitly eroticizes it as sexual practice and to disavow its attraction for them.

That they reach this conclusion despite claiming that their decision to undertake this collection was motivated by reclamation and by the "unfortunate fact . . . that so many of us still lead dispirited, buried lives in which full sexual expression is denied us" (Willis, Martin, and Bell 1992, xxxiii) would seem to mark s/m as a limit test of the black erotic community that the editors seek to create. It is, as Mercer says, "my sense that questions of sexuality have come to mark the interior limits of decolonisation, where the utopian project of liberation has come to grief" (1996, 116). In other words, despite their editorial principles, the "sensitive and sensual" people who practice s/m are not allowed free expression in this book; they haunt the text (just as the Middle Passage installation and the voices in the wall of the museum haunt *The Attendant*) as they remain unseen and unheard in black erotic representation except as instances of the pathologically illicit or "sad." The editors of *Black Erotica* are not alone; they are but one instance of the disavowal of queer, non-heteronormative sexuality. But I wonder if in their revulsion at and disavowal of a set of sexual practices that fall under the rubric of s/m and that may make explicit the very master-slave configurations that haunt us, that make visible slavery within freedom and questions of consent, they end up reifying the very power and pleasure relations that they aim to traverse, especially the real which is encumbered by the other. Clearing a space for s/m, attending to it, might get at precisely what is so disturbing about identification itself. Diana Fuss reminds us in regard to race that "racist practice and racial identity alike are forged through the process of identification" (1995, 14). It seems, then, that to "combat absurd phantasmagoric stereotypes" about blackness one must *not* excise an other that is both external to "us" and internal; one must *not* disavow self-difference.

In their final criterion, not to diminish or demean others, the editors' framing approaches the language of the final clause of the proposed (and

defeated) amendment by Jesse Helms, which was a response to a sched-
uled exhibition of Mapplethorpe's work.[38] In calling for regulation of the
National Endowment for the Arts, Helms focused in particular on Mapplethorpe's images of nude children and on his images of s/m. Though the
obvious intent was to censor homosexuality, there was a clause in the
original amendment that would have denied arts funding to any artist
whose "material . . . denigrates, debases, or reviles a person, group or class
of citizens on the basis of race, creed, sex, handicap, age, or national origin"
(Stychin 1996, 149). The logic of *Black Erotica*'s editors uncannily repeats
Helms's attempt to harness the language of antiracism and antidiscrimina-
tion in order to foreclose representational possibility (what Spillers calls
representational potentialities) of the very people the language purports to
protect. This is the structure, I think, that Spillers has identified recently in
relation to race as "mimetic racism," but which I extend to the structure
exercised here: "Mimetic racism . . . repeats racism 'unconsciously'—it
takes over its presumptions, unexamined, whatever privileges accrue to it
'innocently' as a thing that is simply done" (2003b, 16). Sadism and masochism do appear in *Black Erotica* as everyday straight power—not as s/m's
intended theater of power—in the editors' inclusion of a piece that ana-
lyzes *The Narrative of the Life of Frederick Douglass* and the "blood-stained
gate" of slavery, Captain Anthony's whipping of Aunt Hester.

In "Forbidden Fruits and Unholy Lusts: Illicit Sex in Black American
Fiction," Sandra Govan's contribution to *Black Erotica*, she recounts that
the genesis of her piece was a student's query about all of the "weird sex"
she was reading about in Govan's black literature class. Govan refers to a
number of slave narratives and sadistic scenes, most notably the whipping
of Aunt Hester. She writes:

> Two quick observations. First, Anthony clearly enjoys his task. As his whip is
> curling about the naked flesh of Hester, ripping into her tender breasts as well
> as scoring her "naked back," his "fatigue" or exhaustion comes as much from
> the sexual release as it does from the physical exertion. Second, *Aunt Hester
> either loved pain or loved Lloyd's Ned entirely too much,* for Douglass claims he
> "often" heard her "heart-rending shrieks at the dawn of day." *It seems a clear-cut
> case of a White man who wants "his own" Black woman getting bested, sexually, by
> a Black man while the Black woman "love" object suffers because of their lust.*
> (Govan 1992, 36)

An erotics of power in slavery for the slaveholder and an indication of the forms of *jouissance* are found there for the master and his agents, but in Govan's recounting of the scene she misreads sadism for sadomasochism. This is one powerful example of how *Black Erotica* plays power straight and collapses s/m in the context of black erotica into the monstrous but also everyday relations of terror and power in slavery and into the present.

While Julien and the editors of *Black Erotica* share a similar concern with the means by which "some of the myths of black sexuality are maintained by the unwanted imposition of force from above, and by the very people who are in a sense 'dominated' by them" (Mercer 1994, 136), they approach this concern very differently. The editors of *Black Erotica* engage in the "masochism of self-censorship," and in doing so they maintain dominant representational structures. In the Spanner case and the two precedents that were key to the prosecution of that case, the Offences Against Persons Act of 1861 and a case in 1934 that involved a man caning a woman with her consent for their mutual sexual gratification (Julien 2000a, 81), might we not see points of conjuncture between these precedents that allow us to read the Conservator's relationship to the museum, her containment in her work uniform and evening dress, and her aural voyeurism as additional sites of s/m within Julien's film? The Conservator is invested with mastery in relation to her work and in relation to the Attendant in the opera scenes and also in her position in the museum. (Do conservators see attendants?) The Conservator's clapping hands after the Attendant sings echo the whip cracking, but also point to the ways that she is constrained as she facilitates a certain kind of possibility for the Attendant.

Let's revisit the scene of the Attendant's and Conservator's chaste kiss. In black and white the Attendant slowly descends the stairs, interrupted by a quick cut to the Angel rendered in brilliant colors, then back to the Conservator's and the Attendant's exchange of smiles and their kiss when he reaches the foot of the stairs (again in black and white). The Angel, filmic object of desire, occupier of center stage, and perhaps a phantasmatic incarnation of the Attendant, is between the Conservator and the Attendant, acknowledged by them. Is it not the Angel who is the primary object and subject at whom we love to look and who seems to look directly at us, delivering the most sustained direct look at the camera (the direct look that is both the challenge and the invitation in the pornographic) and therefore at the viewer of the film? Indeed at each moment

15 *The Attendant*, 1993. Isaac Julien, director. Reprinted with permission of Isaac Julien.

that the Conservator seems to associate herself with the Attendant she encounters the Angel: as a shadowy figure framed in the doorway after she hears the Attendant's pleasure/the porn soundtrack/the groans from the basement soundtrack; between them in the cut before the kiss at the base of the stairs; and as the principal focus of the Attendant's lament and her applause in the opera house scene.

The encounter with the white object of desire who enters the museum wearing the plaid cap and who does not recognize the Attendant is repeated differently moments later with the Visitor, who enters the museum bearing the leather bag. Again, in a moment of pleasurable and sustained looking, this Visitor and the Attendant acknowledge their mutual desire (signaled by their reciprocal acknowledgment of the cupids that float around their heads). A similar shot has also inserted itself in the failed recognition with the white museum-goer in the plaid baseball cap, a scene that fades away to the Attendant performing as Dido.[39] At the end of the film the Attendant once again performs as Dido, Queen of Carthage, seduced and abandoned by Aeneas when he sails off to found Rome and make history. As the Snow Queen cum African Queen the Attendant sings to the Visitor/Aeneas while the Conservator (who may be yet another Dido) bears witness. For she too is seduced by the possibilities let loose on the other side of the wall, abandoned, left to her fate as the preserver of tradition and the histories that would fix and erase her while he actively and imaginatively "makes history."

The Attendant's labored singing from the proscenium box in the opera house is to the Visitor as well as to and for the Angel (shots of whom intersperse these scenes), as well as, perhaps, for the Conservator (figure 15). Again the Attendant sings, "When I am laid in earth / May my wrongs create / No trouble / No trouble / In thy breast." In a moment of recognition, though not of shared looking, the Attendant seems to acknowledge the Conservator's burden as they both look toward the stage, where the Angel appears. But the cut to the Angel resolves to a shot of the Visitor stroking his black leather gloved hands in another gesture of remembrance and then, as he acknowledges the Attendant, gesturing as if to wipe away a tear. The Attendant acknowledges the Conservator and her instrumentality in maintaining in the black-and-white spaces of everyday life the illusion of his normative heterosexuality. This time the Conservator stands and claps in the almost empty opera hall, and in her applause one hears the echo of the earlier crack of the whip. The Conservator's claps on the downbeat recall the images of loss and longing that repeatedly punctuate *The Attendant*. Largely unexplored in this film (but explored in *Three: The Conservator's Dream* and *Vagabondia*), the Conservator's position too seems infused with loss, longing, and a failure of fulfillment of desire, if not a failure of its recognition.

Julien characterizes the Conservator's desire as abject; her clapping that echoes the whip cracking is an indication of her resentment at being used as an alibi for her husband. He also portrays the Conservator as a dominatrix in this scene. I want to let her remain in the space of ambivalence in order to allow her pleasure at being a dominatrix, at being an aural witness to the Attendant's desires, pleasure in desires that conserve and resist, that withhold and are withheld. Pleasure at her own ambivalent instrumentality in facilitating his desires, and her pleasure in facilitating the subversion and perversion of the space of the museum that she also conserves.[40] The Conservator is anxiety producing and has proved difficult to attend to in this space, in *The Attendant*. (The black woman who "conserves" as "the conservator" is figured as abject, as a marker for the site of trauma. I turn to this figure in the following chapter on Kara Walker.) I began with Brand and the space of the door and I return to it here in order to leave us positioned in that space of (im)possibility and all of its attendant dangers and pleasures. Julien's *The Attendant* offers a vital space of regeneration and resistance to total incorporation, a map to creating and theorizing within and against sociopolitical and disciplinary regimes, a possible space for retheorizing consent, desire, and transmission.

FOUR

Kara Walker's Monstrous Intimacies

What I discovered was that possessing a black body through which history and fiction coexist was the stuff performances are made of, and I performed a number of parts in a series of vignettes too sordid to relate here to you, my dear audience.

They are scenes better viewed from a great distance.

Suffice to say, I ran. Via a modified underground railroad up from Georgia to a far northern state to pursue a graduate degree in the fine art of painting. . . . The question was, how could I turn this feeling that I had become a blank space into which people projected their fantasies into something concrete? What about the possibility that I might reflect those fantasies back into the projector's unsuspecting eyes, and cause them to want to face the shame of (our) collective psyche? . . .

For every panoramic view I have "taken a likeness of, in silhouette form," there are new questions that arise.

No narrative is ever finished, and very few have proper beginnings.

Am I forever locked into cyclorama-scenes of perpetual battles won–battles lost?

Chained to you at the ankle as a new representative of Negro Emancipation?

Will I be Caged together with every pickaninny bucknigra mammy prissy scarlet Tom Eva, massa, Simon Legree brer rabbit ole missus Huck Finn kunta kinte Hottentot newsreel lynchmob free issue scalawag ever created and ever exhumed to the thrill and horror of audiences all—black and white!? . . .

I think my work . . . mimics the past, but it's all about the present.—**KARA WALKER,** "Kara Walker Speaks: A Public Conversation on Racism, Art, and Politics with Tommy Lott."

Look and See

To see the black silhouettes of the African American visual artist Kara Walker in a gallery installation is to be caught up in the scenes and therefore in the actions of the figures that populate them. Walker's scenes of profound, excessive sexual(ized) violence incorporate all of her viewers and produce a number of anxious, often hysterical responses from some of her critics, both those who applaud her work and those for whom it is regressive, minstrelsy. Each of her (primarily white) critics that I read reading Walker has specific blind spots that appear to me symptomatic of the ways that American post-slavery subjectivity is constituted, conferred, and (not) acknowledged. While each viewer/critic proceeds from the awareness that the subjects depicted in the images are both black and white—given the titles of the work (for example, *The End of Uncle Tom and the Grand Allegorical Tableau of Eva in Heaven*, 1995), the subject of the work (slavery), and Walker's own accompanying explanations—the *black* black figures in her silhouetted work nonetheless tend to become the sole site on which the signifying power of slavery in the past and the present is put to work.

In other words, the majority of critics, readers, and reviewers, regardless of their diegetic reading of the work, locate its signifying effect almost exclusively on black people. Such myopia is unsurprising given that the history of slavery (and race) in the United States tends to be regarded as an issue of and for black people *about* black people and involves a persistent erasure of whiteness. I suspect that it was in order to work against that persistent perceptual repression of the whiteness of the diegetically *white* black figures from her work and therefore remove them beyond the scope of slavery that Walker added to recent installations white figures and gray backgrounds and used light and overhead projection in some of her later silhouette work, additions that make the viewer's, any viewer's/every viewer's, interpellation by the scene much more difficult to disavow. To enter the gallery space is to enter into the exhibit, to step in front of the projector, to always be included, to appear as one of the shadows on the wall; the scene that now *includes* the viewer is transformed into a three-dimensional tableau vivant. In *The Attendant* the tableaux come to life in color out of the *narrative* of the film, which is in black and white; Walker's silhouetted tableaux come to life through their abstraction to a pure black-and-white form.

Walker turns to the silhouette, a domestic art, a prephotographic form that is distant from yet appears familiar to contemporary viewers,[1] in order to pose and then attempt to answer her own questions: "Was it possible for me to make the art that should have been made by a woman like me before the turn of the *last* century? Using just the methods available to her coupled with a 'lofty ambition' and 'checkered past?'" (Saltz 1996, 82). The silhouette is a form of remembering that is a blank form "with its own deep origins in bodily absence and sentimental memory" (Wagner 2003, 94), a popular art form that reached its height in the mid-nineteenth century, at a time coincident with the final years of the institution of slavery, the Civil War, and Reconstruction, but also with the rise of the photographic image and discourses of scientific racism. The silhouette allows Walker to produce the admittedly historically impossible and yet theoretically necessary imaginative work of placing herself and the viewer into the material conditions of the past that is not yet past "using just the methods available to her" in order to better understand the past's omnipresence in the present. We see in her silhouetted slavery tableaux a brutal past that has not been captured fully in language or that has been captured but that we cannot hold; the beating of Aunt H/Esther by Captain Anthony as well as its specific effects on Douglass are two instances of this: the blood-stained gate that on his subsequent rewritings of the narrative Douglass expunges while keeping and invigorating his graphic descriptions of the ritualized beating. Another is our refusal still to really look at Aunt H/Esther. We see in Walker's work, among other things, a visual representation of the slave narratives and neo-slave narratives and their long reach into the present.

These formalized reductions, these would-be stereotypes seem to point away from those enslaved persons who wrote or narrated their own stories of slavery and escape and instead to point to those enslaved people who appear as so many black forms in the background of those narratives as well as in other anti- and pro-slavery texts.[2] In other words, one can read the *black* black figures that populate Walker's work as the black background against which difference (from self and from others) can be erased and constituted. In anti- and pro-slavery narratives these *black* black figures are often the background, the black difference, against which a black individual emerges to write herself or himself as, or to be written as, extraordinary.

One can read Walker's *black* black figures that appear to be devouring themselves and each other, who fuck, fight, stab, shit, suck, puncture, beat, *and survive* and are also fucked, fought, stabbed, shit upon, suckled, punctured, beaten, *and nonetheless survive*, as those transfigured enslaved people (the *black* black background) who were able to survive the violence and brutality *in* the disfiguring institution of slavery. I read Walker's cutouts as representing a violent past that is not yet past in such seductive forms that black and white viewers alike find themselves, as if against their will, looking and looking again.[3] For white viewers this act of looking at Walker's allegories of slavery often entails a seduction by or complicity with violent acts of reading, seeing, naming, and fixing into stereotype that resolves in disavowal and projection. For black viewers this looking can mean encountering shame and violence and sometimes refusing this representation or sometimes being seduced into and complicit with violent acts of reading, seeing, naming, and fixing into stereotype; it means engaging with the disfigurations of black survival that we would prefer to look away from.[4] Walker says that she arrives at her technique by way of acknowledging her "particular upbringing, and by necessity the history which fostered a creature like [her] in the American suburbs": "I thought, here I am, the product of an ambitious black family, pretty well-assimilated—which is code word for 'knows a lot of white people'—and trained in their way of seeing . . . which includes absorbing their racist visions (about me) large and small. There's a certain amount of shame in admitting to this life of mine, and it was shame—the opposite of the pride, black pride in particular—that began to interest me. I thought, for visual resources I should look really in those places where embarrassment lay" (Boerma 2002, 166).[5] This brings me back to the shame (and complicity) involved in looking at, and the dangers involved in circulating, Douglass's description of the violation of Aunt H/Esther. I return to Douglass and H/Esther in this chapter in order to underscore the necessity in *my* grappling with Walker's work, of really looking at those enslaved black people (like Aunt H/Esther)—who are extraordinary *mostly because they survived* a brutality that still cannot be grasped,[6] that is not over, that we may be said to still be surviving (in and dying from)—and of attempting

16 *Gone: An Historical Romance of a Civil War as It Occurred between the Dusky Thighs of One Young Negress and Her Heart*, 1994. Kara Walker. Cut paper (21 paper silhouettes) original and templates with signed certificate. 15 x 50 feet on wall. Installation view at The Walker Art Center, 2007. Image courtesy of Sikkema Jenkins and Co.

to look at shame itself, in order to try to account for its eruption into the present. Put another way, what Walker's work reveals about shame, inasmuch as it is not an individual shame, necessitates also looking at "those places where embarrassment lay," at the shame that "black pride in particular" disavows. At stake are the results of a continued looking away.

Walker's black paper cutouts (figures and forms cut out and then affixed to a white wall) that allegorize the antebellum United States also take the plantation romance of Margaret Mitchell and then David O. Selznick's *Gone With the Wind* at their word, for example, in *Gone: An Historical Romance of a Civil War as It Occurred between the Dusky Thighs of One Young Negress and Her Heart* (1994; figure 16). Walker's work reveals what is everywhere present in the plantation romance, what is in plain sight and denied, and what in its denial functions even still in its remainders. Taken as complicated responses to the conception of and investment in the plantation romance's rewriting of slavery's profound and varied violence as seduction, affection, intimacy, and mutual benefit—or as perfectly natural relationships—Walker's flat black-and-white glyphic forms reveal what the melodrama conceals.

Such highly charged psychosexual violence is everywhere present in the work of Kara Walker. In my discussion of Walker's silhouettes I again want to emphasize the formation of the post-slavery subject that has been the connecting theme of the previous three chapters. While my focus here is on Euro-American and African American post-slavery subjectivity, the post-slavery subject is, of course, not limited to these subject positions. As Toni Morrison reminds us, "The overweening, defining event of the modern world is the mass movement of raced populations, beginning with the largest forced transfer of people in the history of the world: slavery. The consequences of which transfer have determined all the wars following it as well as the current ones being waged on every continent" (1997, 10).

The link that Walker insists on between past and present, seen in the traumatic registers of post-slavery subjectivity (and, for her, specifically a Georgia desegregating with "all deliberate speed"),[7] does not mean that she attempts a naïve collapse of their spatiotemporal distance in her work. Rather her works are allegories for the present; as Walker says, she goes back to this form, this history, "to critique it and to question why it's reoccurring" (Saltz 1996, 82), much the same way that Toni Morrison's *Beloved* can be said to tell about freedoms claimed, granted, assumed, and withheld post-emancipation as well as about desegregation after *Brown v. Board of Education*. The initial "driving force" for Walker's exploration of the past in the present that takes the particular form of the black "burden of representation" was a decision to "investigate interracial desire": "I think it maybe started from that. And the ways in which it seemed, in my life, to challenge set stereotype notions about blackness and whiteness and how they're operating in Georgia, where I was." A personal encounter left her with what she identifies as a desire to understand "the *feeling* of being thrust into history for walking down the street with a white man by some outside force—say a Ku Klux Klan or a guy who leaves a flyer on [one's] car after spotting this illicit liaison. . . . The *feeling* of walking and talking and having to be historical somehow, *bearer of some truth of history*" (1999).

Considering Walker's articulations of self in relation to history, her "walking and talking and having *to be* historical" and bear "some truth of history," I focus a large part of my reading of her work on her construction of the mammy (as the "embodiment of history"), and I argue that that figure is one through which Walker links our antebellum past to our post-slavery, postintegration present. Walker's shadow plays draw our attention to the ways that the act of entering into those other bodies, "playing the slave" (or the master, entering into the ever present traces of the plantation romance), continues to be constitutive of subjectivity for all of those who I am calling post-slavery subjects.

Walker's early self-presentation as "the Negress" and "Missus K. E. B. Walker, a Free Negress of Noteworthy Talent" and her focus on violence, power, and desire in her work and in her statements about her work have been unsettling to many of her viewers, readers, and critics. This is manifest in the extremity of her critical reception: she has been praised lavishly and criticized for her historically informed and deformed, complex and ambivalent representations of self and slavery. As Thelma Golden says, "Kara's work takes from fact but also fantasy and throws on its head any notion we might have of good and bad, right and wrong, black and white. There are no clear dichotomies" (Sheets 2002, 26). Walker's silhouettes depict the centrality of what passes as the underbelly of and vestibular to the plantation romance; she exposes the relationships that construct us all.

Who's(e) Mammy? Whose History?

> The horror of slavery was its absolute domesticity that configured the "peculiar institution" into the architectonics of the southern household.
> —**HORTENSE SPILLERS**, "Changing the Letter"

> Once you get a clear grasp on the fundamentals of history; who's writing it, what emotions are involved in reshaping it, what kinds of people are subjected to it— well, like being the guinea-pig . . . European style enlightenment: "Thems that are most doomed to repeat it are thems that believe in it"—taking history like a faith, a new religion of time and events and more time and more events.—**KARA WALKER**, *Flash Art*

Hortense Spillers begins her essay "Mama's Baby, Papa's Maybe: An American Grammar Book" with a series of meaningful and constitutive displacements, projections, misnamings, and blindnesses that locate the gaze. The one doing the looking insists on the ability to see, to name, and to fix into stereotype black women. "Let's face it," she writes, "I am a marked woman, but not everybody knows my name. 'Peaches' and 'Brown Sugar,' 'Sapphire' and 'Earth Mother,' 'Aunty,' 'Granny,' 'God's Holy Fool,' a 'Miss Ebony First,' or 'Black Woman at the Podium': I describe a locus of confounded identities, a meeting ground of investments and privations in the national treasury of rhetorical wealth. My country needs me and if I were not here, I would have to be invented" (2003c, 203). Her list of names describes a social identity effect that includes but far exceeds any particular impact on individual and collective black women.

To Spillers's list of "confounded identities" and nominative properties I add the encompassing figure of the mammy, who "from her beginnings in southern plantation reality and literature . . . was a sexual and racial symbol that was used by men and women, North and South, white and black, to explain proper gender relationships, justify or condemn racial oppression, and establish class identities (for both whites and blacks)" (Manring 1998, 9). The figure of the mammy is a quintessential example of the national and rhetorical wealth that Spillers articulates. The mammy spans more than a century; pictured on pancake boxes as Aunt Jemima, embodied in salt and pepper shakers, door stoppers, string holders, and memo peg boards—products intimately connected to the U. S. domestic scene—her figure is strangely omnipresent in popular and high culture, advertising, literature, film, and music. There is an uncanny pleasure located in U. S. culture in the Aunt Jemima or mammy figure and her many appearances.

But despite the proliferation of images and objects, who is this mammy? Do we recognize her by her bulk, her headscarf, her mixing bowl and apron, her domestic busyness, simple moral correctness, or simply by her blackness? "It is indisputable," writes M. M. Manring, "that there were slave women called 'mammy,' that these women supervised other house slaves, cooked, and watched children. It is also indisputable that even children and housewives of postbellum America fondly remember a woman called mammy, who played much the same role. But even those who are absolutely certain that they know the person called mammy have trouble explaining everything they think she did" (1998, 19). A house slave and then a domestic, but not fully domesticated, for the viewer she is an(other) indicator of desire and its absence, a placeholder, a cipher. With so much projected into and onto her figure, no wonder the mammy becomes large, superabundant, splits into more of herself. Impossible to contain her in one body, impossible not to see her, she circulates widely but remains invisible nonetheless.[8] Having, as Walker says, no place in the memory of her creators as a creation she becomes a realized figment of collective imagination, an avatar of the collective unconscious. A phantasmatic figure, she is everywhere, in every place.

The mammy is, in Walker's words (specifically in the text of "The Big Black Mammy of the Antebellum South Is the Embodiment of History"), "history as a critical muttering thing, suckling *your* young, and ignored by her creators . . . To all who have fed on the often sour breast milk of the wandering Mammy-as-History it comes as no surprise that history has been declared dead . . . Mammies in popular consciousness cease to exist, She has no place . . . The big black mammy is the object of Oedipal longing within the plantation family romance . . . sucked and fucked she is the ultimate 'earth-mother' wholly submissive yet defiant. . . . she is pairs in opposition she is incomplete and unknown and inconsistent and repressed . . ." (1997; emphasis mine). While the figure of the mammy appears in various forms in much of Walker's work, in this section I focus in particular on an image from the larger work *The End of Uncle Tom and the Grand Allegorical Tableau of Eva in Heaven*. I emphasize that this is an image of at least four figures to allow for the way that Walker's silhouettes, like the blot of figure against ground in Rorschach tests, also bring into focus the white space/figure in the midst of the figure(s) of black suckling women/girls.[9] What is this image, the art critic Jerry Saltz asks Walker, "in the left side of one of the panels . . . this incredible image of four women—girls and women—suckling each other[?] What was this meant as a metaphor for?" (1996, 185; figure 17). Walker responds, "History. My constant need or, in general, a constant need to suckle from history, as though history could be seen as a seemingly endless supply of mother's milk represented by the big black mammy of old. For myself, I have this constant battle—this fear of weaning. It's really a battle that I apply to the black community as well, because all of our progress is predicated on having a very tactile link to a brutal past" (85).[10]

We must keep in mind the visual impact of the large-scale cutout image of the condensed black form of three women suckling each other and the baby attempting to suckle one of the three, and that there is nothing that specifically identifies the women individually or collectively as *the* stereotypical "big black mammy of old." There is an immediate disjunction, a

17 *The End of Uncle Tom and the Grand Allegorical Tableau of Eva in Heaven* (detail), 1995.
Kara Walker. Cut paper and adhesive. 15 × 35 feet on wall. Image courtesy of Sikkema Jenkins
and Co.

gap that opens up, between the perception of the powerful image and
Walker's explanation of it. In what follows I explore Walker's explanation of
the image and the critic Joan Copjec's reading of it in "Moses the Egyptian
and the Big Black Mammy of the Antebellum South: Freud (with Kara
Walker) on Race and History."[11] I consider both Walker's and Copjec's
positioning of the symbolic, historical, and familiar figure of the mammy
not only as history but also as an object that becomes internalized. Finally,
I look at black and white resistance to being interpellated by the scene.

Writing about the image of the suckling women, Copjec cautions, "We must not lose sight of *what is most extraordinary about the portrait; its analogization of history and the maternal breast.* For if we insist on distinguishing the mother from the breast, as I have argued we must, then the analogy becomes both more profound and a more enlightening clue to Walker's artistic project. What does it mean to think of history not as a mother, that is, not as a container that holds subjects as part of its contents, but as an internal object that lives the subject as the double of another?" (2002, 104; emphasis mine). But in addition to distinguishing the mother from the breast, we must also differentiate between the mammy('s breast) and the mother's (maternal) breast, and then again between the breast of the mother substitute and the milk. I do not mean to say that the maternal breast is the same as the mother's breast; I wish instead to turn our focus to the distinction between the mammy (black), who may in deed, if not in law, be a mother (who also might mother white children) on the one hand, and a mother (presumed to be white) on the other hand; a distinction between the wet nurse's (black) breast and the maternal (white) breast. In calling the breast of the enslaved woman a maternal breast, we must remember that she is denied the rights and privileges of both womanhood and motherhood. Such naming would grant her a legal status as well as "a 'feminization' that enslavement kept at bay" (Spillers 2003c, 215). Nonetheless the mammy performs a—often *the*—maternal function in the white household.[12] Connecting this back to Walker's statement, in her description of the vignette, history is not the (maternal) breast; it is the "seemingly endless supply" of "mother's milk represented by the big black mammy of old." Indeed what is most extraordinary about Walker's reading of the portrait (which is not, I think, specifically about the portrait itself) is that what she analogizes is the mammy-as-history-as-mother's-milk. I imagine Walker imagining "the fantasmatic scene of black white suckling, . . . disguised in the generic costume of mammy . . . [in which] the construction of whiteness comes at a cost—the installation of envy of what is posited as blackness in those who take themselves to be white" (St. John 2001, 151).

Likewise when Walker speaks of a "constant battle—this fear of weaning. It's really a battle that I apply to the black community as well, because all of our progress is predicated on having a very tactile link to a brutal past" (quoted in Copjec 2002, 98), I take this to be an articulation of the profound anxiety around the painful emergence of the black object as subject and around the making visible in Walker's installation of something like innocence in the "subject presumed-to-be-white" (St. John 2001, 151).[13] By "innocence" I mean to indicate the absence of the violence in being (mis)seen. In this image of four suckling women/girls in which one can also see in the white ground a phantasmatic white figure suckling the breast of one of the black women, that innocence means the erasure of white suckling through recourse to a readable black (narrative) image or glyph.

In the context of Walker's description of the women/girls and child as *the* big black mammy of old, what Copjec registers in her reading of the repetition of suckling women is "the woman's reencountering of difference from herself" (2002, 103). The "big black mammy" is halved, quartered, redoubled, quadrupled; whichever way we see her, she is constantly reproduced by our need, by the post-slavery subject's need, to be connected to some tangible thing (history, myth) that constitutes us even as we are unable to see it or even as we refuse to acknowledge it. Suckling and being suckled—arranged in a circle, the black figures appear to be of various ages—the women/girls and child are held together as not quite one image and as not yet four as much by the white ground between and around them as by their figures merging with and arising out of each other, their mouths attached to breasts. If one were to break apart Walker's black suckling figures, to sever their "tangible link to a brutal history" that is both past and present, one would see as well the white figure in their midst that has gone unseen because the gaze that is drawn to and reads the black figures as doubly black and endlessly repetitive ignores the white ground.

Let's return to the black figures in Walker's image: three women suckling and being suckled by each other and an infant reaching for a breast, a nipple, that is either just out of reach or hasn't yet been grasped, to ask if this is necessarily, and therefore only, an image of *black* women/girls, and hence only enacted *self*-difference. For if we read the image diegetically, the breast of the black-woman-read-as-mammy that is just out of reach may just as easily be out of the reach of the white infant as out of the reach of the mammy's own child. Mammy, as she is called up in the "white imagination," exists, after all, not to feed the children she gave birth to, but to feed and care for the white children, the white family. Even as the repeated (but different) women suckle each other the breast/milk is out of reach of the white/black infant. We are accustomed to the mammy's inability to feed the black child, trapped as she is in the white household, suckling their young instead of her own, but what of an inability, a refusal to feed the white one? How would we recognize that? How would history account for that possibility? Repeated images that produce the mammy as a comforting presence and comic relief in the white household (as St. John notes, her body a cookie jar, her breast caught in a washing machine wringer, her mouth an ashtray, her behind exposed as she leans over) are matched in number by the images of the mammy's own unsupervised children in all kinds of danger (swallowed up by watermelons, devoured by alligators, left to fend for themselves).[14] And this difference, which is self-difference as well as a blank space that is not a blank space into which difference from an other is projected, is indeed "both more profound and a more enlightening clue to Walker's artistic project" (2002, 104).

Recall that Copjec points out that Walker's response to Saltz's question about the image (that it is "as though history could be seen as a seemingly endless supply of mother's milk represented by the big black mammy of old") is unsatisfying not least of all because the image in question is, of course, not of one black woman but of three women and an infant, none of whom is distinctly recognizable, without Walker's explanation, as the "big black mammy of old."[15] Involved here is also and always a question of the gaze. For some viewers every black woman regardless of age, size, and position may be read as a mammy or as one of the mammy's other incarnations: "God's Holy Fool," "Black Woman at the Podium," "Earth-Mother" (Spillers 2003c, 203). As Copjec notes, Walker's answer *appears merely to restate a popular cliché in which the mother is viewed as a superabundant source from which future generations draw and to which all lines of filiation lead back*" (2002, 98). But such a restating would confuse mammy and mother; more important, it would obscure the ways that lines of filiation and kinship ran for the enslaved, for mammy, not for mother, in which neither blood nor milk ensured familiarity.[16] In relation to the "big black mammy of old" the parental function is repeatedly displaced as the fate of the black child is legally bound to the condition of the enslaved mother, as the ability to mother that child is denied her, *or can always be denied her*, and as the woman legally denied the rights and functions of mother is made to do the mothering of the white children. What Walker states then seems to be something entirely different from the "popular cliché" of mother as superabundant source; she seems to be saying that all lines of descent, all lines of transmission, lead back to the mammy. In Walker's image we might see enacted the introjection of the figure of the mammy.

In this vignette we might see as well the relationship among the four generations of the Corregidora women in Gayl Jones's *Corregidora*, in which the women are held together by their emphasis on reproduction, on passing on evidence, on making the horrors of slavery as "visible as the blood," and in reproducing *for* and reproducing the desires *of* the slave owner whoremonger old man Corregidora. Between them, among them, keeping them attached to each other, ingesting and reproducing this sexually violent history, and suckling the "sour breast milk" is a relationship once legislated and ever present. We see in this image the connection between old man Corregidora and the generations of Corregidora women; we see the defining white ground; we see an image of a *sustaining*, brutal history that the women transmit from generation to generation, ending with Ursa.[17]

Once Copjec has made this connection between the image and Walker's own explanation of it, an explanation that at first seems to refuse exegesis and in fact occasions more questions, she links this plural, otherwise unidentifiable image of the "big black mammy of the antebellum South" to Freud's Egyptian Moses. For Copjec, when Walker invokes the "big black mammy of the antebellum South [who] is the embodiment of history" and Freud invokes the Egyptian Moses, who, according to Freud's own argument, has no basis in recorded history but nonetheless seems theoretically necessary to him to account for the evolution of the myth of Moses into the form that was written down, each participates in "equally scandalous gestures." Each "eschew[s] identification with the traits of empirical (and, one hopes, noble) ancestors as the basis of racial identity, and both begin their inquiry by wondering how the differences separating them from others of their race fail to disqualify them automatically from membership in it" (91–92).

Freud's nonempirical Moses is irreducible (that is, *he* persists even after characteristics that would take him away from the Jews are pared away); in positing him Freud both "den[ies] a people the man whom it praises as the greatest of its sons" (Freud 1939, 9) and insists on the " 'historical truth' of his admittedly hypothetical and undocumentable story of the martyred and resurrected Egyptian Moses and contrast[s] it explicitly with the 'material truth' of 'objective historians' " (Copjec 2002, 91). Copjec's alignment of this Moses with the divided black mammy who is the embodiment of (U.S.) history speaks to the historical and phantasmatic truth of the mammy as an abject and theoretically necessary but impossible figure.

What are the stories of the women whose only remaining trace is the mammy? While there are instances of a historical figure known as Mammy that Walker bases her work on, the parallel that Copjec draws to Freud's Egyptian Moses is instructive both for what it makes visible in Walker's work and for how it exposes one of the blindnesses of Copjec's reading of Walker's work. Although there are mythic and religious accounts of the Egyptian Moses, what most of us know is something more like a Moses-effect, the result of condensations and displacements and resolutions of multiple and conflicting oral traditions laden with thousands of years of elaboration. Likewise, along with the histories of the black women who lived as mammies what we know is something like a mammy-effect, the leftover trace of these historical mammies that continues to circulate phantasmatically and that is continually reproduced as an object that continues to "live the subject as the double of another" (Copjec 2002, 104). In other words, the mammy, however historically based she may be, stands for or in the place of, is laden with what is accepted as history and its effects; the mammy naturalizes blackness in the United States. She is animated according to the work that she is being asked to do: to refute or shore up particular readings of inter- and intraracial violence and affection in slavery, to abet consumption, to internalize and articulate intraracial tensions.[18] Effectively a mythical character, the mammy does not exist, yet she is based on the misseen bodies and labor of real black women. Manthia Diawara writes:

> As a stereotype, the Mammy is the most powerful symbol of the South because she is the only one that is necessary and indispensable to the representation of the entire mythology of the South. To borrow an insight from Roland Barthes, in *Mythologies* (1957), "the Mammy is to the South what the African soldier saluting the French flag on the cover of *Paris-Match* was to the French empire: she forms the identity of the South on the one hand and universalizes the Southern way of life on the other. Dressed in her long dress, apron, head kerchief, and big smile, she becomes as natural as cotton." (1999, 10)

Extending Diawara's insights, the mammy is the mythic figure who forms the identity not only of the South; she comes to be a founding figure of the entire United States.

Resuscitating the mammy in her work and writing as a phantasmatic figure rather than simply as a historical one, Walker would seem to cast off a set of positive features "that ought to have been the tell-tale source" of identity (what was Jewishness for Freud and is blackness for Walker). This casting off, this *animation* of shame ("as the opposite of pride, black pride in particular") is profoundly distressing to any number of Walker's black critics; it is for them Walker's setting back into territory that has already been traversed.[19] It is, though, as Walker herself notes, the exploration of shame that is of particular interest to her (Boerma 2002, 166). This casting off is both the erasure of positive attributes of blackness and it is blackness's signing. In other words, the mammy, her blackness, is analogous to Moses the Egyptian, "a fulginous [*sic*] stain that not only Freud but history and death itself proved incapable of rubbing out" (Copjec 2002, 92). The "fuliginous stain" is residual blackness, blackness that won't be erased, blackness that allows whiteness to (almost) erase itself, and blackness that illuminates what is otherwise unreadable, unseeable. This fuliginous stain, this blackness, works the way that a black light works: it makes white things show up even more brightly. It is also like the ten drops of black liquid that the unnamed protagonist in *Invisible Man* adds to the white paint, the substance that makes "Liberty Paints Optic White" the "right white."[20]

What Walker's work reveals, what it is so adept at revealing, is that there is something in excess of what historical narrative gives us. I suggest that one thing that the figure of the mammy is called up to conceal appears in the chapter "TV Guide" in Phyllis Rose's memoir, *The Year of Reading Proust: A Memoir in Real Time* (1997):

> The colored person who came to live with us when I was eight was Lily McAllistar. Lily came from Starr, South Carolina, where her husband, Taft, was a farmer. *They had three children, but Lily had to leave them in South Carolina to be raised by her mother and Taft's, while she raised me in the North. She sent home the money my parents paid her, along with long letters, written on ruled paper in a hand as rounded and hearty as Lily and a style as cheerful. . . . I had Lily to mother me and only me for several happy years.* Then she told my mother she was

quitting, she was too lonely, and my mother, both in her kindness and in her concern for the good functioning of her household, offered to hire Taft.

So Taft came to live with us, too, and to work as our "chauffeur," although he did not know how to drive and by the time he came to us my brother was away at college and my sister had her own driver's license. . . . It was bad enough to be driven around by a chauffeur, which was "different" at a time when difference was not admired. . . . It was also clear to me, although I had never seen a chauffeur except in the movies, that Taft was not a real chauffeur. *A chauffeur was above all competent and intrepid, whereas Taft was timid and tentative in everything he did.* My mother gave him a chauffeur's hat to wear, but *I knew this was a charade being carried on for the benefit of Taft and Lily for which my father was footing the bill but I was paying the worst price, humiliation.*

In retrospect I envy the well-run household over which my mother presided. Every morning as I got dressed I could hear the sound of Lily or Taft vacuuming the living room carpet. *There was freshly squeezed orange juice for breakfast. Laundry was done on a regular basis.* When I got home from school in the afternoon, Lily would pour me a glass of milk and give me some cookies, or cake, or chocolate pudding. *She was a fine cook, but my mother orchestrated the meals, and under her baton* chopped liver might precede spaghetti with meatballs and Vita herring, Southern fried chicken. Mother and Lily did better on Jewish holidays when the menu was traditional and gefilte fish followed matzoh ball soup and was followed in turn by pot roast or turkey.

Here are Rose's reflections from the analyst's couch, what the analyst helps her realize:

What was unique about me was that no one had hurt me. . . . I never "understood" my childhood because I never understood what a happy childhood it was. *I had my parents' love and attention. There was no story to tell except a happy one,* and I had been led by whatever theories or literary models to think that only unhappy childhoods counted. (1997, 56–57; emphases mine)[21]

The diegetic subject here is a child, Rose, looking back on a childhood that she can now, in the present and with the help of her therapist, recognize and understand to be a happy one. The narrator's reinstallation of innocence, the recovered innocence of the "subject-presumed-to-be-white," is predicated on and structured by the myth of the benevolent patriarchy, the monstrous intimacies of the plantation romance, where the mammy's labor must be accompanied by the affects of cheer and gratitude and not read as labor.[22] Round, hearty, cheerful Lily's subjectivity and labor are erased as she comes to embody a number of contradictions. She is a mother of three away from her children and a disavowed worker ("There was freshly squeezed orange juice for breakfast. Laundry was done on a regular basis": note the use of the passive voice), who mothers a child who is not her own; her body is put in the space of the hyphen that would otherwise mark the site of the interpellation of the subject as white. As Maria St. John writes, "Mammy's cheerful width covers over the fact that people who identify as white have no essential claim to the privilege we enjoy by assuming that identity. When mammy appears to broadcast her natural blackness, she functions to shore up the category 'white'" (2001, 137–38).

We learn from reading Rose how this mythologizing and shoring up happen and how they are maintained; we see black people and black labor elided in Rose's romance just as white people are elided from many readings of Walker's slavery silhouettes. As part of Rose's construction of her family romance she displaces onto Lily and Taft the weight of shame and of class, race, gender difference, and this displacement in turn is part of what allows her in the present to remember and understand her childhood as a happy one.[23] The erasure of Lily's work and of her loneliness is part of the "architectonics of the southern [and northern] household" (Spillers 2003a, 178) that the dismantling of the institution of slavery does not do away with. That Lily takes care of the narrator, "and only her for three years," means that Lily's children have a profoundly different experience of mothering, a childhood marked by the absence of their mother. Indeed the mammy's presence often indicates the mother's absence—the white mother from the white home or the tasks of mothering, the black mother from the black home—and the transfiguration of the black mother into the mammy in the home of the white woman. Disguised as or hidden behind good management, intimacy, affection, and even love, a monstrous intimacy is at the center of the production of white subjectivity vis-à-vis the introjection of the figure of the mammy. The mammy becomes an object that circulates, with effects. Rose's story has in it the innocence of those millions of people who consume the comforting and familiar phantasmatic aura of Aunt Jemima.

According to Rose's narrator, the "worst price" of Lily's and Taft's labor is not their absence from their own home, not Lily's cheerful caretaking of her in the face of loneliness, but the narrator's own *humiliation* at the "charade being carried on" for the "benefit of Taft and Lily." Again the gaze is crucial to observe here. What makes being chauffeured to school the worst price for the narrator is that driven to school by Taft, she is suddenly in the position of *seeing others seeing her* dropped off at school by him. Not only is Taft an unwanted chauffeur, but the "timid and tentative" Taft is not even a real chauffeur. In the narrator's seeing and being seen lies the recognition of Lily's and Taft's labor, of class, race, power, and gender that must be concealed, kept at home in order to produce a narrative of a happy (innocent) childhood. It is this that Rose (and the therapist) need to cover over, and that Walker attempts to make visible.

For a white subject to be seen (to see oneself) as a white subject in the Walker vignette on which this chapter focuses would fracture the fantasy that constructs the mammy as (like) part of the family. This is a fracturing that simply cannot be allowed. Whatever humiliation the narrator feels from being seen having servants must be buried under the force of nostalgia encouraged by her therapist. The pursuit of happiness with which Rose's tale ends does not extend to the unremarked-upon childhoods of Lily's and Taft's children. The cruelty of Rose's reflection (the monstrous intimacy) is that in remembering she seeks to erase what she experienced as a child being driven to school by Taft when her anxiety emerged for the reasons she details and as a symptom of that experience. Her recognition of Lily and Taft remains disavowed.

There is thus an "exorbitant pleasure" (Copjec's term) in Rose's looking back and in her innocence here that repeats the erasure of the mammy, which in fact confirms Walker's rendition of the mammy in that particular vignette, as circulating, introjected. There is a similar pleasure to be found on the part of those (white) (re)viewers of Walker's work who absent themselves from her dialectical practice while rehearsing a whole catalogue of names and acts for the black characters in the silhouettes. Both positions involve a retrospective assumption of nostalgic innocence that allows Rose to understand her childhood as a happy one by the covering over of black characters to save her innocence and also allows (white) viewers and critics of Walker's work to insist that her images are "about" black people, thereby covering over the white characters to preserve "white innocence." There is, however, no plantation romance or plantation slavery without white people, and Walker's silhouettes contain many diegetically white characters in the black cutouts as well as in the white ground.

This brings me back to Copjec's reading of Freud's Egyptian Moses and Mammy and to her erasure of white figures, white people, from Walker's work. Again, I suspect that this persistent erasure is why some of Walker's later work includes overhead projectors and light so that the gallery visitors cast shadows. It is a didactic tool, Walker notes, that reinforces each viewer's participation in the scene unfolding before him or her. There are other, not so happy stories to tell here; one of them might be about how the U.S./American "subject-presumed-to-be-white" becomes white and the presumptive U.S./American subject stays white. The post-slavery subject—black, white, male, female—stems from the mammy in the mode of the ancient Hebrews stemming from Moses; both are a reconciliation of competing and contradictory historical characters and historical perspectives into a consolidated myth.

Reading White from Black

> How can a would-be white subject consciously entertain and thus work through envy of the black female figure when the cultural "fact" of her worthlessness is reinforced at every discursive and institutional turn? In what image can he recognize his love of her when her reproduction is synonymous with her debasement? How can he speak of her inestimable value to him when her devaluation constitutes the very basis on which the economy he was born into perpetuates itself?
> —MARIA ST. JOHN, "'It Ain't Fittin': Cinematic and Fantasmatic Contours of Mammy in *Gone with the Wind* and Beyond"

When Jerry Saltz asks Walker how the silhouette functions in her work, she replies, "It's a blank space, but it's not at all a blank space, it's both there and not there" (Saltz 1996, 82). The silhouette is projection; it is what remains after something has been cut away, and it is the thing that has been cut away. The silhouette is also like the stereotype, "blank in [its] generality, and yet powerfully present in [its] introjection by the stereotyped subjects and their racial others" (Joselit 2000, 31). For Walker the silhouette is also about "indirection," an "avoidance of the subject."

In her descriptions of Walker's most well-known and recognizable work, Copjec writes, "Composed of black paper, all the human figures are, technically, black, though we are able to distinguish the diegetically white 'folk' from the diegetically black on the basis of their stereotypical profiles, postures, and clothing. Glued to the walls the figures become part of their flat surface rather than standing out in front of them as they would had they been mounted on canvas" (2002, 83). In comparing Mammy to Freud's Moses, Copjec in one way explicates what Rose's therapist allowed Rose to avoid. And while she is aware that some of the characters in the cutouts are white, nevertheless Copjec repeats what is standard in white critics' readings of Walker: the (white) viewer ascribes race to the black figures that adhere to the wall through a calculation of features (hair texture and style, profile, clothing, etc.) into a racial equation of, in Copjec's words, "Hottentot harlots, sambos, mandingos, Uncle Toms, churls and scallywags of every sort [who] *engage nonchalantly* in violent and licentious acts of parturition, sodomy, cannibalism, and coprophany, as well as *in other acts we have no idea how to name*" (2002, 93).

Race, like slavery, is read as entirely about black people, and everyday reading practices become reified in these descriptions. In other words, we are taken away from the fact that race is read through "a calculation of features" all of the time. Mark Reinhardt writes, "With a knowing inversion of the one-drop rule that labels even the palest skin 'black,' Walker first brings before the viewer the usually unnamed and unseen codes of racializing vision" (2003, 113). Aware of the existence of the diegetically *white* black figures, Copjec's reading is caught up by Walker's cutups in a way that she herself would call symptomatic. Copjec knows that these characters represent black and white people of various classes, slave and free, but she proceeds to list only diegetically black characters and to discuss the actions of the cutouts as if they were only black performances:

> The "plantation family romances," as Walker calls her vignettes, have not been warmly received by everyone. In the black community, particularly, they remain controversial, with many blacks fiercely agitating against the work and even mounting letter-writing campaigns to protest her exhibitions. The problem for these protestors is that rather than narratives confirming the dignity of the race or reflecting the actual achievements and steady integrity of a downtrodden but spirited people, rather than positive and uplifting images of defiant or self-sacrificing and virtuous blacks, Walker's nursery-rhyme raunchy vignettes offer a fulguration of uncouth "sex pickaninnies." Hottentot harlots, sambos, mandingos, Uncle Toms, churls and scallywags of every sort *engage*

nonchalantly in violent and licentious acts of parturition, sodomy, cannibalism, and coprophany, as well as *in other acts we have no idea how to name.* The charge made against Walker is both that her representations are sexually and racially derogatory and that they have no basis in fact but simply recycle stereotypes found in that racist memorabilia or Americana that Walker, like many other blacks, admits to collecting. What she calls her "inner plantation,"[24] this criticism implies, has been implanted in her by white racists; she owes it to herself, and her race, not to recreate these fictions, but to exorcise them through a recovery of her actual, truthful, and by the way, glorious origins. (2002, 84–91; emphasis mine)

We might ask why it is important that these acts (which Copjec has "no idea how to name") have a name, and what it might mean that Walker represents acts for which we, or at least Copjec, who names with such deliberateness, have descriptions but no names. Naming is, I suspect, a way to refuse an act or a position, much like Copjec's description of Walker's black critics fixes into stereotype varied objections and interventions under the label of "protestors."

The black artist and art historian Howardeena Pindell is one person who has been critical of Walker's work and its circulation. About the controversy over Walker's work Pindell reflects on two groups and their responses: black people in the art world and black people from "more conservative sectors." She writes:

Recently there has been a swift negative response from a number of African-American artists, art historians, and museum curators to the rapid embrace of Kara Walker. . . . There has been, however, a muffled, restrained, fearful response from more conservative sectors of the African-American community, perhaps fearful because of the ostracism and trivialisation of those who object, by those behind the trend. . . .

I feel that artists who use racial stereotypes without critique become complicit. They are reinforcing the old stereotype as if to say the fabricated image is their true experience. Thus, in the visual industries' uneven playing field these artists entertain, titillate, mesmerise and amuse their European/European-American admirers. (2002)

Pindell, Betye Saar, and other black artists, curators, and academics who have spoken and written critically (sometimes negatively and sometimes personally) about stereotypes in Walker's work and the presentation and reception of Walker, her work, her writing, and statements about her work, have all too often been lumped together and summarily dismissed. Should we ignore the set of power relations on display here and in Pindell's and others' critiques, that an often uncritical embrace and dissemination of Walker's work seeks to place her, the work, and the art establishment itself outside of a particular history of art world inclusion and exclusion and a broader history of institutionalized racism and white supremacy?[25]

This too is the ground of Walker's work. What Walker finds in the form of the silhouette is, she says, "a near perfect solution to a complex project that [she] set for [herself] to try and *uncover the often subtle and uncomfortable ways racism, and racist and sexist stereotypes influence and script our everyday lives*" (quoted in Obrist 1998–99).[26] I suggest that while Walker looks to familiar figures, her work is not simply the *recycling* of stereotypes. The forms are identifiable as stereotypical through naming, through association (Topsy, Uncle Tom, Mammy, Eva, plantation master and mistress, overseer, etc.), through scene and scenery, but that the figures engage in actions that one can describe and not name (as Copjec says) and that sometimes one can barely describe seems to me a step away from the readily assignable roles and postures of the stereotype and a step toward throwing them into relief against what they conceal.

Walker's work seems to revel in (and this reveling is painful to witness) this kind of disfiguration of blackness and whiteness, in what one reviewer terms "finely cut nastiness" (Steffen 2002, 98). This reveling is coupled with a refusal to disavow the monstrous pleasures—pleasures that (depending on the position from which one sees the thing) one sees as well in antislavery writings and visual arts—that Walker depicts in her work, a monstrosity that black and white viewers alike find themselves, perhaps in different ways, participants in. This unwilling interpellation into the scenes of slavery (past and present) is, I think, what has drawn the ire of a number of (art) critics and academics: their confrontation with their participation in the scene, through recognition, denial, identification, and through collapsing horror and pleasure, humor and pain.

Once Copjec describes Walker's black and white figures, as she begins to read the violent scenes that Walker stages among them, her description shifts, like that of many critics, to one in which all of the human characters are, for all intents and purposes, diegetically or otherwise black.[27] Black and white viewers alike erase the *white* black figures. But if we accept, as I think we must, that part of what Walker's work takes on is the transmission and effects of profound interracial (sexual) violence (as well as intraracial violence) in, for example, *The End of Uncle Tom and the Grand Allegorical Tableau of Eva in Heaven*, from which the vignette of the four women/girls is drawn, how are we to read these scenes as scenes of slavery (and its traumatic return) without those white characters who are its primary agents (master, mistress, young master, young mistress) and their agents (driver, overseer)? The very ways that we see, and following from the visual cues the critical conversations that we have about Walker's shadows and their acts, at first inclusive of actors who are white and black, are projected onto and then become internal to those *black* black figures who thereafter appear to be fucking, fighting, shitting, eating, and otherwise violating and sometimes pleasuring each other and themselves all to themselves. To erase the white characters is to repress and then to repeat the profound national, visual, and rhetorical violence that Walker's allegories of slavery attempt to make visible. The subject (black and white) doing the erasing (of self and other) is unable to see that erasure as the site of slavery's traumatic insistence. Without the white characters we see nonchalance and not horror in these black performances; without the white characters and with no memory of the conditions under which such acts are compelled, the excessive sex and violence that we see might well be described as that phenomenon called "black-on-black crime."

When Copjec, Robert Hobbs, and others write about the "racist memorabilia or Americana that Walker, like many other blacks, admits to collecting," the focus on black collecting appears to me to be another instance in which Euro-American post-slavery subjects erase the scene of their own production through profound violence. That is, (white) critics who, on the one hand, locate the emergence of Walker's images as coincident with the increased numbers of black people (what Hobbs calls "upscale African Americans") collecting racist memorabilia, on the other hand do not mention the fact that the majority of such objects not only circulate among and are owned by, but are produced by, nonblacks, principally whites, of *all classes*.[28]

But what is it in Walker's work and its circulation that produces such visceral responses, such passionate refusals, from some black viewers who may or may not collect racist memorabilia?[29] Might this discomfort point to their awareness of the conditions of "freedom within unfreedom" in which we live now, present conditions that are coincident with and structured by the past that is not yet past? Walker's work, along with the work of Michael Ray Charles, Beverly McIver, Fred Wilson, Robert Colescott, Carrie Mae Weems, and Josephine Tarry (in conjunction with Bradley McCallum), among others, is another instance of the return of an African American repressed in the form of an exploration of *black* blackface minstrelsy. Is it a discomfort related to the very unspeakability of the conditions that are still compelling such black performances? While I do not explore this here, it's worth repeating Michele Wallace's caution: "The case of extensive black participation in blackface minstrelsy needs to be accepted and interrogated since it means, it seems to me, that there are crucial aspects to the form that have somehow been overlooked in the haste to condemn it as hopelessly racist, and to erase all memory of it" (2000, 145).

I return to Copjec, who slips too easily into stereotype, dismissal, and disavowal (her language of a "downtrodden but spirited people," "self-sacrificing and virtuous blacks," etc). This easy slippage, this spatiotemporal erasure of whites from the scene of slavery, its excesses, and the persistence of its traces in the present may be part of what makes those whom Copjec identifies simply as Kara Walker's black "protesters" so upset with the art establishment's embrace of Walker and her narrative cutouts. Copjec's look at the black critics' reading of Walker's work repeats the gesture of erasure, like the one that erases whites from the scene of producing slavery and from producing and collecting racist memorabilia. It erases the ways that Walker's work circulates among, adorns the walls of, and is in conversation most often with the (largely white and largely nonblack) art establishment (buyers, curators, gallery owners, collectors, art historians). Given the general agreement that Walker's images are allegories of profound violence in slavery and in the present, there is significantly less attention given to the ways these images traffic in different spaces and produce a variety of responses (not to mention subjects) precisely as an effect of the blankness of the silhouette form. Walker's cutouts and the narrative pieces that sometimes accompany them appear for a number of her critics to be too loose, too unframed, and too close to minstrelsy.[30] That in her work and in her statements about her work Walker quite openly references ante- and postbellum images, image making, and viewing practices does not mitigate this view. For example, in

Walker's frequent focus on the conjunction of horror and pleasure I see traces of François-Auguste Biard's antislavery painting *Slaves on the West Coast of Africa* (1833). One of the scenes from *Slaves* that was frequently reproduced by abolitionists and pro-slavery advocates alike depicts a black woman being branded by a French sailor. We see in this image, its reproduction, and circulation the meeting of libidinal philanthropic and sadistic investments. While Walker acknowledges her indebtedness to the long and very problematic traditions of minstrelsy and the Tom show, her cutouts are, I would argue, not simply or merely her "cutting-up." They are not, or at least not simply, Walker being an art world opportunist or the product of art world hype. Connected as they are to minstrelsy these silhouetted vignettes should, indeed must tell us something about the inter- and intraracial relations that minstrel shows, their antecedents, and progeny reflect and produce. So while Walker's disturbing allegories of the antebellum United States seem to some critics to be minstrel show capering and to others a "cakewalk," I suggest that they are an uncanny sideways look (her black-eyed squint, what she calls an unreliable look) at slavery that ruptures history.[31]

It is just such attention to the look and what it reveals that brings me to "Kara Walker's Cakewalk," the art historian Donald Kuspit's vitriolic review of Kara Walker: Excavated from the Black Heart of a Negress (2003). Kuspit writes:

> Kara Walker's wall works are a kind of cakewalk—"a musical promenade of black American origin with the prize of a cake awarded to couples who demonstrated the most intricate or imaginative dance figures and steps," according to the dictionary. They certainly take the cake for imaginative brilliance and strutting wit, but what's the ideological point, beyond the fancy art footwork, for doing a cakewalk these days? The civil rights surge of the 1960s has passed into history. Prejudice remains—against Asians, Jews, women and gays as well as blacks—and, these days, *perhaps most of all against heterosexual white males*, but there's no special pleading on their behalf.[32]

Kuspit asks, "What is the ideological point, beyond the fancy art footwork, for doing a cakewalk these days?" The cakewalk being his own trope for Walker's work, Kuspit posits the black American origin of the trope, then relies for an answer on a definition of the cakewalk that rhetorically erases the conditions of this black American art form's production and the different audiences for whom this performance is staged. He attempts to completely erase Walker's point as he turns this history into a cakewalk that posits white heterosexual males as its final and actual victims, victims for whom there is no appeal. During slavery cakewalks were dances that were encouraged, supported, or compelled by the master; they were also sites of recuperation, sites where enslaved people could access some pleasure that enabled survival within slavery, sites from where the enslaved could stage some resistance, and also sites from where the master could sustain the "consent" of the enslaved to their lot.[33]

> [The] Cakewalk developed as a pastiche of the dance slaves witnessed their white masters and mistresses performing in the Big House. Certain meanings were encoded and although apparent to those in the know (the slaves), were read differently by white people who had the slaves perform this dance for them. For these spectators, the Cakewalk was an amusing attempt at sophistication on the parts of their slaves, rather than a mockery of their lifestyle. . . . "They [the enslaved people] did a take-off on the high manners of the white folks in the 'big house,' but their masters who gathered around to watch the fun, missed the point." (George-Graves 2000, 60)

Calling Walker's work a cakewalk thus turns our attention to the gaze to highlight Kuspit's, and a larger audience's, desire to see a particular "black performance" rendered transparent.[34] Missing the point, or perhaps getting it and erasing the evidence of that understanding, Kuspit continues: "The installation as a whole is a kind of pastiche spectacle—a theater of the absurd, in which the spectator, standing in the center, is assaulted by a buckshot of texts and overwhelmed by the big screen-size image. The change in scale, medium and import is disorienting, adding to the sense of victimization: *one is forced to identify with blacks—forced into their position*" (2003; emphasis mine). Kuspit's entirely symptomatic (mis)reading of Walker's work seems to arise from this crucially accurate reading of a forced identification with blackness (this blackness and these blacks) that this spectator (any spectator) may experience as profound, disorienting violence ("assaulted by a buckshot of texts," "overwhelmed by the big-screen image"). Kuspit's complaint stems from the fact that Walker's work works all too well. On the one hand he is correct: one *is* in a position of reading "white through black" and thus in the position of an identification of sorts with blackness, if not with black people. On the other hand the diegetically black characters do not provide the only point of entry into the scene.[35] Forced to identify with *these* blacks,[36] forced into "*their* position," what Kuspit experiences, and I suspect an audience of both black and white viewers may experience, is a too close association with a "fuliginous" blackness that must immediately be met with a violent disavowal. There are, of course, other disavowals here as well: Kuspit's admitted horror at being forced to identify with the black characters in the vignettes serves to protect him from acknowledging his forced identification with the *white* ones, and, for some black as well as white spectators, an unwilling identification with disfigured blackness.[37]

For Kuspit this work is an "ideological failure" because in spite of being assaulted by blackness he "experienced no pity and terror—no catharsis despite the stressful drama—nor did [he] feel particularly enlightened with new insights into the situation or mentality of black America, if there is any single situation or frame of mind that defines it (doubtful)" (Kuspit 2003). But Kuspit does feel the terror of identification, and the anxiety that arises in his work is all about the power of signification. Certainly the work is successful at revealing Kuspit's ideology: "Prejudice remains . . . perhaps most of all against heterosexual white males, but there's no special pleading on their behalf" (2003). His response to his unsettling interpellation into the scene of slavery and its incarnations in the present seems to me *not* indicative of the ideological failure of Walker's work but of its ideological and artistic success. He continues:

> Walker's work is certainly high drama, weirdly tragicomic, with a deft narrative twist, but it has less to do with social reality than black rage, resentment and bitterness. The mural suggests a futile attempt—or is it a deliberate refusal?—to come to terms with past history, suggesting that there is a regressive dimension to the sense of being a victim. Walker seems obsessed with the past, as though to preclude a vision of the future, perhaps because it is a generalized American future rather than a specifically black one. Is she holding on to black difference in defiant fear of American sameness (which is more of a myth than reality)?

Kuspit, it seems, reads this backwards, for there is no myth of "American sameness" without black difference. Once again we have black-on-black crime, this time a drive-by shooting. This rhetorical move repeats what I identify as the white critics' anxiety when confronted by Walker's cutouts: it exposes a desire to put black and white back in their "proper" places.

Kuspit then proceeds to buttress his argument by inserting a quotation from Adorno on jazz, without mentioning that it is a notoriously problematic (mis)reading. Despite possessing some technical brilliance, for Kuspit Walker's work, "however artistically eloquent, remains haunted by T. W. Adorno's dialectical view of the jazz performer":

> It is well known that jazz is characterized by its syncopated rhythm, thus by a displacement which inserts apparent beats within the regular measures, comparable to the intentionally clumsy stumbling of the eccentric clown, familiar enough from the American film comedies. A helpless, powerless subject is presented, one that is ridiculous in his expressive impulses. Now the formula of jazz is this, that precisely by virtue of his weakness and helplessness this subject represented by the irregular rhythms adapts himself to the regularity of the total process, and because he, so to speak, confesses his own impotence, he is accepted into the collective and rewarded by it. Jazz projects the schema of identification: in return for the individual erasing himself and acknowledging his own nullity, he can vicariously take part in the power and the glory of the collective to which he is bound by this spell. (Adorno, "Sociology of Art and Music," quoted in Kuspit, 2003)

Kuspit allows himself to maintain his blindness by projecting it onto Walker and her work and by repeating without qualification Adorno's reading of jazz, which is structured by a similar blindness. Indeed might we not read in Walker's vignette of the four suckling figures, her "big black mammy" as "the embodiment of history," precisely the means by which the (white) individual erases himself or herself so that he or she can take part in "the power and the glory of the collective" (Kuspit 2003)?

Perhaps part of the cause of Kuspit's discomfort (his argument is representative in its symptoms) lies in Walker's *explanation* about her choice of the silhouette form that spoke to her "in the same way that the minstrel show does—it's middle class white people rendering themselves black, making themselves somewhat invisible, or taking on an alternate identity because of the anonymity. . . . You can play out different roles when you're rendered black, or halfway invisible" (1999). Not black people's self-erasure or white people "blacking up," but white people making themselves white through a rewriting of the one-drop rule (in which a little blackness makes you whiter).

Of course in Walker's work there is an intraracial conversation going on as well as an interracial one, but many critics would have us believe that it is wholly intraracial, that what Walker depicts is all and only about black, or constructively black, people, as if race, slavery, and racist memorabilia are of relevance predominantly, if not exclusively, to the African American post-slavery subject as the one who wears the shadow of the "blood-stained gate." Let's review Copjec's list of characters in Walker's work: "pickanin-nies," "Hottentot harlots, sambos, mandingos, Uncle Toms, churls and scal-lywags," black folk all of them, with the exception of the scallywag,[38] a white figure outside of whiteness, a "nigger-lover," a white person who is seen by white people through a lens of derision to be counted with black people, blackened, an example of unassimilated whiteness. Each term signals a slippage that on the one hand acknowledges and on the other hand repudiates Kara Walker's "ironic and giddy, half-vulgar attempt . . . to suggest that everything is akin to blackness" (Hobbs 2001, 81). Put another way, Copjec's slip indicates that she uncannily misses Walker's point of rendering everything black, and yet her elision makes both her own point and Walker's point all too well: that black bodies are "bodies occupied, emptied and occupied" (Brand 2001, 38) and that too close association with blackness produces uncanny effects; on the one hand it makes white-ness unreadable, and on the other hand it makes whiteness more readable. It is not that " 'blackness' is only visible in and against the 'whiteness' of its containing ground" (Wagner 2003, 96). Rather, reversing the title of Rob-ert Hobbs's and Michael Corris's discussion of Walker's work ("Reading Black from White"), is it possible to read white from black? Is it possible, given the history of the United States, to read whiteness any other way?

Indeed, Walker's furious cuts refuse to disavow that everything (every-one) is kin, family to blackness, not reducible to the *black* black figures on the wall except through eliding the "diegetically white folk" with the white wall against which it is only blackness that becomes visible. Conflating the *white* black figures with the *black* black figures is part of the process of reading Walker's work, and the collapse of one into the other is, I think, an indication of the interior limit of post-slavery Euro-American subjectivity. For the white post-slavery subject the black figure, and in this instance the "big black mammy of the antebellum south," that bearer of abject subjec-tivity, is always seen to be on the outside, constitutive of difference, not internal to subjectivity, always the not me.[39]

Copjec writes in "Moses the Egyptian and the Big Black Mammy of

the Antebellum South: Freud (with Kara Walker) on Race and History,"
"Freud removed his notion of race from this problematic of identification;
he stripped it of ideality. In the process he uncovered an *anonymous root of
racial identity, in a useless, exorbitant pleasure*" (2002, 106–7). Walker's
work connects this *jouissance*, this inaccessible kernel, to the more manifest version that Françoise Vergès articulates in relation to slavery. For
Vergès slavery tells us something about the master's exorbitant pleasure:
"The forms of domination instituted by slavery constituted new ways of
being whose exploration might open up interesting perspectives upon the
jouissance of power and violence" (1999a, 3). I would argue, however, in extending Copjec's link to Walker and to the mammy as the embodiment
of U.S. history, that the exorbitant pleasure that one locates in relation
to the mammy is not entirely exorbitant and certainly is not useless.[40]
The mammy (as the embodiment of U.S. history) is often recuperated
fully within the scope of the law, called up to perform a multitude of
functions. The pleasure identified with her is still useful, like the pleasure
Copjec identifies in relation to the construction of the Aryan ideological
"machine-body," and it is, I think, an example of *usufructus*.[41]

The mammy in all of her incarnations is useful. On the level of direct
signification she stands for domestic usefulness. We might see as well the
uses to which she has been and is put in countless commercial applica-
tions, from the extracted labor of black women in white households to the
(melo)dramatic ideological appeal of the loving mammy in slavery that
covers over legal and other violence, to the versatile marketing appeal of
Aunt Jemima on a box of pancake mix. Mammy is so pervasive because she
is useful in so many ways in maintaining, justifying, and euphemizing
social subjugation. Copjec, in focusing on an exorbitant, nonrecuperable
pleasure (*jouissance*) that pertains in these relations, overlooks the material and social pleasures of use and profit. Nonetheless her point about
jouissance is valid, for there are "no limits, no borders to the kind of
pleasure, of *jouissance*, that [the enslaved persons'] owners were seeking. It
went beyond a desire for economic benefit, beyond a desire to be served.
The unnecessary excesses of violence testified to the obscene quality of
enjoyment experienced by the masters. . . . [This was] a world in which
beating, violence, was addictive, in which terror was the order of things.
Yet it would be wrong to think that it was exceptional behaviour" (Vergès
1999a, 5). There is an unmetabolized terror and pleasure (though not

18 *The End of Uncle Tom and the Grand Allegorical Tableau of Eva in Heaven*, 1995. Kara Walker. Cut paper and adhesive. 15 x 35 feet on wall. Image courtesy of Sikkema Jenkins and Co.

necessarily for the same subjects) in Walker's silhouettes that haunts and constitutes the post-slavery subject; its excesses circulate still.

What is so effective about Walker's work is that she opens up those monstrous excesses. Isn't it this effectiveness that drives Kuspit's excessive denial? The more Kuspit denies, the more it becomes apparent that his humiliation is the same humiliation that at once stimulates Rose's symptom and also "requires" that she repress it.

Copjec concludes with the following about Walker's work:

Allowing her work to be haunted by the traumatic event of the antebellum past, that is, by an event that neither she nor any other black American ever lived but that is repeatedly encountered in the uncanny moment, she opens the possibility of conceiving racial identity as repeated self-difference. *What she shares with all the other members of her race* is not simply a number of common experiences but this impossible-to-experience event that keeps tearing them apart from themselves, a historical rupture that cannot be "metabolized," but keeps depositing itself in those little piles of shit that turn up everywhere in the Walker silhouettes. (2002, 107; figure 18; emphasis mine)

19 *World's Exposition* (detail), 1997. Kara Walker. Cut paper and adhesive. 10 x 16 feet on wall. Image courtesy of Sikkema Jenkins and Co.

Here Copjec succeeds in completely erasing the *white* black figures in Walker's cutouts, making it all, once again, about black people. If Walker's work is, like Freud's Moses, "stripped of identification" it is for Copjec only so for black people. This erasure, this inability to see herself in the mammy, allows Copjec to miss her own point: that this figure is the "anonymous root" of "racial subjectivity." That is, it is not just Walker and "the other members of her race" who share in this "impossible-to-experience event," but also the white viewers who white themselves out of the scenes, out of any relationship to a common past. There is an excess in Walker's work to which critics and viewers react variously: Saar and Pindell see the work as succumbing to the past, as playing in slavery (playing the slave) for the white art world and not as a performance for some other end; Copjec, in the end, erases whites from the scenes and symptoms of

20 *Cabinetmaking*, 1820–1960, from *Mining the Museum: An Installation by Fred Wilson*, The
Contemporary and Maryland Historical Society, Baltimore, 4 April 1992–28 February 1993.
© Fred Wilson. Courtesy PaceWildenstein, New York.

(post) slavery; Kuspit both denies any implication in the scene and re-
emphasizes all the other repressions; and the (white) art patron, as we will
read, cleans up all the shit.

The insistence that race equals black and that black, and not white,
equals slavery means that one New York art patron can, "for her children's
sake," censor "the scatological content of Kara Walker's mural Worlds
Exposition" (Vogue 2003, 481) (figure 19).[42] Without the little piles of shit,
points of entry into Walker's "nursery rhyme raunchy" vignettes that a
child might indeed latch onto, what remains are any number of disturbing
scenes: a black woman painting a tree from which she is hanging by her
tail as she defecates (shit excised but mouth still open to receive) into the
open mouth of a black child impaled on a white man/statue;[43] a black
child about to penetrate with a stick a white/black woman whose legs are
hooked over the tree branch that she hangs upside down from as she drops
bananas to a black man down on one knee below her; a white/black child
sucking on the breast of a topless black woman who wears what looks like
a grass skirt. The art patron's erasure of the shit, for the sake of her
children, seems to be the same kind of erasure that, again, allows Copjec

to miss her own point in reading Walker's "Big Black Mammy of the Antebellum South."[44] Nonetheless Walker's work succeeds in catching up all of her critics. If old man Corregidora is positioned as the father of them all, in Walker's work the figure of the mammy is the "anonymous root" of "racial subjectivity." And just as Freud insisted on the universality of psychoanalysis (it was not, he maintained, a Jewish science), so do I read Walker's positioning of her big black mammy, her "anonymous root," as the mother, the "mythic source" of *all* U.S./American post-slavery subjects.

Introduction. Making Monstrous Intimacies

1 The "door of no return" is that door through which captive Africans were taken on their way to the New World
as chattel. Brand writes, "The Door of No Return is of
course no place at all but a metaphor for place . . . a place
where certain transactions occurred, perhaps the most
important being the transference of selves" (2001, 18).

2 See Alexander 1995, 90–110; Hartman 1997; Moten
2003.

3 Hartman writes:

> I have chosen not to reproduce Douglass's account of
> the beating of Aunt Hester in order to call attention
> to the ease with which such scenes are usually reiter-
> ated, the casualness with which they are circulated,
> and the consequences of this routine display of the
> slave's ravaged body. Rather than inciting indignation,
> too often they immure us to pain by virtue of their
> familiarity—the oft-repeated or restored character of
> these accounts. What interests me are the ways we are
> called upon to participate in such scenes. Are we wit-
> nesses who confirm the truth of what happened in the
> face of world-destroying capacities of pain, the distor-
> tions of torture, the sheer unrepresentability of terror,
> and the repression of dominant accounts? . . . What
> does the exposure of the violated body yield? Proof
> of black sentience or the inhumanity of the "peculiar
> institution"? (1997, 3)

4 Jesse Jackson, Interview with Anderson Cooper 360 Degrees, 2 September 2005.

5 It is a blood transaction because of the familial relations
involved here and because of contemporary understandings of *amalgamation* and *miscegenation*.

6 The most widely circulating understanding of intimacy is that it is about the innermost, something that is at the very core of subjectivity and that is private to a (sexual or other) relationship. In many understandings of intimacy, sexual relations mean intimate relations. Intimacy is also defined as "closeness of observation, knowledge, or the like"; "close in acquaintance or association; closely connected by friendship or personal knowledge; characterized by familiarity (with a person or thing)" (OED). For Lauren Berlant intimacy "involves an aspiration for a narrative about something shared, a story about both oneself and others that will turn out in a particular way" (2000, 1). Because intimacy is also spatial and temporal, I use it to think through the configurations of relations that arise out of domination and that continue to structure relations across race, sex, ethnicity, and nation. Intimacy is always about desire—and perhaps specifically about what Ann Laura Stoler (1995) calls the "education of desire"—and the structures that organize and constitute the relationships between past and present and possible futures.

   The word *monstrous* too signifies desire and has multiple meanings that range from "unnatural" and "strange" to "excessive." From the OED: "Of a thing (material or immaterial): deviating from the natural or conventional order; unnatural, extraordinary"; "of a person: strange or unnatural in conduct or disposition"; "of, relating to, or characteristic of a monster; having the appearance or nature of a monster, esp. in being hideous or frightening"; "used as a colloquial intensifier: very great, excessive, 'tremendous.'" These monstrous intimacies also end up being interracial intimacies, as the monster is also normally part animal and part human (polygenesis), "a mythical creature."

7 I trace several meanings of transaction to underscore the multiple understandings that I bring to the word. Transaction is defined in the OED as "the adjustment of a dispute between parties by mutual concession; compromise; hence *gen.* an arrangement, an agreement, a covenant"; "the action of transacting or fact of being transacted; the carrying on or completion of an action or course of action; the accomplishment of a result"; "a physical operation, action, or process"; "the action of passing or making over a thing from one person, thing, or state to another; transference. *Obs*"; "the record of its proceedings published by a learned society."

8 I will return to this relationship between antagonism and identification in detail in chapter 1.

9 While I mean monstrous intimacies and post-slavery subjectivity to include everyone, here I am talking about the black subject. (I turn to white subjects in the United States in chapter 4, on Kara Walker's work.) And while I recognize that blackness (who is and who is not black) is contested and a space of identification and nonidentification, when I talk about black subjects I am talking about people descended from Africa.

   I use *blackened* to refer to those people (of recognizable African descent and not) who because of a proximity to blackness (specifically a proximity to the shame, violence, etc. that black bodies are made to wear) are covered by the shadow of blackness, are, like the "scalawag" in Kara Walker's work (chapter 4), blackened. *Blackened* then allows for the overlap of self-identified and imposed; it is a marker of proximity that positions one as not properly white or nonblack. It acknowledges the movement of bodies, the myriad meanings attached to African populations, the residues of raced and class signifiers that locate one within or without (visually) African-descended communities. As well as indicating those whose material conditions and circumstances position them with blackness, *blackened* can also mean those African-descended people who have moved away visually from blackness.

I offer an anecdote. In 2004 I taught Dorothy Allison's fictionalized autobiography *Bastard out of Carolina* (1992) to a group of students who had never heard of it or her. Despite my work to locate the book in time and space before the first class meeting in which we would discuss the text and Allison's descriptions of the Boatwright family, one-third of the class believed the Boatwrights were black. That is, the Boatwrights were "blackened" in their location as "poor whites," and also because in those students' imaginations it was inconceivable that this family living in and with a particular kind of poverty and violence, living in what are considered pathological (read culture of poverty) ways, could be white, that they could be anything but black.

10 Hester Bailey, who is the sister of Douglass's mother, Harriet Bailey, is part of what Douglass refers to in *My Bondage and My Freedom* as the "kitchen family" (1855/2003a, 60). Captain Anthony is sometimes reported to have been Douglass's father. About this Douglass writes, "My father was a white man. He was admitted to be such by all I ever heard speak of my parentage. The opinion was also expressed that my father was my master; but of the correctness of this opinion I know nothing, the means of knowing was withheld from me" (1845/2003b, 42).

11 In "Love of God, Love of Man, Love of Country," a speech on American slavery given on 24 September 1847 in Syracuse, New York, Douglass said:

If the Gospel were truly preached here, you would as soon talk of having an uncle or brother a brothel keeper as a slaveholder; for I hold that every slaveholder, no matter how pure he may be, is a keeper of a house of ill-fame. Every kitchen is a brothel, from that of Dr. Fuller's to that of James K. Polk's (Applause). I presume I am addressing a virtuous audience—I presume I speak to virtuous females—and I ask you to consider this one feature of Slavery. Think of a million of females absolutely delivered up into the hands of persons in any way they see fit. And so entirely are they at the disposal of their masters, that if they raise their hands against them, they may be put to death for daring to resist their infernal aggression.

12 See, for example, Maurice Wallace, who writes, "The threat to young Douglass posed by Covey is the same threat realized by Anthony on Hester" (2002, 91). See especially his chapter "Constructing the Black Masculine: Frederick Douglass, Booker T. Washington, and the Sublimits of African American Autobiography."

13 The phrase "monstrous features" comes from Lydia Maria Child's introduction to Jacobs's text (1987/1861, 4).

14 Queen Esther, the beautiful passing Jewish wife of King Ahasuerus of Persia, risks the king's displeasure (he is bored with her) by appearing before him with information supplied by Mordecai of a plot against his life. Ahasuerus has ordered the slaughter of the Jews in Persia, an order that he cannot withdraw, but in gratitude to Esther he issues another edict that allows the Jews to take up arms and fight back. For an extensive reading of Queen Esther and black speech, see Nero 2003. In 1833 the black abolitionist and proto-feminist Maria W. Stewart asked her Boston audience, "What if I am a woman; is not the God of ancient times the God of these modern days? . . . Did not queen Esther save the lives of the Jews?" (quoted in Nero 2003, 5). Stewart also encouraged enslaved people to rebel.

15 Louis Agassiz was also a student of Baron Georges Cuvier, whom I discuss briefly in chapter 2 in his role as the father of modern biology and the man who dissected Saartje Baartman's body. Agassiz also wrote about the connection between incest and amalgamation, a connection that is central to chapter 1.

16 Two years later (1857) the Dred Scott decision, written by Chief Justice Taney, stated that blacks are not citizens and have "no rights which the white man was bound to respect."

17 See also Paul Gilroy's The Black Atlantic, especially chapter 2, "Masters, Mistresses, Slaves, and the Antinomies of Modernity" (1993).

18 "Justice is an experience of the moment, [the] definition [of which] will continue to shift depending on the time and location we are in" (Dent 1992, 16).

19 Strom Thurmond died without ever publicly acknowledging his relationship to Essie Mae Washington-Williams. In an interview with Terry Gross on Fresh Air (National Public Radio, 1 February 2005), Washington-Williams said that after Thurmond retired it would have been nice if he'd acknowledged her because at that point, doing so would have done nothing to harm his career. But she demurs that it was probably out of concern for his family that he remained silent. The Thurmonds, like many southern families, had a white branch and a black branch that were well known throughout the community. See Brent Staples, "Senator Strom Thurmond's Not-So-Secret Black Daughter," New York Times, 18 December 2003.

20 Quoted in Jeffrey Gettleman, "'At Last I Am Completely Free,' Thurmond Daughter Says," New York Times, 17 December 2003; emphasis mine.

21 A notable exception is Kimberle Crenshaw, who writes in The Nation in March 2004:

> The possibility that Thurmond's transgression might have gone beyond statutory rape to include the use of force has not even been raised. Yet consider what is known about Thurmond. In 1924 he had already developed a reputation in college for his sexually aggressive conduct—and this was with white women. Thurmond's sexually inappropriate behavior didn't end there; stories abound about his groping women in the Capitol, including a senator and a

government agent. If Thurmond was not above the unwelcome fondling of some of America's most powerful women long after the women's movement established that such boorish behavior was unacceptable, is it such a stretch to imagine him ignoring the protests of a powerless black teenager in 1925?

Perhaps most insistent in mainstream media was Dan Rather, who repeatedly returned the focus of his interview with Washington-Williams to the nature of the relationship between Butler and Thurmond. An article in the *New York Times* reported on Reverend Jesse Jackson's reaction:

> He was struck by the similarities between Mr. Thurmond's situation and that of Jefferson, asserting that they reflected "a deep and ugly Southern tradition" of white men taking advantage of young black women in their employ.
>
> "By day, they are bullies," Mr. Jackson said. "By night, they manipulate race to their advantage." Referring to Mr. Thurmond and Ms. Washington-Williams, he added: "The point that strikes me the most is that he lived 100 years and never acknowledged his daughter. He never let her eat at his table. He fought for laws that kept his daughter segregated and in an inferior position. He never fought to give her first-class status. Thomas Jefferson did pretty much the same." (Michael Janofsky, "Thurmond Kin Acknowledge Black Daughter," *New York Times*, 16 December 2003)

See also Terry Gross's interview with Washington-Williams on *Fresh Air*, 1 February 2005.

22 A conventional reading would be that Washington-Williams's declaration of freedom was the result of speaking the truth, of bearing witness to and bearing the scrutiny of such revelations, of achieving closure. I read this differently.

23 Even in his notes to her, Thurmond never refers to her as his daughter, never refers to himself as her father. He is always circumspect.

24 Retha Hill, "Sex and Race in the American South: The Story of Strom Thurmond and His Black Maid," MSNBC, 4 January 2004.

25 Washington-Williams does not write that she's struck by his whiteness. While "fairness" here refers to the lightness of Thurmond's skin, "fair" skin is often used to describe "lighter-skinned" people of African descent. Fairness also introduces the question of justice—which links Judge Thurmond to old man Corregidora in chapter 1, who is a magistrate—and making evidence (in)visible.

26 At the end of a later visit in which Thurmond suggests that she come south to attend all-black South Carolina State College, he gives her an envelope with five hundred dollars in it. Washington-Williams writes, "I went shopping at Macy's and bought myself a dress. I felt I had earned it" (2005, 98). Part of this feeling of having earned the money is caught up with her disappointment that although Thurmond never refers to her as a Negro (though South Carolina State is a Negro college) she is, according to law and custom, a Negro. She writes, "My father saw me as a *Negro*. I may have been half white and half black, but the rule in the courts was a drop of blood made you black. I don't know what I was expecting. I had lived my whole life as a Negro, but to hear it from my white father, and a judge at that, made it a brutal ruling, and one with no appeal" (96–

97). By the end of the narrative Washington-Williams has framed an appeal in the language of biracialism.

In her review of *Dear Senator*, Adele Logan Alexander writes, "At the same time, the money kept coming—never enough to support her fully but always enough to keep her quiet. Washington-Williams, however, maintains that money was never the point. Rather, she argues, she felt a devoted daughter's need to protect her father, his political career and his reputation. We can see in their awkward and distorted dance only a mismatched couple, trapped in an unholy, symbiotic alliance in which they gave and received endless bribes that neither of them could call what they really were" (Adele Logan Alexander, "The Still Untold Story of the Senator's Child," *Washington Post*, 25 January 2005).

27 In a piece in *The New Yorker* in 1996 called "My Best White Friend: Cinderella Revisited," Patricia J. Williams writes with complexity about an exchange with her "best white friend": "You see, part of the problem is that white knights just don't play the same part in my mythical landscape of desire. If poor Cinderella had been black, it would have been a whole different story. I tell my best white friend the kind of stories my mother raised me on: about slave girls who worked their fingers to the bone for their evil half sisters, the 'legitimate' daughters of their mutual father, the master of the manse, the owner of them all; about scullery maids whose oil-and-ashes complexions would not wash clean even after multiple waves of the wand" (94).

That this is about accessing the white father—and through him, the symbolic—was clarified in Caroline Weber's *New York Times* book review of Heidi Ardizzone's *An Illuminated Life: Belle da Costa Greene's Journey from Prejudice to Privilege*: "Belle could not have achieved the social and professional prominence she did at the turn of the 20th century had she been completely open about her background." When Belle changes her name from Greener to Greene, Weber writes, it is to

> distance Belle from her father, Richard Greener, renowned as "the first black graduate of Harvard College" and "the first colored librarian and professor at the University of South Carolina." Although "Belle probably developed . . . her fascination with rare books from her father," *she may have feared that his high racial profile would marginalize her at a time when black and white communities were becoming even more segregated and distinct than they had been at the start of his own career.* Conveniently, Greener left the country in 1898 to assume a consular post in Vladivostok, Russia. After this move, which also effectively ended her parents' marriage, Belle and her mother shortened their last name, "crossed the color line and began to live as white." (Caroline Weber, "Long Time Passing," *New York Times*, 22 July 2007; emphasis mine)

Heidi Ardizzone writes, "As Belle da Costa Greene, of mysterious exotic origins, rumored to be from Cuba, Portugal, New Orleans, suspected to have some black ancestry, Belle gained far greater privilege and freedom than that which Belle Marion Greener, daughter of the first black man to graduate from Harvard College, could ever have inherited in this period of history." In other words, it is

Greene's father's recognition as a successful black man that limits her freedom. His education, academic success, and position are not enough *because* he is known to be black. (Sam Roberts, "Reading New York; Brooklyn Murders, Depression Love, a Glamorous Librarian," *New York Times*, 24 June 2007).

28 "As Coatesville hunkered down for war, I tried my hardest to put Strom Thurmond out of my mind. Yet like a moth to a flame, I couldn't stop reading about South Carolina and the *Gone With the Wind* world that was at least half my birthright, but that was a birthright I could not claim" (Washington-Williams and Stadiem 2005, 56).

What compels Carrie Butler to introduce Essie Mae to Thurmond, and why does she wait until their daughter is sixteen to do so (the same age Butler was when she gave birth to Essie Mae)? Was it at Thurmond's instigation or her own? (Is this Thurmond demanding access to her? Or is it Butler arranging a meeting in order to give her daughter access, the passing on and passing her on to this configuration of power? Some combination of both? What mechanisms of violence, protection, transmission, etc. are at work in this particular repetition?)

29 In an interview on CBS on 17 December 2003 Dan Rather asked Washington-Williams, "What was your relationship with your mother?" She replied, "My mother had to work. And she had my aunt to take care of me."

Early on in *Dear Senator* Washington-Williams explicitly links her relationship with Thurmond to a history of exploitation by white men of black women: "What Strom Thurmond was doing with me, then, was part of a long Edgefield tradition. *Another aunt told me that Judge Thurmond was supporting my mother; that was why she didn't have to work.* I didn't ask her about the arrangements" (2005, 39; emphasis mine).

30 In chapter 4 I discuss the ideological and actual work performed by the black woman in the house called "Mammy."

31 John McWhorter, "Thurmond's Daughter Offers an Example of Progress," *All Things Considered*, NPR, 11 February 2005. Washington-Williams also said, "I may have called it 'closure,' but it was much more like an opening, a very grand opening." Quoted in Amy Geier Edgar, "Thurmond's Daughter Tells Story in Book," *Associated Press*, 11 December 2004.

32 In her review of *My Confederate Kinfolk: A Twenty-first Century Freedwoman Discovers Her Roots* by Thulani Davis (2006), Renee Graham writes, "At its core, this is the story of Davis's great grandparents—Chloe Tarrant Curry, a former slave, and William Argyle Campbell, the son of a wealthy white Missouri family for whom she worked in Mississippi. Davis's grandmother described her parents as 'contented companions' who remained devoted to each other for the rest of their lives, though they never married." Renee Graham, "In 'Kinfolk,' Another Greatest Generation," *Boston Globe*, 2 January 2006. It is while Davis is working on the script for a Broadway show on Sally Hemings and Thomas Jefferson that she recalls that her family "had its own Sally Hemings story." See Terry Gross's interview with Thulani Davis on *Fresh Air*, National Public Radio, 17 January 2006.

Likewise, in an interview with Charlie Rose on PBS on 26 January 2004 about the series and book *America Behind the Color Line: Conversations with African Americans*, Henry Louis Gates Jr. speaks about Jane Gates, his grandfather's mother who was a slave: "Jane Gates' lover, who was the father of her children, was an Irishman named Brady, and I don't know what kind of relationship they had but I do know that in 1860 she's still a slave and in 1870 she owns 200 acres of prime bottom land on the south branch of the Potomac River." Consideration about the cost, to her, of this inheritance, the cost by which she comes to be in possession of "200 acres of prime bottom land," is covered over with laughter in the conversation between Rose and Gates.

33 The entire quotation appears in Jacqueline Rose's framing of Lucille Angellier, the protagonist of Irene Némirovsky's *Suite Française*, who in sheltering and contemplating making love with a German soldier at first resists the "pull of blood" of the French Resistance—the only proper way to understand resistance in this context. Rose writes, "She has burdened her desire for him with the meaning of freedom. Not the superficial freedom to travel or leave her house, 'even though that would be unimaginably blissful,' but freedom of the mind: 'I'd rather feel free inside—to choose my own path, never to waver, not to follow the swarm'" (2007, 1).

34 After she tells her children who their maternal grandfather is they briefly meet him in the reception line after he speaks at an all-white church in southern California. Washington-Williams writes, "When Ronald [her son] decided to go to medical school, his grandfather arranged for him to get a commission in the Navy that paid for his entire education. He did lots of smaller favors for our family. And he continued, through his nephew Thurmond Bishop, to send us money, perhaps not as much as Julius [her son] would have liked, but to me an extremely generous amount as a token of his affection for us" (2005, 198).

35 She writes, "I believe he loved me, after his fashion. It was an unspeakable love, forbidden by the 'culture and custom' of the South, as he called it. The money was speaking it for him. It wasn't hush money; it wasn't a bribe. It was the governor's own outpouring of love and shame and frustration. He had no other way to demonstrate his affection" (Washington-Williams and Stadiem 2005, 148).

The role of father and the role of lover are constantly confused in Washington-Williams's own retelling. She writes, "He didn't give me any envelopes of money on those college visits. As my room and board were paid for, there was no need for any. I don't think he wanted the president [to] see him passing me cash. That might have implied a different relationship, and my father, lawyer, judge, and now governor, had to be above reproach. Yet I did find it rather bold for a man of his position to risk all kinds of scandal by coming to see me. It was so gallant. It was chivalrous. It was daring. I loved it. What woman wouldn't respond to a great man taking such great risks for her." The next sentence begins, "My connection to my father was hardly fatherly however. It remained as distant as when I had visited him with my two mothers" (118).

36 Washington-Williams maintains that Thurmond never asked for her silence about their relationship. This places her on the inside as familial caretaker of his reputation, political career, and white family and repeats the role of the black caretaker who is "like" family.

37 Washington-Williams first met Thurmond in 1941. In 1948, during his presidential run under the banner of the States Rights Democratic Party, better known as the Dixiecrats, he will say, "All the laws of Washington and all the bayonets of the army cannot force . . . the southern people to break down segregation and admit the Negro race into our theaters, into our swimming pools, into our homes and into our churches" (Cohodas 1993, 146).

38 There are times in the narrative when Washington-Williams expresses her anger at and frustration with Thurmond's segregationist policies. But most often she stifles her anger in the name of preserving her relationship to him.

39 The mythic space occupied by another person in the kitchen is that of the mammy, whom I discuss in chapter 4. Washington-Williams writes of a conversation with her mother:

    It was 1925. He was twenty-three. She was fifteen. She and her sister made beds, cleaned, and did basic housekeeping, "He was known for having an eye for the ladies, and he was handsome, as you can see. He was always running in the road, half naked, at the crack of dawn, because that was part of his health routine. I couldn't help but notice."

    "And he noticed you?"

    "Only after his brother did. Mister Will, that's what I called him, the big brother, was going to medical school, and he would come home and flirt with me like crazy. I think he saw too many cadavers. And Mister Strom would see this, and I think he got jealous." (Washington-Williams and Stadiem 2005, 41)

    This seems to point to the sexual violation hidden in the figure of the mammy and to the continuing vulnerability of the black women in that position. I discuss this further in chapter 4.

40 In "Uncommon Ground: Diary of a Mad Law Professor," Patricia J. Williams writes:

    When Essie Mae Washington-Williams stepped forward and revealed that she was Strom Thurmond's daughter, the very first news accounts almost universally described her as "a black woman" who claimed to be his daughter. Once his family admitted the relationship, however, she quickly became "mixed-race," specifically "half-black" or "biracial." But clearly, "biracial" doesn't really mean much in terms of biological heritage in a country where almost anyone who's been here more than two or three generations is not just biracial but multiracial and multicultural—words, alas, that seem to have become nothing less than dirty in the recent culture wars.

    It's worth looking at the hidden layers of meaning behind the quietly polarizing category of "biracial": It seems to be emerging as a term reserved for those who are the product of recent rather than historical unions between one socially "black" parent and one socially "white" parent, and where the white parent acknowledges the child, either by marriage or—as with the Thurmond family—by admission." (Williams, *The Nation*, 18 March 2004)

41 In "We Need to Learn More about Our Colorful Past," *New York Times*, 31 July 2004, Maurice A. Barboza and Gary B. Nash write, "Reared apart from her father, Ms. Washington-Williams did not have the same privileges as Mr. Thurmond's white children during his life, yet she is seeking the right to some of the privileges of her lineage."

Chapter One. Gayl Jones's *Corregidora*

1 Quoted in Genovese 1976, 418 (emphasis mine). Hughes is called the first American sociologist.

2 In *A Treatise on Sociology* Hughes argued that what was called slavery in the South was no longer slavery but had evolved into warrenteeism. For Hughes the key difference between warrenteeism and slavery was that the warrantor (formerly called the slave owner) did not own the person of the warrantee (the slave) but the labor of the warrantee. He also argued that warrenteeism was the ideal labor situation: unfree labor was necessary and the southern United States practiced a particular kind of ethnic warrenteeism. Later, however, he continued to speak and write about slavery in a positive light. See Ambrose 1997. I say that this is a precursor to *Plessy v. Ferguson* because Hughes insisted that the way to ensure harmony was for whites to "mentalise" and blacks to "manualise," a division that is akin to "separate but equal."

3 Kimberly Magowan notes, "In response to the charge by abolitionists that slavery was a sin, slavery advocates recast the peculiar institution from a necessary evil to a 'positive good'" (1999, 2). Likewise Hughes's argument arises in relation to increasing anxiety about the end of chattel slavery and the prospect of black freedom, specifically that political amalgamation led to sexual amalgamation. Anticipating the end of slavery, Hughes's work to remake slavery as warrenteeism speaks to the fears of black incorporation—political amalgamation would lead to the graver ill of ethnic amalgamation—a fear that was shared by many antislavery advocates as well.

4 This is not an uncommon coupling. For Louis Agassiz, "sexual intercourse between blacks and whites . . . was the moral and biological equivalent of incest," and "the production of half-breeds is as much a sin against nature, as incest in a civilized community is a sin against purity of character" (quoted, respectively, in Menand 2002, 114, and Gould 1996, 80). For more on how Hughes has been read, see Saks 2000, 71. Doreen Fowler writes, "In the American South, with its history of racial slavery, the prohibition against miscegenation replaces the prohibition against incest (2004, 432). George B. Handley cites "Eric Sundquist [, who] has argued that 'the miscegenation between white masters and black slaves . . . made conceivable forms of incest that paradoxically could not be defined as such since the intimate family relationships incest assumes were,

by further definition, utterly invalid" (2004, 179). See also Harkins 2003, and Magowan 1999.

5 Joan Dayan (1999) compellingly illustrates how this works. See also Karla Holloway's introduction to *Passed On* (2002).

6 Butler (2002, 15) writes:

> When Lévi-Strauss makes the argument that the incest taboo is the basis of culture and that it mandates exogamy, or marriage outside the clan, is "the clan" being read in terms of race or, more specifically, in terms of a racial presupposition of culture that maintains its purity through regulating its transmissibility? Marriage must take place outside the clan. There must be exogamy. But there must also be a limit to exogamy; that is, marriage must be outside the clan but not outside a certain racial self-understanding or racial commonality. So the incest taboo mandates exogamy, but the taboo against miscegenation limits the exogamy that the incest taboo mandates. Cornered, then, between a compulsory heterosexuality and a prohibited miscegenation, something called culture, saturated with the anxiety and identity of dominant European whiteness, reproduces itself in and as universality itself.

See Rowell 1982, 42. In "Seduction by Law," Harkins (2003, 143) looks at similar configurations in Carolivia Herron's *Thereafter Johnnie* (1991): "In place of the subjective property of testimony, then, [*Thereafter Johnnie*] articulates a mythic collective storytelling in which the history of U.S. racial slavery is represented as a family affair whose divine or pre-historical origins lie in the epic emplotments of Lot, John the Baptist, Leda and the Swan, King Lear, and a host of other Biblical and mythic icons of founding violence."

7 One primal scene that is often written about occurs in *The Narrative of Frederick Douglass* when he enters "the blood-stained gate of slavery" by being a "witness and participant" to the sadistic beating of Aunt Hester by Captain Anthony. In *Corregidora* one such primal scene is Great Gram's being forced to sleep with the master/father and mistress from the ages of thirteen to eighteen.

8 While Jones is familiar with Freudian theory, my point here is not that she maps out the Oedipus complex. Rather, I suggest that the work Jones does in *Corregidora* is analogous to and complementary to the work Freud does with his Oedipus complex. If the Oedipus complex maps out a constellation of desires in family relationships constituted around the theoretical violation of the incest taboo, then the "Corregidora complex" would map out a constellation of desires in family relationships that include, in addition to patriarchy and incest, miscegenation and slavery. The Oedipus story and the Corregidora story both hinge on disavowed sex with a parent.

> Foucault (1980, 113) reminds us of the Oedipus complex's production:
> At a time when incest was being hunted out as a conduct, psychoanalysis was busy revealing it as a desire and alleviating—for those who suffered from the desire—the severity which repressed it. . . . The discovery of the Oedipus complex was contemporaneous with the juridical organization of loss of pa-

rental authority. . . . Freud was uncovering the nature of Dora's desire and allowing it to be put into words . . . [that is, expressly semiotic, while] the father was elevated into an object of compulsory love, but . . . if he was a loved one, he was at the same time a fallen one in the eyes of the law. Psychoanalysis, as a limited therapeutic practice, thus played a differentiating role with respect to other procedures, within a deployment of sexuality that had come into general use. Those who had lost the exclusive privilege of experiencing more than others the thing that prohibited it and of possessing the method which made it possible to remove the repression.

9 Tracey Sedinger writes, "Kinship relations are not themselves biological or natural; rather, kinship intervenes in nature and therefore converts nature into a real that eludes the scientific and symbolic discourses that would presume to represent that real as something knowable" (2002, 66).

10 I say "at least" because the text indicates that Great Gram is also the daughter of Corregidora. In the first half of the text Ursa says of her great-grandmother, "I thought of the girl who had to sleep with her master and mistress. *Her father, the master*" (Jones 1975/1986, 57). I return to this later in the chapter.

11 All quotations from Jones's *Corregidora* are from the 1986 reprint by Beacon Press.

12 Here I think of the decision that Mama has made: what *she* doesn't reveal, what *she* wouldn't give her mother, and so on.

13 Quoted in Simon 1997, 101.

14 What Great Gram points to is what Marianne Hirsch calls the curious power of camera images and still photographs to act as "precisely the medium connecting first- and second-generation remembrance, memory and postmemory. . . . The fragmentary sources and building blocks of the work of postmemory, they affirm the past's existence and, in their flat two-dimensionality, they also signal its insurmountable distance." In this writing about still photographs and their relationship to Holocaust memory and trauma—that is, to a future reckoning with the Holocaust—Hirsch distinguishes between the memory of a "directly" experienced trauma and what she terms "postmemory," a narrated or second-generation experience of trauma (1999, 10). Later Hirsch writes, "That is not, of course, to say that survivor memory itself is unmediated, but that it is more directly—chronologically—connected to the past" (2001, 9).

15 See Rushdy 1999, 2001 for more on the neo–slave narrative.

16 Hammond settled in Edgefield, South Carolina, later the hometown of Senator Strom Thurmond.

17 Louis D. Rubin writes in the foreword to *Secret and Sacred*:
As might be suspected, Hammond was nobody's gentle and kind slaveholder. He worked his slaves hard, so much so that, particularly at the outset of his career as a planter, they experienced an appalling mortality rate. Hammond's views in the "Mud-sills" Speech were genuinely held. Africans were in every way an inferior race, designed for his *use*. . . . Indeed, as Dr. Bleser makes clear,

not only did such usage include concubinism, but—and nothing could offer greater proof of Hammond's attitude toward the human inferiority of blacks—Hammond took for his mistress an eighteen-year-old slave with a one-year-old female child, and then when the child reached the age of twelve he made her his mistress as well! (Bleser 1988, xi)

18 James Henry Hammond, "Speech of Hon. James H. Hammond, of South Carolina, On the Admission of Kansas, Under the Lecompton Constitution: Delivered in the Senate of the United States, March 4, 1858," Washington, D.C., 1858.

19 "Relationship" appears here in quotation marks to acknowledge that there is no term adequate to the complexity of those sexual and other relations between enslaved people and those who claimed ownership over them, to acknowledge that it is precisely the nature of such relationships that is at issue here.

20 James W. Loewen writes, "His reputation for cruelty lasted more than a century in the black community" (1999, 271).

21 The full text of the letter reads:

My Dear Harry: In the last will I made I left to you, over and above my other children Sally Johnson the mother of Louisa and all the children of both. Sally says Henderson is my child. It is possible, but I do not believe it. Yet act on hers rather than my opinion. Louisa's first child *may* be mine. I think not. Her second I believe is mine. Take care of her and her children who are both of *your* blood if not of mine and of Henderson. The services of the rest will I think compensate for an indulgence to these. I cannot free these people and send them North. It would be cruelty to them. Nor would I like that any but my own blood should own as Slaves my own blood or Louisa. I leave them to your charge, believing that you will best appreciate and most independently carry out my wishes in regard to them. Do not let Louisa or any of my children or possible children be slaves of Strangers. Slavery *in the family* will be their happiest earthly condition. Ever affectionately, J. H. H. (Bleser 1988, 19)

Hammond's wife, Catherine, leaves him for a period of two years beginning in November 1850. Louisa is twelve in 1850 and Hammond begins having sexual relations with her.

22 "On November 1, 1843 Governor James Henry Hammond of South Carolina received a fateful letter from his brother-in-law Wade Hampton II, one of the wealthiest men in the state. In his letter, Hampton accused the governor of trying to seduce his nineteen-year-old daughter Catherine" (Bardaglio 1998, 3). The nieces were Catherine's sister's children. Confessing to "every thing short of direct sexual intercourse," Hammond does not recover his social standing and none of the Hampton daughters ever marry, as "no man who valued his standing could marry one of the Hampton girls" (Faust 1982, 242).

23 For more on property and kin, see Spillers 2003c; Hartman 1997; Harkins 2003.

24 In *Celia: A Slave* Melton McLaurin offers another reading: "Senator James Henry Hammond of South Carolina was engaging in sexual relationships with two slave women, mother and daughter. He later gave both women to his

legitimate son, Harry, who was also apparently involved in an affair with the daughter and who had fathered a child by her, as the elder Hammond admitted he may have done" (1991, 23).

25 Drew Gilpin Faust (1982, 87–88) writes:

Clearly Hammond was involved in something quite different from sex. He felt strong, troubling emotions about these women and their offspring. But for Sally and Louisa, the situation must have been even more painful. They confronted not only the sexual and emotional demands of both their master and his son and the implicit, if not explicit, threat of physical coercion but also the bitter resentment of Hammond's wife, who discovered his liaison and attempted to end it by demanding the sale or effective banishment of his slave mistresses. The two black women were, moreover, prevented from entering their own marriages. During the period of their relationship with Hammond, neither Sally nor Louisa lived in a household with a black man. Instead, they shared a cabin together with their children. The complex and tangled ties amongst a father and son and a mother and daughter would be bewildering even outside the context of race and power that surrounded it in this slave society. But whatever the specific import of this relationship, whether it was representative of others of a similar type, whether such liaisons were unique or commonplace, whether they usually were long-standing involvements or more episodic and casual encounters, the reality and impact of white sexual demands upon slave life and family at Silver Bluff is beyond doubt. . . . Sally and Louisa's household, almost unique at Silver Bluff in its lack of a resident male, must have served as a searing reminder to the other slaves of the full significance of Hammond's ownership of their bodies and their lives.

26 Sexual violence is obscured or authenticated by white editors, like Lydia Maria Child in her introduction to Harriet Jacobs's *Incidents in the Life of a Slave Girl*. Child writes, "I am well aware that many will accuse me of indecorum for presenting these pages to the public; for the experiences of this intelligent and much-injured woman belong to a class which some call delicate subjects, and others indelicate. This peculiar phase of Slavery has generally been kept veiled; but the public ought to be made acquainted with its monstrous features, and I willingly take the responsibility of presenting them with the veil withdrawn" (Jacobs 1987/1861, 3–4).

27 Although they live in the segregated Jim Crow South the women do not account for what's at stake in their reproducing the wounds of slavery in the current time and place and making them "as visible as the blood." As Gina Dent reminds us in her introduction to *Black Popular Culture*, we must be attentive to the fact that "our choices are always overdetermined," that "justice is an experience of the moment, [the] definition [of which] will continue to shift depending on the time and location we are in" (1992, 16).

28 For more on this, see Lauderdale Graham 1991: "Honorata was but one of dozens of slave women encouraged by police to come forward to tell their stories and to make audacious bids for freedom as part of a crackdown against

procuring slaveowners during the late summer and early autumn of 1871" (669). Ashraf Rushdy (2001) also writes about slave masters in Brazil prostituting enslaved women.

29 The Corregidora women specifically anticipate giving birth to daughters. The bearing witness is intimately tied to reproduction.

30 I return to these questions throughout the chapter. Two examples of the common reading of Gram as enslaved: Jennifer Cognard-Black writes, "Ursa's Great Gram and Gram were repeatedly raped by the same slave master and made to work as prostitutes" (2001, 44), and Elizabeth Swanson Goldberg writes, "I would also suggest expanding this problematic of survival to refer not only to Great Gram/Gram's survival of the sexual violence of slavery" (2003, 465).

31 As Spillers writes, "We might well ask if [the] phenomenon of marking and branding actually 'transfers' from one generation to another, finding its various symbolic substitutions in an efficacy of meanings that repeat the initiating moments?" (2003c, 207).

32 For more on passing on memories as an ethical decision, see Hartman 1997; Bal 1999.

33 The name Irene (which I contend is Mama's name) appears once in the context of the lyrics of the song "Good Night, Irene" (41). For reasons that reflect her position in the family history, I argue that it is only Gram who has neither a proper name nor a nickname.

34 Jones has published two stories with a character named Eudora, both called Dora. In her collection of short stories White Rat (1977b), Dora appears in "The Return: A Fantasy" and "Version 2" (a rewriting of "The Return"). This succession of names, titles, and significations emphasizes Jones's articulation of hysteria.

35 Corregidora too invests some symbolic power in the enslaved women. After a stroke that he interpreted as the result of a curse, "they say he was praying and calling in his niggers and telling them he'd give them such and such a amount of money if they take it off him but they all say they didn't put it on him" (11).

36 This brings me back to the enslaved woman, Celia, and the court case Celia v. Missouri. Celia was raped by Robert Newsom from the age of fourteen to the age of eighteen. Raped the first day he purchases her, having borne two children by him, sick and pregnant with a third, with a lover of her own choosing, Celia warns Newsom to stay away from her. When Newsom arrives at her house later in the evening Celia murders him. She is tried, found guilty, and sentenced to death. The death sentence is carried out after she gives birth. For more on Celia, see Hartman 1997; McLaurin 1991.

37 One such incident involves Harold, May Alice's boyfriend. Harold comes by Ursa's house with some of his male friends and bangs on the door, saying, "Let us in, Ursa. . . . Let us in so we can give you a baby. Don't you want a baby?" (42, 138). These early experiences of sex, accompanied by violence and threats of various kinds of visibility and its repercussions, combine with the stories transmitted by Ursa's foremothers to convey the complexity of sex in the world that Jones creates.

38 See Cognard-Black 2001 for an extensive reading of the silences in Corregidora.

39 In *Beloved* Sethe tells her daughters, Beloved and Denver, about the time when her mother, whom she rarely saw, showed her the brand that she bore under her breast. She remembers her mother explaining why she was showing her the brand: " 'This is your ma'am. This,' and she pointed. 'I am the only one got this mark now. The rest dead. If something happens to me and you can't tell me by my face, you can know me by this mark.' " In other words, the "mark" is what will distinguish her (mother) from the other enslaved women (not mother). When Sethe asks her mother, "Mark the mark on me too," not knowing that she is already marked and that the mark signifies slavery, her mother slaps her. For Sethe the mark did not mean *slavery* but *mother,* the last living woman on the plantation to bear that particular mark. And Sethe believes that with her own mark, specifically a mark like her mother's, she will not only be able to identify her mother but will be identified with a mother whom she rarely sees. An older Sethe, herself now a mother, bears her own scar (the "chokecherry tree" on her back), and she has marked her daughters (internally and externally). Beloved (the girl and the ghost) has a mark under her chin (that Sethe won't or can't recognize), and Denver, traumatized by the death of her sister and the danger of rememory, won't leave the yard, is unable to step off the porch of their house. The "This is not a story to pass on" at the end of *Beloved* is a refusal of marking and the fact that the marking occurs, an antidote to the "making evidence as visible as blood" in *Corregidora* (T. Morrison 1987, 275).

40 The blues are centrally important in *Corregidora,* but they are not the focus of this chapter. See, for example, A. Davis 1998. For an important reading of the blues in *Corregidora,* see Rushdy 2001. Rushdy writes, "What is most important in the blues, Jones argues, is that they contest primary ideological premises in the national narrative that make sex into commerce and black women's bodies into fungible items" (2001, 64).

Chapter Two. Bessie Head, Saartje Baartman, and *Maru*

1 A note on terms: I use "Masarwa" the first time with quotation marks and thereafter without and when I am quoting from the text of *Maru.* I use "Bushmen" and "Bushman" (the first time with quotation marks and thereafter without) when I am quoting a text and when I need to indicate that the terms refer to the same groups of people known as the Masarwa. I use the term "KhoiSan" at all other times. In the long quotation from *Maru* that is the first epigraph to this chapter, Head uses the word Bushmen, but she otherwise uses the word Masarwa (occasionally Mosarwa).

On Bushman "racial difference" David Chidester writes, "Interested in classi-fication . . . natural scientists reinforced an emerging colonial distinction be-tween 'Hottentots' and 'Bushmen,' in which colonists referred to 'Bushmen' as 'Chinese' or 'Chinese Hottentots,' terms designating what colonists perceived as their absolute strangeness" (1996, 54). For more on Bushman and Masarwa difference, see also Motzafi-Haller 2002; Strother 1999.

2 A good example of national disease is in the novel *God's Stepchildren* by the white South African novelist Sarah Gertrude Millin (1924). For more on Millin's fiction, see Clingman 1991. For more on the use of the KhoiSan at various moments in South African history (including currently), see Coombes 2003.

3 An article titled "In Bushmanland, Hunters' Tradition Turns to Dust" by Donald G. McNeil Jr. appeared in the *New York Times* on 13 November 1997. Moses Xoma responds to the interviewer's question: "People romanticize this area. . . . I had one lady tell me she wanted to see a Bushman. I said, 'I'm a Bushman.' She said, 'No, a wild Bushman, with a tail.' We have to educate them: We need to make it clear: if you come, yes, you'll see people hunting—and you'll see people herding cattle. We don't live as we did 200 years ago." On 18 January 1996 the article "Kagga Kamma Journal: Endangered Bushmen Find Refuge in a Game Park" by Suzanne Daley appeared in the *New York Times*. Daley reports a tourist child asking, "Where are the Bushmen babies? I want to see the Bushmen babies."

> Soon, five Bushmen children, ranging in age from 2 to 7, arrive in a Jeep. Some are naked and some have leather aprons. They are taken to a patch of grass beside the dining-room windows, where they giggle and play in a lawn sprinkler that has been provided for their amusement. Several visitors pull up chairs to watch.

> For five years now, a group of about 40 of South Africa's dwindling population of Bushmen has been a tourist attraction here. It is a business deal, one that rescued them from the squalor of a shantytown on the edge of the Kalahari Desert. In a country that has treated them savagely for centuries, being in what feels very much like a zoo may seem like a step up.

4 Like many former colonial governments France claimed stewardship over Baartman's remains. From what I have been able to find out, the plaster cast of Baartman made by Cuvier remains in France in the Musée de l'Homme.

5 Saartje Baartman (1789–1815) is variously identified as Khoi, KhoiSan, Bushman, Hottentot, and Khoikhoi. Her first name is spelled Saartjie, Saatjie, Saartje, Sara, and Sarah and her surname Baartman, Bartman, and Bartmann. I will retain the spelling Saartje Baartman unless I am quoting from another text.

6 To differentiate the novel's two Margaret Cadmores, mother and adopted daughter, I use the designations "Mrs. Cadmore," "Margaret Cadmore Sr." and "Margaret Cadmore Jr.," and also "Margaret Sr." and "Margaret Jr." When it is clear that I am talking about the daughter I use simply "Margaret."

7 In the chapter "Ethnicizing Gender, Engendering the Ethnic Other," Pnina Motzafi-Haller discusses the ways that a group of women who are indistinguishable, to the outsider, from their neighbors have been positioned as Basarwa and excluded on the basis of that positioning. Her analysis includes a reading of *Maru* in which she says, "In 1971 Bessie Head placed the outcast position of the Basarwa at the center of her moving short novel *Maru*. The story of a Mosarwa girl, adopted by a white woman, who faces prejudice and humiliation once her Sarwa origin is known, enables a sensitive exploration of contemporary Tswana

cultural constructions of the Sarwa as the despised Other" (2002, 165). She writes as well about the village in which the women labeled Basarwa live: "In Tamasne, Sarwa identity was so despised that it was a downright insult to openly ask a person (known in the community as a Mosarwa), 'Are you a Mosarwa?' Such identity was almost always attributed by others and rejected whenever possible by its bearers" (166).

8   She wrote *Maru* directly in response to her son's victimization. "Eventually," she wrote to Randolph Vigne, "he got assaulted by children twice his age, apparently on the grounds that he is a usurper into the race of Motswana, or some filthy specimen." Head says of herself, "I look like a Bushman, who is a despised tribe here. . . . I am short in height" (Vigne 1991, 64).

9   Kobena Mercer rightly argues, "When U.S. Black Power activist Stokely Carmichael exalted the name of Fanon at the Dialectics of Liberation Conference at London's Roundhouse in 1967, the sense of jubilation unleashed in the reversal of oppressor and oppressed was no doubt felt as an authentic experience of empowerment, yet from another point of view, such as that of Bessie Head, . . . how could this have been a genuine change if victim and victimiser were merely trading places in the same binary structure of 'Manichean delirium' " (1995, 22).

10 For more on this, see Magubane 2001.

11 For more on the genealogical project, see C. Coetzee 1998; Robins 1998; Abrahams 2003.

12 From the OED.

13 From the OED.

14 For more on this, see Wicomb 1998. One headline reads, "Return of 'Hottentot Venus' Unites Bushmen" (*Guardian*, 6 May 2002):

    Chief Little believes the event is a signal for all those of Khoisan descent to reclaim their identity.

    "She's brought to the fore that we need to be proud of our identity instead of hiding behind the classification of 'coloured' which was given to us by the racist apartheid regime," he added.

    Matty Cairncross, a member of the Khoisan community, agrees with Chief Little. "She's a symbol of our history that's been taken away from us. We have a rich history and culture which needs to be revived and shown to the world. We need to hear more stories about forgotten people like the Khoisan in books and theatre to correct the imbalances created by the previous system of apartheid," she said.

    "The return of Saartje Baartman to South Africa is a victory for all South Africans and indigenous peoples of the world. It's an historic moment for everyone, especially for women in South Africa. She can be a unifying symbol for us," she added.

15 See the website of amagugu.

16 Wicomb notes that for the people of Soweto, "her burial in the western Cape can hardly seem an appropriate site for a national symbol of cultural reconstruction" (1998, 91).

17 Shaun Irlam (2004, 700) also writes about redemption in relation to Baartman. Kai Easton writes, "Krotoä-Eva was a servant in the house of Jan van Rie-beeck.... She became fluent in Dutch and Portuguese, and acted as a translator between the Dutch and Khoikhoi, marrying the Danish surgeon Pieter van Meerhoff in 1664. . . . When van Meerhoff died in a slaving expedition to Madagascar, however, Krotoä-Eva found herself on the outside of both cultures, 'rejected by both Khoi and Company.' . . . Though baptised as a Christian, and the mother of van Meerhoff's children, she was banished to Robben Island, where she died from alcohol abuse in 1674" (2002, 239). For more on Krotoä, see Pamela Scully, 2005; C. Coetzee 1998; Robins 1998; Abrahams 1996b; Wicomb 2001.

18 Krotoä, Baartman, and Head have each been linked to alcohol abuse, death in poverty, and prostitution; on Head, see Nixon 1998. I note this not to declare the truth of these claims but to draw attention to the similarity of the narratives that frame them.

19 Carli Coetzee writes, "In current versions of Krotoä's life, she is being con-structed as the mother of us all, the mother of the nation who was banished but can now be reconstituted. The political gain of this move is the acknowl-edgment of mixed blood and the Khoi contribution to South Africa. . . . The dangers are clear: Krotoä's life serves as the image of a promised sense of fullness and completeness, a return to origin, to fulfillment and reconciliation" (1998, 114–15).

20 Mbeki writes, "The Khoi people of our country and the descendants of the Khoi have every right solemnly to celebrate the return of one who was their daughter. They have every right to demand that this historic act of redress should be given its true meaning by the restoration to the Khoi and the San their place of pride as Africans equal to all other Africans" (website of the African National Con-gress, 2002).

21 "'Hottentot Venus' comes home." *Cape Times*, 3 May 2002.

22 In a really interesting analysis Neville Hoad reads Mbeki's speeches at the Z. K. Matthews Memorial Lecture at Fort Hare (12 October 2001) and his speech at the funeral of Saartje Baartman (9 August 2002) to think through the place-ment and repetition of Cuvier's diagnosis of Baartman and Mbeki's position on AIDS in relation to "the place of African sexuality in an African Renaissance." Specifically, reading Mbeki's speeches and his "implied critique of the sexuality of racism" in relation to Baartman, Hoad argues in relation to Mbeki's reluctance to respond to the "AIDS pandemic facing [South Africa's] citizens," and I agree, that "there is an archive in the present and closer to home that needs to be brought to bear on intellectual attempts to rediscover and reframe" (2005, 126).

Writing about redemption, Janell Hobson (2005, 56) argues:

Baartman has also energized a nation to reclaim an oppressive symbol in the midst of such postcolonial projects as ending South Africa's racial apartheid system and envisioning peaceful approaches to the racial injustices of the past, as dramatized in the Truth and Reconciliation Commission. What is a more powerful act of "truth and reconciliation" than that of confronting Baartman's history, locating her physical remains at the Musée de l'Homme in Paris, and demanding her return to South Africa? When a choir of 100 women sang out to welcome Baartman home, and the state buried her bones on National Women's day on August 9, 2002, we witnessed the redemption of history. What does it mean when the dispossession continues? In Botswana in 2005 the First People of the Kalahari were stripped of their rights to their ancestral homeland, the Central Kalahari Game Reserve.

23 The majority of South African writers forced into exile found themselves living and working in Europe and, less frequently, in North America.

24 Head writes, "It is on record that the British did not want Botswana. In their despatches they called it 'a God-awful country to live in.' It was grim and unproductive" (1990, 71).

25 For more on this, see Olaogun 2002. On remembering slavery in Ghana, see Aidoo 2001.

26 The material consequences of these representations continue to be felt in the twenty-first century. KhoiSan people's land rights and claims were still not protected under South Africa's new democratic constitution. See, for example, P. Coetzee 1999, 68.

27 In addition Jacqueline Rose says, "One way to come at the concept of universality might be to note, on each separate occasion, the history which provokes it" (1996, 103). Head invokes the "universally" disliked white man who "applied the technique of the wild jiggling dance and the rattling tin cans to any one who was not a white man." She writes of Maru (representative of the Dilepe Batswana elite), "How was it that he had inherited so much blood money and so many slaves. . . . It was African. It was horrible. But wherever mankind had gathered itself together in a social order, the same things were happening. There was a mass of people with no humanity to whom another mass referred: Why they are naturally like that. They like to live in such filth. They have been doing it for centuries" (1971, 11, 68).

28 See Wicomb 1998 for more on Baartman's contested ethnicity.

29 See Abrahams 1996a, 89 and 1998. See also Strother 1999.

30 Wayne Dooling writes, "Dr. John Philip of the London Missionary Society was representative of many when he wrote in his famous Researches in South Africa that the legislation of 1809 consigned the 'Hottentots . . . to universal and hopeless slavery'" (2005, 50).

31 Quoting "Humanitas" in The Examiner, 28 October 1810, Yvette Abrahams writes, "Auntie Sarah was making at least one Englishman think, not only about her state of slavery in the metropolis but also about the state of Khoekhoe slavery in the colony" (2003, 20).

32 See, for example, Brown 2003, 157; Gardner 1986.

33 Head writes, "In a country where the rest of the oppressed groups are hounded day in and day out [the coloured] has been able to live in relative peace and

move about as freely as he wished" (1990, 10). This is achieved with what Head refers to as an uneasy "compromise" with the ruling party. Though this is a double exclusion, it is an exclusion that is complemented by the promise of *more* inclusion than for black South Africans (10). Head maintained this solidarity at least during the time that she was writing *When Rainclouds Gather* (1968) and *Maru*.

34 For more on this, see Nixon 1998.

35 How else, in the same essay, can Susan Gardner write, "I regularly sent her new reviews and one of my students translated those in Afrikaans; Afrikaans-speaking newspapers treated her with seriousness and respect, but *paradoxically* she detested the language" (1986, 125; emphasis mine). Gardner herself might not detest Afrikaans, but why does she find it strange, even pathological, that Head does? Head left South Africa in 1964, and it is reasonable that she would have a strong response to Afrikaans. Although Afrikaans was the first language of much of the coloured population in the Cape, Head did not speak it. The Soweto uprising of 1976 was at least in part in response to the decree that Afrikaans would be the language of instruction in black schools. Gardner conducted this interview with Head in 1983, seven years after the Soweto uprising.

36 For more on this, see Jacqueline Rose's "Black Hamlet" in *States of Fantasy* (1996). Head does indeed talk about herself as mad, but to write about her work and her madness in isolation from apartheid, ethnocentrism, and poverty is to diminish those circumstances and to diminish the lucidity of Head's critiques of power.

37 Defined in the OED as a "protuberance of the buttocks, due to an abnormal accumulation of fat in and behind the hips and thighs, found (more markedly in women than in men) as a racial characteristic of certain peoples, esp. the Hottentots and Bushmen of South Africa." Etymology: " 'abnormal accumulation of fat on the buttocks of certain races,' 1822, Mod. L., from steato- 'fat, tallow,' from Gk. stear (gen. steatos) 'solid fat, suet' + Gk. pyge 'buttocks.' " Scientists, however, were not in agreement about this "fact." "*It is not a fact*, that the whole of the Hottentot race are thus formed; neither is there any particular tribe to which this steätopyga, as it may be called, is peculiar" (1822 W. J. Burchell Trav. S. Afr. I. xi. 216 note). In other words, to accept the diagnosis and then to racialize it is to erase the debate of the era, including Cuvier's remark, "It is hardly safe to affirm that these peculiarities are universal in the Bush race" (1817, 201).

38 The quotations are from, respectively, Strother 1999, 23; Wallace, 2005, 426; Lindfors 1983, 100. Punning, Lindfors repeats the kind of categorizing of Baartman that elsewhere he would seek to correct, while, T. Denean Sharpley-Whiting writes, "Literally carrying her fortune behind her, Baartman and her protuberant charms found themselves again in the limelight upon her arrival in Paris in September 1814" (1999, 18).

39 "The Hottentot was within the cage; . . . on being ordered by her keeper, she came out, and . . . her appearance was highly offensive to delicacy. . . . The Hottentot was produced like a wild beast, and ordered to move backwards and forwards, and come out and go into her cage, more like a bear than a human being. . . . She frequently heaved deep sighs; seemed anxious and uneasy; grew sullen, when she was ordered to play on some rude instrument of music. . . . And one time, when she refused for a moment to come out of her cage, the keeper let down the curtain, went behind, and was seen to hold up his hand to her in a menacing posture" (quoted in Lindfors 1983, 86–87).

40 Consider this: "When an American literary journal innocently sent Head a questionnaire about her writing habits, she responded ruefully: I am usually terrorized by various authorities into accounting for my existence; and filling in forms, under such circumstances acquires a fascination all its own" (Nixon 1998, 120).

41 In her introduction to the catalogue for the Miscast exhibition Marilyn Martin, director of the SANG, writes, "Saartje Baartman puts the descendants of the Khoisan populations at the centre of contemporary political and cultural debates—debates with national and international implications and ramifications" (Skotnes 1996, 9). Annie Coombes notes, "What interests me about 'Miscast' is that this reflection on a traumatic history took place at a critical time in the emergence of the new democratic nation. Yet again, the KhoiSan and their representation figure as a central mediator at the moment of nation building, just as in 1952 they had figured as a mediator for the apartheid state at the Jan van Riebeeck Tercentenary Festival" (2003, 236).

42 Skotnes 2001, 310. See also Skotnes 1996.
   Yvette Abrahams writes, "I had seen the infamous plaster casts first, naturally, the ones which had been taken of Khoisan bodies by the South African Museum in the early part of this century and which had lain, ever since, in one of their storerooms until Pippa Skotnes decided to bring them out. . . . Had it not been for those casts, I have little doubt that the Skotnes exhibition would have passed us by unscathed. But those highlighted genitals got on our nerves and are there still. They became an issue waiting for expression" (website of the University of Ulm 1996).

43 I am relying on various articles about the exhibition Miscast: Negotiating Khoisan History and Material Culture and on my reading of the catalogue Miscast: Negotiating the Presence of the Bushmen (Skotnes 1996). "This was the case especially for the design of one of the galleries of the exhibition, constructed so that viewers could not avoid walking on images of the aboriginal KhoiSan people. Angry KhoiSan responses challenged the use of these images and of fragmented body parts as a reenactment, not a critique, of colonial violence." Thomas Blom Hansen and Finn Stepputat, eds., States of Imagination: Ethnographic Explorations of the Postcolonial State (Durham, N.C.: Duke University Press, 2001), 197. Analogously, on a recent trip to the South African Museum,

when I went to see the infamous Bushman diorama I encountered instead a plywood wall with the following text: "The Diorama is now closed. After many years of debate the diorama was closed to the public on 3 April 2001. It will be left in place while a process of consultation with affected communities takes place. We are working in partnership with Khoisan people in developing new exhibitions." I was not allowed to see behind the wall but was directed to the computers upstairs, where I could look at the website with the images of the diorama. See "Debating the Diorama" and "Bushman Diorama: Questions and Answers" on the Iziko Museums of Cape Town website, http://www.iziko.org.za/.

44 For more on this, see the website of the University of Ulm.

45 For Brown nationalists (who trace their ancestry to coloured, Khoisan, and Afrikaner) the return of Baartman's bones to South Africa constitutes a large part of their claims for restoring the nation.

46 Further connecting Head and Baartman in my reading is Skotnes's reminder, "By the end of the nineteenth century bushman bodies had been the subject of dozens of photographic 'essays.' Most of these photographs were part of scientific projects that examined racial differences" (2001, 309–10).

47 For more on this, see Strother 1999, 31. See also a number of essays in Skotnes 1996.

48 In *Maru* we read that there was a "church, a school, and a hospital in the village, all founded by a series of missionaries" (12).

49 For more on this subject, see Strother 1999; Abrahams 1997, 1998; Wiss 1994; Skotnes 1996, 2001.

50 Early accounts of the Khoikhoi use this same language. See Chidester 1996.

51 Again, Head refused the designation of "coloured" in South Africa.

52 Head, who resisted the category of coloured in South Africa and who wrote this text in part because her son was derided for being coloured, not a Motswana, could hardly present passing into the category of coloured as a resolution for Margaret Cadmore Jr. For more on this unspeakability, see Motzafi-Haller 1994.

53 For more on this, see Motzafi-Haller 1994.

54 The title of this section comes from Brand 2001, 29.

55 Head would come to believe that she was punished for telling the truth.

56 Yvette Abrahams writes, "Guess you want me to tell you about the Khoekhoe too? We are First Nations people and the indigenous inhabitants of South Africa. We have had 350 years of colonialism, 250 years of slavery, 50 years of segregation, 48 years of apartheid—and then we had structural adjustment. . . . So if I tell you that the post-apartheid struggle of the Khoekhoe has been to bury the bodies of our ancestors with respect, then it is possible that I need not tell you very much more about our history than this" (2003, 13). For Abrahams, that "no scientist can ever again get a look at [Baartman's] body" is a revolution, which she defines as "a qualitative change in circumstances and structures which cannot be undone" (14).

Chapter Three. Isaac Julien's *The Attendant*

1 For more on this conversation between contemporary black artists and Fanon's *Black Skin, White Masks,* see two important collections: Read 1996 and Bailey 1995.

2 The painting was given to Sir Thomas Fowell Buxton to commemorate the abolition of slavery. It went to hang in Wilberforce House in 1840, seven years after Wilberforce's death. For more on the Biard painting and its history, see Honour 1989; Wood 2000.

3 For more on the distinction (or lack of distinction) between the art museum and the ethnographic historical museum, see Bal 1996.

4 For more on this, see Mercer 2003.

5 Here Bal uses Mark Rothko's work as an example. Repetition has a different function in Kara Walker's work.

6 In this chapter I am primarily concerned with the Attendant, the Conservator, and the Visitor.

7 Henry Purcell was considered England's greatest composer and Wilberforce was one of England's greatest reformers.

8 Julien also refers to the basement rooms of the Wilberforce House Museum in his talk for the Turner short list at the Tate Gallery. See Wood 2000, 296.

9 On this aspect of Biard's work, see Wood 2000.

10 In "Black Is, Black Ain't" Julien says, "I want to raise ambivalent questions about the sexual and racial violence that stems from the repressed desires of the Other within ourselves," but this film does much more than this (2000d, 76).

11 For more on the unspeakable, see Delany 1999, 58–59.

12 I borrow this statement from Kara Walker and I will return to it in chapter 4.

13 An obvious instance of this entering into black bodies is minstrelsy, which I discuss in chapter 4 in relation to Kara Walker's work.

14 See also Wood 2000.

15 Thackeray is not alone in this. This scene was much reproduced for abolitionist tracts. See Wood 2000; Honour 1989.

16 Many critics focused on the "absurdity" of the leg in the foreground of the Turner painting. There is a similar gesture in one of Kara Walker's installations that places her work in conversation with Turner as well as with Biard. In particular see the foot on the brown paper bag in *Presenting Negro Scenes Drawn upon My Passage through the South and Reconfigured for the Benefit of Enlightened Audiences Wherever Such May Be Found.*

17 For more on this, see Gaines 1992.

18 See also Bailey 1995, 57–80.

19 For Wayne Koestenbaum, Dido's punctuating "ah" indicates "I am taking my time, protracting my dying, turning it into a gorgeous cortege" (1993, 234).

20 Wilson figures all of the guards as male, which erases the also ubiquitous (at least in the northeastern United States) black female guards.

21 For more about this experience and about the site-specific exhibition, see Corrin 1994, introduction.

22 Stuart Hall's presence in particular indicates that he is not solely a participant in those viewing relations "dictated by the aesthetics of high culture," but an active participant in black British cultural production. Recognized as themselves, both Hall and Kureishi are simultaneously constructed in these spaces and they construct meaning in them. For the viewer who knows, Hall's presence is a nod to his own contributions to cultural studies and to Julien's previous visual and written work, such as "De Margin and De Center" (Julien and Mercer 2000d).

23 Silverman is describing an exchange of looks in *Looking for Langston*. This argument may be extended to the scene between the Visitor (John Wilson), who is also in *Looking for Langston*, and the Attendant (Thomas Baptiste).

24 Devin Orgeron writes, "What are these angels? One has a devil's pitchfork and the other a cupid's bow and arrow." He notes that the costumes of these angels are "simultaneously 'angelic' and 'perverse.' Wings are kept in place by leather harnesses and the angels carry bows and arrows or pitchforks" (2000, 36).

25 In "Confessions of a Snow Queen" Julien writes, "For instance, the Other in Marlon Riggs's powerful video of *Tongues Untied* is the 'white gay subject.' In the video, Riggs explains how he was himself 'saved' by a white boy with blue eyes, who then became a curse. I have always been disappointed that this representation of interracial desire was then undermined by the tape's Afrocentric gay ending, reinforced by one's 'extra-filmic' knowledge of Riggs's longtime relationship with a white boyfriend. To remain closeted on the subject of interracial desire has its dangers: the undermining of its avowed political project, risking exposure to the meta-discourse of gossip, e.g., 'Oh, did you know that she has a white boyfriend, so how can she talk about black men loving black men as *the* revolutionary act' " (2000a, 82).

26 Rotimi Fani-Kayode's photographs in *Black Male/White Male* (1988), a collaborative project with his white partner, Alex Hirst, engage Mapplethorpe's *Black Males*. Hirst writes that these photographs were at first rejected as being "simply imitative" of Mapplethorpe's. Fani-Kayode's photographs of black men, which included self-portraits, were not given the same kind of space as Mapplethorpe's images of black men. Hirst writes:

>   It is a one-sided discourse, a tale of desire: Africa–Europe–America: fantasy-continents in which these images find some of their contexts, not least of which being the triangle of trade in finished goods, raw materials, and slaves. . . .
>
>   This collection of photographs is one version of the perilous dash through fantasy which is the only distinction between ourselves and the baboons. We may perceive in it a certain tragic freedom in the grand manner, where the premodern collides with the post-modern for a few moments of bewildering intimacy. (1988, 3)

Mark Sealy writes, "In Golden Phallus the phallus is both illuminated and bound, gilded and bandaged, 'free' and yet delicately tethered" (2001, 40).

27 "What interests us are the contradictory experiences in which the porno-phototext implicates us, as pornography is one of the few spaces in which erotic images of other black men are made available" (Julien and Mercer 2000c, 58).

28 We can think here of the uniformed headless black men in Fred Wilson's *Guarded View*.

29 See Hall and Sealy 2001.

30 The following is a brief summary. For more on *Regina v. Brown*, see Hanna 2000–2001.

31 See Weeks 1995, 127–30.

32 This allegation comes from the European Convention for the Protection of Human Rights and Fundamental Freedoms (Hanna 2000–2001, 266).

33 See the website www.sexuality.org.

34 See Wood 2000.

35 Touko Laaksonen, the creator of Tom of Finland, quoted in Michael Alvear, "The Man Who Made Gays Macho," *Salon*, 8 April 2000.

36 Although included in the preface, "In(se)duction: Out of the Closet and into the Bedroom," is the following exchange: "Like last summer when Roseann got pissed off at Miriam's bossiness. 'Just listen to yourself, girl: "We need your intros by next week." "We got to get this to the typist by June 30." Makes me sick! Whaddya think we are, workhorses? Um gonna buy you a whip!' To which Miriam replied, a devilish gleam in her eye, 'Oh boy, and what about some black garters and high-heeled boots to go with that whip?'" They seem to be playing with s/m play, and in the context of the sadomasochism of everyday life (Willis, Martin, and Bell xxiii, xxxiii).

37 For more on s/m sex and politics, see Califia 1994; G. Rubin 1993; Bersani 1988; McClintock 1993.

38 See Stychin 1996.

39 Julien says that the Attendant remembers his past as an opera singer.

40 In 2000 Julien created *Vagabondia*, a film that again features Cleo Sylvestre, who plays the Conservator in *The Attendant*. This film, set in Sir John Soane's Museum in London, "expand[s] the fantasmatic realms of objects on display and the jumbled incoherent spaces that they inhabit through the eyes of the black conservator" (Julien 2001).

Chapter Four. Kara Walker's Monstrous Intimacies

1 The popularity of the silhouette waned as the daguerreotype came into existence in 1839. For more on the silhouette and the stereotype, see Hobbs 2001.

2 I draw on several examples here. First, in Harriet Beecher Stowe's *Uncle Tom's Cabin* Topsy is the foil to Uncle Tom, Aunt Chloe, Eliza, George, and Harry. Stowe describes Topsy as monstrous:

> She was one of the blackest of her race; and her round shining eyes, glittering as glass beads, moved with quick and restless glances over everything in the room. Her mouth, half open with astonishment at the wonders of the new Mas'r's parlor, displayed a white and brilliant set of teeth. Her woolly hair was

braided in sundry little tails, which stuck out in every direction. The expression of her face was an odd mixture of shrewdness and cunning, over which was oddly drawn, like a kind of veil, an expression of the most doleful gravity and solemnity. She was dressed in a single filthy, ragged garment, made of bagging; and stood with her hands demurely folded before her. Altogether, there was something odd and goblin-like about her appearance.... The black, glassy eyes glittered with a kind of wicked drollery, and the thing struck up, in a clear shrill voice, an odd negro melody, to which she kept time with her hands and feet, spinning round, clapping her hands, knocking her knees together, in a wild, fantastic sort of time, and producing in her throat all those odd guttural sounds which distinguish the native music of her race; and finally, turning a summerset or two, and giving a prolonged closing note, as odd and unearthly as that of a steam-whistle, she came suddenly down on the carpet, and stood with her hands folded, and a most sanctimonious expression of meekness and solemnity over her face, only broken by the cunning glances which she shot askance from the corners of her eyes. (1982, 352)

Second, writing about an older enslaved man whom she teaches to read at great risk to both of them, Harriet Jacobs says, "I knew an old man, whose piety and childlike trust in God were beautiful to witness." The man, old uncle Fred, tells Jacobs: "Honey, it 'pears when I can read dis good book I shall be nearer to God. White man is got all de sense. He can larn easy. It ain't easy for ole black man like me. I only wants to read dis book, dat I may know how to live; den I hab no fear about dying" (1987, 73).

Third, as Michele Wallace writes in "Uncle Tom's Cabin: Before and After the Jim Crow Era," "Apparently, black middle-class and educated audiences were repelled by blackface minstrelsy, surmising that it was such buffoonish blacks whom whites wanted to lynch and exterminate. But the facts show that the lynching whites were after the uppity blacks, not the old buffoons and blackface performers who presumably 'knew their place.' It may even be that black people as a group owe some portion of their survival to such performances of 'race'" (2000, 145; emphasis mine).

3 Walker says that she wants "to lure her viewers into something 'totally demeaning and possibly very beautiful'" (quoted in Juliette Bowles 1997, 9).

4 This does not exhaust the range of possibilities of either white or black responses, but it is these responses that I examine in this chapter.

5 We can see in Walker's declared interest in "shame—the opposite of pride, black pride in particular," an echo of Gayl Jones's much earlier assertion that "there's a lot of imaginative territory that you have to be 'wrong' in order to enter" (quoted in Rowell 1982, 42). The "choices" are, of course, in concert with a present use of history to shore up belief in freedom or self-determination but have little to do with what it was like to live and survive within slavery. There is much to be explored in those places.

6 See, for example, the National Geographic website's interactive learning unit on the Underground Railroad. The text reads: "You are a slave. Your body, your

time, your very breath belong to a farmer in 1850s Maryland. Six long days a
week you tend his fields and make him rich. You have never tasted freedom. You
never expect to. And yet . . . your soul lights up when you hear whispers of
attempted escape. Freedom means a hard, dangerous trek. Do you try it?" And
you are presented with two choices: "Yes. I want to go!" and "No! I'll stay here."
In this simulation, if you choose "No! I'll stay here," the next page offers the
following text: "Most slaves chose not to run away. Historians estimate that only
a fraction fled slavery. Millions more lived in bondage, where they fought slavery
in subtle ways: work slowdowns, sabotage, and 'sickness.' Take a journey on the
Underground Railroad by clicking here and choosing YES. Or use the pull-down
menu above to explore other areas of this site." But this text is the end of the
simulation for this option. While the site is dedicated to the Underground
Railroad, a fuller story of those "millions more" (against which the story of the
exceptional is set) might have led to other interactive options than going back
and choosing "YES."

7 Walker says, "One day I finally realized that I was actually participating actively
in a mythological narrative that is maybe more pronounced in the South. There's
such a rich history, a rich tradition if you will, of racism and racial subjugation in
the South, and when I was growing up in the South, this narrative was very
pronounced" (T. Lott 2000, 73).

8 The persistence of descriptions of the mammy as asexual hide the fact that it is
likely that neither her size, age, nor position in the household would protect the
woman-read-as-mammy from sexual assault. See, for example, Richard Wright's
story "Man of All Work" (1989, 109–54); Marjorie Garber, *Vested Interests: Cross-
Dressing and Cultural Anxiety* (New York: Routledge, 1997).

9 We might think here of Frantz Fanon and Mayotte Capecia and what he calls the
process of lactification.

10 Gwendolyn Dubois Shaw writes the following about this image of four suckling
figures:

> With the attention [the women] give to their erotic activity, they all but forget
> the infant. To emphasize the sexual nature of the women, rather than their
> nurturing side, Walker has not cut their forms to resemble the grossly cor-
> pulent body of the mammy. Unlike the stereotype of the mammy, Walker's
> women do not focus their attention outward, seeking the satisfaction of white
> others, but toward each other instead. Having rejected maternal action, they
> are orally fixated on nursing. . . .
>
> This orgiastic carnality speaks of a racialized transgression of sexual and
> gender roles. No longer are their bodies to be used by others, by men, or by
> babies; now they are to be enjoyed by the self and *one's own kind*, now they
> are themselves the objects of desire as they consume the bodies of their
> analogues. . . .
>
> Walker's *slave women live in the immediate moment in which their needs are
> being fulfilled.* (2004, 47–48)

Shaw's reading of this vignette effectively denies multitudes of other possibilities in favor a positive (i.e., recuperative) reading. Walker's description of the image as "the big black mammy of old" might disrupt Shaw's reading of the figure (of at least four forms) as not-mammy because not congruent with a particular stereotype of mammy. Nancy Spector describes this image as one in which "three bare breasted 'mammies' suckle each other in a circular pose reminiscent of the Three Graces" (2000, 37).

11 Copjec performs this reading of Walker's work largely without availing herself of reference to other black artists or to all of the work that African Americanist art historians and other African Americanists (black or not) have done on Walker, on positioning her production in relation to a history of black and white artistic production.

12 Dilsey in William Faulkner's *The Sound and the Fury* is a perfect example of the black woman performing the maternal function in a white household.

13 Anne Wagner writes, "Speaking of Walker's achievement as an artist, [Henry Louis Gates] writes 'the black object has become the black subject in a profound act of artistic exorcism.'" Wagner adds, "Yet liberation into subjectivity clearly has its risks—or so the critical chorus seems to insist. Walker offers a *staging of self and identity in which the chorus wants no part.* Such reaction suggests that what Walker's art cultivates is the complex and discomfiting subjection of viewers to a radically destabilizing form of consciousness. *And if white viewers value that experience, some reasons for such dubious pleasure clearly still need to be found*" (Wagner 2003, 93; emphases mine). Wagner's reading here is fascinating; she never quite explores why this radical destabilization is an experience in which white viewers find some dubious pleasure, though I suspect the answer is found in her own erasure of whites from Walker's allegorical scenes of slavery and slavery's presence in the present.

14 For more on these pleasures of ownership, see St. John 2001, 151.

15 Copjec writes, "What makes Walker's reply most unsatisfying is its failure to respond to the question posed to her: why are there *four* girls and women in this vignette rather than just the *one* superabundant mammy her answer implies? Why this duplication, this replication of women, suckling not their young (the descendants of the race whose source they are supposed by the cliché to be), but each other?" (2002, 98). The explicit question is not why are there four women, but what are the four women a metaphor for. There should arise from Walker's answer a new set of questions about the general and specific need to suckle from history, the fears and dangers of weaning, the split within, and the internal circularity in what we consider to be the mammy. I think here of Toni Morrison's *Song of Solomon* and "Milkman" Dead, so named because he is seen breastfeeding at the age of six. What might it mean to be denied the ability to suckle? And what might it mean to suckle too long?

16 Spillers writes, "I am suggesting that even though the enslaved female reproduced other enslaved subjects, we do not read 'birth' in this instance as a

reproduction of mothering precisely because the female . . . has been robbed of the parental right, the parental function" (2003c, 224).

17 Walker's focus on the fear and necessity of weaning ("For myself, I have this constant battle—this fear of weaning. It's really a battle that I apply to the black community as well, because all of our progress is predicated on having a very tactile link to a brutal past") seems to be what Ursa enacts through the end of reproduction in *Corregidora*.

18 Consider that Betye Saar resurrects her "revolutionary mammy," *The Liberation of Aunt Jemima* (1972), in order to counter Walker's creations. See Wilson 2003, 24.

19 In "Diaspora/Realities/Strategies," for example, the African American visual artist Howardeena Pindell writes, "I feel it is tragic when black artists further *'invigorate'* the stereotype. Their work is, I fear, catering to racism, misogynistic at times, and self-loathing in both its subtle and more gross forms. Very few African-American artists with affirmative stereotype-busting images/messages are allowed in the same venues. I feel that artists who use racial stereotypes without critique become complicit. They are reinforcing the old stereotype as if to say the fabricated image is their true experience. Thus, in the visual industries' uneven playing field these artists entertain, titillate, mesmerise and amuse their European/European-American admirers" (2002).

20 This is a reference to Ralph Ellison's *Invisible Man* and the Invisible Man's encounter with Lucius Brockway in the basement of the Liberty Paint Factory. For more on optic whiteness, see Mullen 1994. "Ralph Ellison's 'Optic White,' that drop of black, that irreducible invisibility necessary to make white appear as such" (Lindberg, 851).

21 This is precisely the problem that many people have with American ego psychology. When Rose goes to the analyst these anxiety-producing events are pushed further down.

22 This is then transposed in Rose's text into twentieth-century Euro-American domesticity. The white housewife's "emancipation" is in no small part constructed on the disavowed labor of the mammy. See Berlant 1991.

23 The mammy operates beyond sex; if the image of the mammy confuses and fuses black and white women, it also confuses and fuses black women and black men and extends to include Lily's "timid and tentative" husband, Taft. (Again Richard Wright's remarkable short story "Man of All Work" comes to mind here.)

24 The inner plantation, Walker says in an interview, is "a place in the collective unconscious which continues to fight the Lost Cause and revel in the futility of it. This place is inhabited by familiar and forbidden ghosts acting out the debacle we call History. Confederate soldiers, downtrodden and defeated, mingle with tawny and seductive Creole belles who arouse the suspicion of Scarlett. Fearful 'free-issue niggers' stumble over little Eva, the puritanical martyr. Wicked

Topsy butts a Yankee. *The consumptive mistress demands satisfaction from her old Mammy*" (Saltz 1996, 82).

25 Anne Wagner writes, "What we might well prefer to take as evidence, however limited and circumscribed, of the art world's belated integration becomes, in the eyes of some viewers, pandering, voyeurism and worse. Business as usual" (2003, 92).

26 Joan Copjec describes Walker's images as "on the contrary an erotic dissembling of [stereotypes], a mad tussle away from their stale scent and heavy burden" (2002, 107).

27 Once again we see the inability to continue to see or read white characters once they are located in their black forms. What is it that is making one not see?

28 In the museum catalogue *Kara Walker Slavery! Slavery! The 25th International Bienal of São Paulo, Brazil* Robert Hobbs writes, "Walker's art . . . has proven particularly offensive to Civil Rights–era blacks who have regularly availed themselves of the modern propensity to essentialize and reify identity in their ongoing battle against racist images by creating in their art paragons of African-American morality. . . . Although her art has not been viewed in terms of the relatively recent post–Civil Rights fascination with black collectibles by upscale African-Americans, it is in part predicated on their reevaluation of this material" (2001, 11).

29 A few responses: "*I am writing you, seeking your help, to spread awareness about the negative images produced by the young African American artist, Kara Walker.*" *Betye Saar* (Betye Saar, quoted in Juliette Bowles 1997, 4).

Bowles writes: "During the summer of 1997 she sent out over 200 letters and packets to writers, artists and politicians containing information about Walker, samples of her work, and a statement which asked: 'Are African Americans being betrayed under the guise of art? Is this white backlash, art elitist style?' " (Bowles 1997, 4).

Howardeena Pindell: "It's skewing the view of the African American community. Mostly white people are coming to see this show with imagery that gets imbedded into their consciousness. The (Kara Walker) exhibit, for example, shows an African American woman having intercourse with a horse." 2002.

30 A symposium in summer 1998 at Harvard University on Walker's work addressed some of these concerns.

31 The black-eyed squint is that person whose perceptions run contrary to the expectations of others (Aidoo 1977/1997).

32 This is yet another instance in which a white critic erases whites as participants. Hobbs says, "While no one is suggesting that Walker does not believe deeply that racial stereotyping is abhorrent and a key element of racist thought, *it is interesting to me that the artist's use of such stereotypes has been most vehemently contested by an older generation of African-Americans. To my knowledge, no white commentators have taken issue with her use of stereotypical imagery*" (2003, 429; emphasis mine). Donald Kuspit is one exception to this.

33 Of the holidays, and spells of relative leisure of which the cakewalk might be a part, Frederick Douglass writes, "To enslave men successfully and safely, it is necessary to have their minds occupied with thoughts and aspirations short of the liberty of which they are deprived. A certain degree of attainable good must be kept before them. These holidays serve the purpose of keeping the minds of the slaves occupied with prospective pleasure, within the limits of slavery" (1855/2003a, 56).

34 The cakewalk was taken up by white minstrels, who imitated blacks imitating whites, and then again by whites imitating blacks imitating whites.

35 One of the images from the show that accompanies the review is titled *Beats Me* (2001). It shows two silhouetted white men standing side by side, one with his shoulders raised and palms up ("beats me") and the other (the one who beats) stands with his hands on hips and holding what looks like a riding crop in his left hand. To their left is a silhouetted naked black man or woman lying face down, draped over a low standing shed or outbuilding, after having been beaten or about to be beaten. The "beats me" of the title is both a declarative sentence (they/he "beat[s] me") and an idiomatic expression of bafflement. Kuspit could enter into the frame not as the black figure who is beaten but as the white men doing the beating or expressing puzzlement over the scene.

36 "These black people," as opposed to the individuals whom Kuspit names or signals to in his review. He writes, "But the place of blacks in American society has changed for the better—Colin Powell, Condolezza [*sic*] Rice and the heads of Coca Cola and AOL suggest as much (they seem more than establishment tokens)—however many problems remain for them" (2003).

37 I think here of Elizabeth Alexander's articulation of black suffering for public consumption in " 'Can You Be BLACK and Look at This?' Reading The Rodney King Video" (1995).

38 The OED defines a scallywag as "a native white of the southern states who was willing to accept the reconstructionary measures."

39 One might argue that contemporary white youth culture's appropriation of black culture, what gets read as "black identity," offers a counterexample to this. But I think this appropriation produces a rewriting of whiteness: those young white (and nonblack) people are not really rendered black; their performance of blackness functions to further reify black and white.

40 The OED defines exorbitant as "not coming within the scope of the law," "exceeding one's rights" (obs), and "grossly or flagrantly excessive." I want to bring to bear both senses of exorbitant as excessive and outside of the law.

41 In his interview with Walker, Saltz asks, "Why is one breast exposed?" Walker says, "Implying suckling, implying childhood, implying history resides there. A shack in the background also refers to the black woman in this world as an anonymous root" (1996, 84).

42 Indeed the photograph and review of Jeanne Greenberg's installation of the Walker piece, displayed with "Maxime old tables and mid-century orchestra chairs," bears a striking resemblance to Fred Wilson's installation "Cabinetry"

from *Mining the Museum* (figure 20). The chairs arranged around a whipping post are a visual analogy to the dining table in front of the scenes I describe above.

43 The black children that appear with such frequency in Walker's work also appear with regularity in the work of numerous nineteenth-century artists and in work by other African American artists. Fred Wilson in *Mining the Museum*, for example, examines the ways that blackness itself is used as a frame in so much of art history.

44 This erasure might also be seen in the title of Copjec's chapter "Moses the Egyptian and the Big Black Mammy of the Antebellum South: Freud (with Kara Walker) on Race and History" (2002). Why this bracketing of Walker when the chapter both begins and ends with her work?

BIBLIOGRAPHY

Abel, Elizabeth, Barbara Christian, and Helene Moglen, eds. 1997. *Female Subjects in Black and White: Race, Psychoanalysis, Feminism*. Berkeley: University of California Press.

Abrahams, Yvette. 2003. "Colonialism, Dysfunction, and Disjuncture: Sarah Bartmann's Resistance (Remix)." *Agenda* 58, 12–26.

——. 1998. "Images of Sara Bartman: Sexuality, Race, and Gender in Early-Nineteenth-Century Britain." *Nation, Empire, Colony: Historicizing Gender and Race*, edited by Ruth Roach Pierson and Nupur Chaudhuri, 220–36. Bloomington: Indiana University Press.

——. 1997. "The Great Long National Insult: 'Science,' Sexuality, and the Khoisan in the 18th and Early 19th Century." *Agenda* 32, 34–48.

——. 1996a. "Disempowered to Consent: Sara Bartman and Khoisan Slavery in the Nineteenth Century Cape Colony and Britain." *South African Historical Journal* 35, 89–114.

——. 1996b. "Was Eva Raped? An Exercise in Speculative History." *Kronos* 23, 3–21.

Abreu, Martha. 1996. "Slave Mothers and Freed Children: Emancipation and Female Space in Debates on the 'Free Womb' Law, Rio de Janeiro, 1871." *Journal of Latin American Studies* 28 (3), 567–80.

Aidoo, Ama Ata. 2001. "Of Forts, Castles and Silences." *Facing Up to the Past: Perspectives on the Commemoration of Slavery from Africa, the Americas and Europe*, edited by Gert Oostindie, 29–34. Kingston, Jamaica: Ian Randle.

——. 1997. *Our Sister Killjoy: Or Reflections of a Black Eyed Squint*. 1977. New York: Longman.

Akomfrah, John, and Kass Banning. 1993. "Feeding off the Dead: Necrophilia and the Black Imaginary: An Interview with John Akomfrah." *Border/Lines* 29–30, 28–38.

Alexander, Elizabeth. 1995. " 'Can You be BLACK and

Look at This?' Reading the Rodney King Video." *Black Male: Representations of Masculinity in Contemporary Art*, edited by Thelma Golden, 90–110. New York: Whitney Museum of Art.

———. 1994. "Memory, Community, Voice." *Callaloo* 17 (2), 408–21.

———. 1990. *The Venus Hottentot*. Charlottesville: University Press of Virginia.

Allen, Donia Elizabeth. 2002. "The Role of the Blues in Gayl Jones's *Corregidora*." *Callaloo* 25 (1), 257–73.

Altick, Richard D. 1978. *The Shows of London: A Panorama History of Exhibitions, 1600–1862*. Cambridge, Mass.: Harvard University Press.

Ambrose, Douglass. 1997. *Henry Hughes and Proslavery Thought in the Old South*. Baton Rouge: Louisiana State University Press.

Bailey, David A. 1995. "Mirage: Enigmas of Race, Difference and Desire." *Mirage: Enigmas of Race, Difference and Desire*, edited by David Bailey, 57–80. London: ICA.

Bal, Mieke. 1999. Introduction to *Acts of Memory: Cultural Recall in the Present*, edited by Mieke Bal, Jonathan Crewe, and Leo Spitzer, vii–xvii. Hanover, N.H.: University Press of New England.

———. 1996. "The Discourse of the Museum." *Thinking about Exhibitions*, edited by Reesa Greenberg, Bruce W. Ferguson, and Sandy Nairne, 201–18. New York: Routledge.

Baldwin, James. 1987. *The Fire Next Time*. 1963. New York: Vintage.

Bardaglio, Peter. 1998. *Reconstructing the Household: Families, Sex, and the Law in the Nineteenth-Century South*. Chapel Hill: University of North Carolina Press.

Barnett, Ursula A. 1983. *A Vision of Order: A Study of Black African Literature in English (1914–1980)*. Amherst: University of Massachusetts Press.

Barrett, Lindon. 1998. *Blackness and Value: Seeing Double*. Cambridge: Cambridge University Press.

Bell, David, and Gill Valentine, eds. 1995. *Mapping Desire: Geographies of Sexualities*. New York: Routledge.

Bell, Vickie. 1999. "On Speech, Race and Melancholia: An Interview with Judith Butler." *Theory, Culture and Society* 16 (2), 163–74.

Bending, Tim. 2002. "Power versus Love: The Production and Overcoming of Hierarchic Oppression." *Alternatives* 27, 117–42.

Benjamin, Jessica. 1988. *The Bonds of Love: Psychoanalysis, Feminism, and the Problem of Domination*. New York: Pantheon.

Bergner, Gwen. 2005. *Taboo Subjects: Race, Sex, and Psychoanalysis*. Minneapolis: University of Minnesota Press.

Berlant, Lauren. 2000. *Intimacy*. Durham, N.C.: Duke University Press.

———. 1991. "National Brands, National Body." *Comparative American Identities: Race, Sex, and Nationality in the Modern Text*, edited by Hortense Spillers, 110–40. New York: Routledge.

Bersani, Leo. 1988. "Is the Rectum a Grave?" *Aids: Cultural Analysis, Cultural Activism*, edited by Douglas Crimp, 197–222. Cambridge, Mass.: MIT Press.

Bleser, Carol. 1988. *Secret and Sacred: The Diaries of James Henry Hammond, a Southern Slaveholder*. New York: Oxford University Press.

Blessingame, John, ed. 1979. *The Frederick Douglass Papers*, vol. 2. New Haven: Yale University Press.

Boerma, Silke. 2002. "Kara Walker Interview with Silke Boerma." *Kara Walker: Kunstverein Hannover,* edited by Stephan Berg, 165–73. Hanover, Germany: Modo Verlag.

Bowles, John P. 2001. "Blinded by the White: Art and History at the Limits of Whiteness." *Art Journal* 60 (4), 38–67.

Bowles, Juliette. 1998a. "Editor's Response." *International Review of African-American Art* 15 (2), 50–51.

———. 1998b. "Stereotypes Subverted." *International Review of African-American Art* 15 (2), 44–50.

———. 1997. "Extreme Times Call for Extreme Heroes." *International Review of African-American Art* 14 (3), 3–15.

Brand, Dionne. 2006. *Inventory*. Toronto: McClelland and Stewart.

———. 2002. *Thirsty*. Toronto: McClelland and Stewart.

———. 2001. *A Map to the Door of No Return: Notes to Belonging*. Toronto: Doubleday Canada.

Briggs, Laura. 2000. "The Race of Hysteria: 'Overcivilization' and the 'Savage' Woman in Late Nineteenth-Century Obstetrics and Gynecology." *American Quarterly* 52 (2), 246–73.

Brody, Jennifer DeVere. 2001. "Black Cat Fever: Manifestations of Manet's Olympia." *Theatre Journal* 53, 95–118.

Bronfen, Elisabeth. 2000. "The Language of Hysteria: A Misappropriation of the Master Narratives." *Women: A Cultural Review* 11 (1–2), 8–18.

Brown, Coreen. 2003. *The Creative Vision of Bessie Head*. Madison, N.J.: Fairleigh Dickinson University Press.

Butler, Judith. 2002. "Is Kinship Always Already Heterosexual?" *Differences: A Journal of Feminist Critical Studies* 13 (1), 14–44.

———. 1993. *Bodies That Matter: On the Discursive Limits of "Sex."* New York: Routledge.

———. 1990. "The Force of Fantasy: Feminism, Mapplethorpe, and Discursive Excess." *differences* (2), 105–25.

Califia, Pat. 1994. *Public Sex: The Culture of Radical Sex*. San Francisco: Cleis Press.

Cameron, Dan. 1997. "Rubbing History the Wrong Way." *On Paper,* September/ October, 10–14.

Caruth, Cathy. 1996. *Unclaimed Experience: Trauma, Narrative, and History*. Baltimore: Johns Hopkins University Press.

———. 1995. "Recapturing the Past: Introduction." *Trauma Explorations in Memory,* edited by Cathy Caruth, 3–13. Baltimore: Johns Hopkins University Press.

Castronovo, Russ. 2000. "Political Necrophilia." *Boundary 2* 27 (2), 113–48.

Cheng, Anne Anlin. 2000. *The Melancholy of Race*. New York: Oxford University Press.

Chidester, David. 1996. "Bushman Religion: Open, Closed, and New Frontiers." *Miscast: Negotiating the Presence of the Bushmen,* edited by Pippa Skotnes, 51–65. Cape Town, South Africa: University of Cape Town Press.

Christianse, Yvette. 2003. "Passing Away: The Unspeakable (Losses) of Post Apartheid South Africa." *Loss: The Politics of Mourning,* edited by David L. Eng and David Kazanjian, 372–96. Berkeley: University of California Press.

Clabough, Casey. 2005. "Speaking the Grotesque: The Short Fiction of Gayl Jones." *Southern Literary Journal* 38 (3): 74–96.

Clingman, Stephen. 1991. "Beyond the Limit: The Social Relations of Madness in Southern African Fiction." *The Bounds of Race: Perspectives on Hegemony and Resistance,* edited by Dominick LaCapra, 231–54. Ithaca, N.Y.: Cornell University Press.

Coetzee, Carli. 1998. "Krotoä Remembered: A Mother of Unity, a Mother of Sorrows?" *Negotiating the Past: The Making of Memory in South Africa,* edited by Sarah Nuttall and Carli Coetzee, 112–20. Cambridge: Oxford University Press.

Coetzee, Paulette. 1999. "Bushman Women in Bessie Head's *Maru* and Daphne Rooke's *Margaretha de la Porte.*" *Current Writing* 11 (1), 67–78.

Cognard-Black, Jennifer. 2001. " 'I Said Nothing': The Rhetoric of Silence in Gayl Jones's *Corregidora.*" NWSA *Journal* 13 (1), 40–61.

Cohodas, Nadine. 1993. *Strom Thurmond and the Politics of Southern Change.* New York: Simon and Schuster.

Comaroff, Jean, and Joan Comaroff. 1991. *Of Revolution and Revelation,* Vol. 1: *Christianity, Colonialism, and Consciousness in South Africa.* Chicago: University of Chicago Press.

Coombes, Annie E. 2003. *History after Apartheid: Visual Culture and Public Memory in a Democratic South Africa.* Durham, N.C.: Duke University Press.

Copjec, Joan. 2002. *Imagine There's No Woman: Ethics and Sublimation.* Cambridge, Mass.: MIT Press.

Corrin, Lisa. 1994. *Mining the Museum: An Installation by Fred Wilson.* New York: New Press.

Cowie, Elizabeth. 1997. *Representing the Woman: Cinema and Psychoanalysis.* Minneapolis: University of Minnesota Press.

Crenshaw, Kimberle. 2004. "Was Strom a Rapist?" *The Nation,* 15 March.

Crimp, Douglas. 1993. *On the Museum's Ruins.* Cambridge, Mass.: MIT Press.

Cruz, Amanda. 2000. "Introduction." *The Film Art of Isaac Julien,* edited by Amanda Cruz et al., vi–ix. Annandale-on-Hudson, N.Y.: Bard College, Center for Curatorial Studies.

Cuvier, Georges. 1817. In P. Kirby, "More about the Hottentot Venus." *Africana Notes and News* 10, 124–34.

Cvetkovich, Ann. 2003. *An Archive of Feelings.* Durham, N.C.: Duke University Press.

Davis, Angela. 1998. *Blues Legacies and Black Feminism: Gertrude "Ma" Rainey, Bessie Smith, and Billie Holiday.* New York: Pantheon.

Davis, Thulani. 2006. *My Confederate Kinfolk: A Twenty-first Century Freedwoman Discovers Her Roots.* New York: Basic Civitas Books.

Dawson, Ashley. 2001. "Surveillance Sites: Digital Media and the Dual Society in Keith Piper's Relocating the Remains." *Postmodern Culture* 12 (1), n.p.

Dayan, Joan. 1999. "Held in the Body of the State: Prisons and the Law." *History, Memory, and the Law*, edited by Austin Sarat and Thomas Kearns, 183–248. Ann Arbor: University of Michigan Press.

Dean, Carolyn J. 2003. "Empathy, Pornography, and Suffering." *Differences: A Journal of Feminist Cultural Studies* 14 (1), 88–124.

Decosta-Willis, Miriam, Reginald Martin, and Roseann P. Bell. 1992. *Erotique Noire/Black Erotica*. New York: Anchor.

Deitcher, David. 2000. "A Lovesome Thing: The Film Art of Isaac Julien." *The Film Art of Isaac Julien*, edited by Amanda Cruz et al., 11–23. Annandale-on-Hudson, N.Y.: Bard College, Center for Curatorial Studies.

De Kock, Leon. 2001a. "Sitting for the Civilization Test: The Making(s) of a Civil Imaginary in Colonial South Africa." *Poetics Today* 22 (2), 391–412.

———. 2001b. "South Africa in the Global Imaginary: An Introduction." *Poetics Today* 22 (2): 263–98.

Delany, Samuel. 1999. *Shorter Views: Queer Thoughts and the Politics of the Paraliterary*. Hanover, N.H.: University Press of New England.

Deleuze, Gilles, and Guattari, Félix. 1994. *Anti-Oedipus: Capitalism and Schizophrenia*. Minneapolis: University of Minnesota Press.

Dent, Gina. 1992. "Black Pleasure, Black Joy: An Introduction." *Black Popular Culture*, edited by Michelle Wallace and Gina Dent, 1–19. Seattle: Bay Press.

Desai, Guarav. 1997. "Out in Africa." *"Sex Positives?": The Cultural Politics of Dissident Sexualities,* Genders 25, edited by Thomas Foster, Carol Siegel, and Ellen E. Berry, 120–43. New York: New York University Press.

Diawara, Manthia. 1999. "The Blackface Stereotype." *David Levinthal: Blackface*, edited by Manthia Diawara, 7–17. Santa Fe, N. Mex.: Arena Editions.

Dooling, Wayne. 2005. "The Origins and Aftermath of the Cape Colony's 'Hottentot Code' of 1809." *Kronos* 31, 50–61.

Douglass, Frederick. 2003a. *My Bondage and My Freedom*. 1855. New York: Penguin Classics.

———. 2003b. *Narrative of the Life of Frederick Douglass, An American Slave, Written by Himself.* 1845. Boston: Bedford/St. Martin's.

Dovey, Theresa. 1989. "A Question of Power: Susan Gardiner's Biography versus Bessie Head's Autobiography." *English in Africa* 16 (1), 29–38.

Driver, Dorothy. 2001. Afterword to *David's Story*, by Zoë Wicomb, 219–71. New York: Feminist Press.

———. 1996. "Transformation through Art: Writing, Representation, and Subjectivity in Recent South African Fiction." *World Literature Today* 70 (1), 45–53.

Easton, Kai. 2002. "Travelling through History, 'New' South Africa Icons: The Narratives of Krotoä-Eva and Saartje Baartman in Zoë Wicomb's *David's Story*." *Kunapipi* 24 (1–2), 237–50.

Edelman, Lee. 1994. *Homographesis: Essays in Gay Literary and Cultural Theory*. New York: Routledge.

Eilersen, Gillian Stead. 1996. *Bessie Head: Thunder behind Her Ears: Her Life and Writing*. Portsmouth, N.H.: Heinemann.

Eng, David. 2001. *Racial Castration: Managing Asian American Masculinity*. Durham, N.C.: Duke University Press.

Fanon, Frantz. 1967. *Black Skin, White Masks*. 1952. New York: Grove Press.

Faust, Drew Gilpin. 1982. *James Henry Hammond and the Old South: A Design for Mastery*. Baton Rouge: Louisiana State University Press.

Fausto-Sterling, Anne. 1995. "Gender, Race, and Nation: The Comparative Anatomy of 'Hottentot' Women in Europe 1815–1817." *Deviant Bodies*, edited by Jennifer Terry and Jacqueline Urla, 19–48. Bloomington: Indiana University Press.

Foucault, Michel. 1980. *The History of Sexuality*. Trans. Robert Hurley. New York: Vintage Books.

Fowler, Doreen. 2004. "Faulkner's Return to the Freudian Father: *Sanctuary* Reconsidered." *Modern Fiction Studies* 50 (2), 411–35.

Freud, Sigmund. 2003. *The Uncanny*. Edited by David McLintock. 1919. New York: Penguin Classic.

——. 1939. *Moses and Monotheism*. New York: Vintage Books.

Fusco, Coco. 1995. *English Is Broken Here: Notes on Cultural Fusion in the Americas*. New York: New Press.

Fuss, Diana. 1995. *Identification Papers*. New York: Routledge.

Gagiano, Annie. 2000. *Achebe, Head, Marechera: On Power and Change in Africa*. Boulder, Colo.: Lynne Rienner.

Gaines, Jane. 1992. "Competing Glances: Who Is Reading Robert Mapplethorpe's *Black Book*?" *New Formations* 16, 24–39.

Gardner, Susan. 1986. " 'Don't Ask for the True Story': A Memoir of Bessie Head." *Hecate* 12 (1–2), 110–29.

Garrett, James M. 1999. "Writing Community: Bessie Head and the Politics of Narrative." *Research in African Literatures* 30 (2), 122–135.

Gates, Henry Louis, Jr. 1997. *Thirteen Ways of Looking at a Black Man*. New York: Random House.

Genovese, Eugene D. 1976. *Roll, Jordan, Roll: The World the Slaves Made*. New York: Vintage.

George-Graves, Nadine. 2000. *The Royalty of Negro Vaudeville: The Whitman Sisters and the Negotiation of Race, Gender and Class in African American Theatre, 1900–1940*. New York: Palgrave Macmillan.

Giddings, Paula. 1992. "The Last Taboo." *Race-ing Justice, En-Gendering Power: Essays on Anita Hill, Clarence Thomas and the Construction of Social Reality*, edited by Toni Morrison, 441–70. New York: Pantheon.

Gilman, Sander. 1995. *Difference and Pathology: Stereotypes of Sexuality, Race and Madness*. Ithaca, N.Y.: Cornell University Press.

——. 1989. "Black Bodies, White Bodies: Toward an Iconography of Female Sexuality in Late Nineteenth-Century Art, Medicine and Literature." *Race, Writing and Difference*, edited by Henry Louis Gates Jr., 223–61. Chicago: University of Chicago Press.

Gilmore, Leigh. 2001. *The Limits of Autobiography: Trauma and Testimony*. Ithaca, N.Y.: Cornell University Press.

Gilroy, Paul. 1993. *The Black Atlantic: Modernity and Double Consciousness.* Cambridge, Mass.: Harvard University Press.

Goddard, Horace I. 2000. "Liberation and Self-Understanding: Bessie Head's Female Characters." *Kola,* 1 January.

Golbourne, Harry. 2001. "African Slaves and the Atlantic World." *Facing Up to the Past: Perspectives on the Commemoration of Slavery from Africa, the Americas and Europe,* edited by Gert Oostindie, 127–32. Kingston, Jamaica: Ian Randle.

Goldberg, Elizabeth Swanson. 2003. "Living the Legacy: Pain, Desire, and Narrative Time in Gayl Jones's *Corregidora.*" *Callaloo* 26 (2), 446–72.

Golden, Thelma, ed. 1994. *Black Male: Representations of Masculinity in Contemporary American Art.* New York: Whitney Museum of Modern Art.

Good, Kenneth. 1993. "At the Ends of the Ladder: Radical Inequalities in Botswana." *Journal of Modern African Studies* 31 (2), 203–30.

Gopnik, Adam. 2002. "New York Journal: A Purim Story: The Funny Thing about Being Jewish." *New Yorker,* 18 February, 124–31.

Gordimer, Nadine. 1983. "Living in the Interregnum." *New York Review of Books,* 20 January, 21–22, 24–29.

Gordon, Avery F. 1997. *Ghostly Matters: Haunting and the Sociological Imagination.* Minneapolis: University of Minnesota Press.

Gordon, Robert J. 1984. "The !Kung in the Kalahari Exchange: An Ethnohistorical Perspective." *Past and Present in Hunter Gatherer Studies,* edited by Carmel Schrire, 195–224. Orlando, Fla.: Academic Press.

Gordon-Reed, Annette. 2008. *The Hemingses of Monticello: An American Family.* New York: Norton.

Gottfried, Amy S. 1994. "Angry Arts: Silence, Speech, and Song in Gayl Jones's 'Corregidora.'" *African American Review* 28 (4), 559–70.

Gould, Stephen J. 1996. *The Mismeasure of Man.* New York: Norton.

——. 1985. *The Flamingo's Smile: Reflections in Natural History.* New York: Norton.

——. 1982. "The Hottentot Venus." *Natural History* 91 (9), 20–27.

Govan, Sandra. 1992. "Forbidden Fruits and Unholy Lusts: Illicit Sex in Black American Literature." *Erotique Noire/Black Erotica,* edited by Miriam Decosta-Willis, Reginald Martin, and Roseann P. Bell, 35–43. New York: Anchor.

Gray, Herman. 2000. "Cultural Politics as Outrageous." *Black Renaissance/Renaissance Noire* 3 (1), 92–101.

Grundmann, Roy. 1995. "Black Nationhood and the Rest in the West: An Interview with Isaac Julien." *Cineaste* 21 (1–2), 28–31.

Guldimann, Colette. 2003. "Bessie Head's *Maru*: Writing after the End of Romance." *Critical Essays on Bessie Head,* edited by Maxine Sample, 47–71. Westport, Conn.: Praeger.

Gunner, Liz. 1994. "Mothers, Daughters, and Madness in Works by Four Women Writers: Bessie Head, Jean Rhys, Tsitsi Dangarembga and Ama Ata Aidoo." *Alif: Journal of Comparative Poetics Civilization/Al-Junun wa al-Hadarah* 14, 136–51.

Halberstam, Judith. 2005. *In a Queer Time and Place: Transgender Bodies, Subcultural Lives.* Durham, N.C.: Duke University Press.

Hall, Stuart. 1998. "What Is This 'Black' in Black Popular Culture?" *Black Popular Culture*, edited by Michelle Wallace and Gina Dent, 21–37. Seattle: Bay Press.

———. 1997. "Fetishism and Disavowal." *Representation: Cultural Representations and Signifying Practices*, edited by Stuart Hall, 264–69. London: Sage.

———. 1996. "New Ethnicities." *Black British Cultural Studies: A Reader,* edited by Houston Baker, Manthia Diawara, and Ruth H. Lindeborg, 163–72. Chicago: University of Chicago Press.

Hall, Stuart, and David A. Bailey. 1992. "The Vertigo of Displacement: David A. Bailey and Stuart Hall Explore the Shifts in Black Photographic Practices in the 80s." *Ten 8: Critical Decade: Black British Photography in the 80s* 2 (3), 15–23.

Hall, Stuart, and Mark Sealy. 2001. "A Historical Context." *Different: A Historical Context,* edited by Stuart Hall and Mark Sealy, 4–32. London: Phaidon.

Handley, George B. 2004. "Oedipus in the Americas: *Lone Star* and the Reinvention of American Studies." *Forum for Modern Language Studies* 40 (2), 160–181.

Hanna, Cheryl. 2000–2001. "Sex Is Not a Sport: Consent and Violence in Criminal Law." *Boston College Law Review* 42, 239–90.

Harkins, Gillian. 2003. "Seduction by Law: Sexual Property and Testimonial Possession in *Thereafter Johnnie.*" *Discourse* 25 (1–2), 138–65.

Hartman, Saidiya. 2007. *Lose Your Mother: A Journey along the Atlantic Slave Route.* New York: Farrar, Straus, and Giroux.

———. 2002. "The Time of Slavery." *South Atlantic Quarterly* 101 (4), 757–77.

———. 1997. *Scenes of Subjection: Terror, Slavery, and Self-Making in Nineteenth-Century America.* New York: Oxford University Press.

Head, Bessie. 1995. *The Cardinals, with Meditations and Short Stories.* Edited by M. J. Daymond. Portsmouth, N.H.: Heinemann.

———. 1990. *A Woman Alone: Autobiographical Writings.* Edited by Craig MacKenzie. Portsmouth, N.H.: Heinemann.

———. 1989a. "Bessie Head Interviewed by Michelle Adler, Susan Gardner, Tobeka Mda, and Patricia Sandler." *Between the Lines: Interviews with Bessie Head, Sheila Roberts, Ellen Kuzwayo, Miriam Tlali,* edited by Craig MacKenzie and Cherry Clayton, 5–30. Grahamstown, South Africa: National English Literary Museum.

———. 1989b. *Tales of Tenderness and Power.* Edited by Gillian S. Eilersen. Portsmouth, N.H.: Heinemann.

———. 1977. *A Question of Power.* Portsmouth, N.H.: Heinemann.

———. 1971. *Maru.* Portsmouth, N.H.: Heinemann.

Heron, Gil Scott. 1978. "Bicentennial Blues." *The Mind of Gil Scott Heron.*

Hirsch, Marianne. 2001. "Surviving Images: Holocaust Photographs and the Work of Post-memory." *Yale Journal of Criticism* 14 (1), 5–37.

———. 1999. "Projected Memory: Holocaust Photographs in Personal and Public Fantasy." *Acts of Memory: Cultural Recall in the Present,* edited by Mieke Bal, Jonathan Crewe, and Leo Spitzer, 3–23. Hanover, N.H.: University Press of New England.

Hirst, Alex. 1988. Introduction to *Black Male/White Male,* by Rotimi Fani-Kayode. Hong Kong: South Sea International Press.

Hoad, Neville. 2005. "Thabo Mbeki's AIDS Blues: The Intellectual, the Archive, and the Pandemic." *Public Culture* 17 (1), 101–27.

Hobbs, Robert. 2003. "Reading Black through White in the Work of Kara Walker." *Association of Art History* 26 (3), 422–41.

———. 2001. *Kara Walker Slavery! Slavery! The 25th International Bienal of Sao Paulo, Brazil.* Museum catalogue, 9–48. São Paulo: International Arts and Artists.

Hobson, Janell. 2005. *Venus in the Dark: Blackness and Beauty in Popular Culture.* New York: Routledge.

Hochberg, Gil Zehava. 2003. "Mother, Memory, History: Maternal Genealogies in Gayl Jones's *Corregidora* and Simone Schwarz-Bart's *Pluie et vent sur Telumee Miracle.*" *Research in African Literature* 34 (2), 1–12.

Holland, Sharon Patricia. 2000. *Raising the Dead: Readings of Death and (Black) Subjectivity.* Durham, N.C.: Duke University Press.

Holloway, Karla. 2002. *Passed On: African American Mourning Stories: A Memorial.* Durham, N.C.: Duke University Press.

Honour, Hugh. 1989. *The Image of the Black in Western Art IV: From the American Revolution to World War I, Slaves and Liberators.* Cambridge, Mass.: Harvard University Press.

hooks, bell. 1996. *Reel to Real: Race, Sex and Class at the Movies.* Boston: South End Press.

hooks, bell, and Isaac Julien. 1991. "States of Desire." *Transition* 53 (3), 168–84.

Horvitz, Deborah. 1998. " 'Sadism Demands a Story': Oedipus, Feminism, and Sexuality in Gayl Jones's 'Corregidora' and Dorothy Allison's 'Bastard out of Carolina.' " *Contemporary Literature* 39 (2), 238–62.

Ibrahim, Huma. 1996. *Bessie Head: Subversive Identities in Exile.* Charlottesville: University Press of Virginia.

Irlam, Shaun. 2004. "Unraveling the Rainbow: The Remission of Nation in Post-Apartheid Literature." *South Atlantic Quarterly* 103 (4), 696–718.

Jacobs, Harriet A. 1987. *Incidents in the Life of a Slave Girl: Written by Herself.* 1861. Edited by Jean Fagan Yellin. Cambridge, Mass.: Harvard University Press.

Jenkins, Sidney. 1995. *Look Away! Look Away! Look Away!* Annandale-on-Hudson, N.Y.: Bard College, Center for Curatorial Studies.

Jimenez, Marilyn. 1999. "Naked Scene / Seen Naked: Performing the Hott-En-Tot." *Looking Forward, Looking Black*, edited by Jo Anna Isaak, 11–15. Geneva, N.Y.: Hobart and William Smith Colleges Press.

Jones, Gayl. 1991. *Liberating Voices: Oral Tradition in African American Literature.* Cambridge, Mass.: Harvard University Press.

———. 1986. *Corregidora.* 1975. Boston: Beacon Press.

———. 1985. "About My Work." *Black Women Writers*, edited by Mari Evans, 233–35. London: Pluto Press.

———. 1977a. *Eva's Man.* Boston: Northeastern University Press.

———. 1977b. *White Rat.* Boston: Northeastern University Press.

Joselit, David. 2000. "Notes on Surface: Toward a Genealogy of Flatness." *Art History* 23 (1), 19–34.

Julien, Isaac. 2002. "The Long Road: Isaac Julien in Conversation with B. Ruby Rich." *Art Journal* 61, 50–67.

——. 2001. Tate Gallery talk. Availabe online at http://channel.tate.org.uk/media/25802205001.

——. 2000a. "Confessions of a Snow Queen: Notes on the making of *The Attendant*." *The Film Art of Isaac Julien*, edited by Amanda Cruz et al., 79–82. 1993. Annandale-on-Hudson, N.Y.: Bard College, Center for Curatorial Studies.

——. 2000b. "Black Is, Black Ain't: Notes on De-Essentializing Black Identities." *The Film Art of Isaac Julien*, edited by Amanda Cruz et al., 73–77. 1992. Annandale-on-Hudson, N.Y.: Bard College, Center for Curatorial Studies.

——. 1999. *Three (The Conservator's Dream)*. 6 mins. color/sepia 16mm to video.

——. 1997. "Resisting Representations." University of Vienna website.

——. 1996a. *Trussed*.

——. 1996b. "Black British Cinema—Diaspora Cinema." *New Histories*. Exhibition catalogue, 60–64. Boston: Institute of Contemporary Art.

——. 1993. *The Attendant*. 8 mins. black and white/color.

Julien, Isaac, and Kobena Mercer. 2000a. "True Confessions." *The Film Art of Isaac Julien*, edited by Amanda Cruz et al., 57–61. 1986. Annandale-on-Hudson, N.Y.: Bard College, Center for Curatorial Studies.

——. 2000b. "De Margin and De Center." *The Film Art of Isaac Julien*, edited by Amanda Cruz et al., 62–71. 1988. Annandale-on-Hudson, N.Y.: Bard College, Center for Curatorial Studies.

——. 1988. "Race, Sexual Politics and Black Masculinity: A Dossier." *Male Order: Unwrapping Masculinity*, edited by Rowena Chapman and Jonathan Rutherford, 97–164. London: Lawrence and Wishart.

Katrak, Ketu. 1995. " 'This Englishness Will Kill You': Colonialist Education and Female Socialization in Merle Hodge's *Crick Crack, Monkey* and Bessie Head's *Maru*." *College Literature* 22 (1), 62–78.

Keegan, Timothy. 1997. *Colonial South Africa and the Origins of Racial Order*. Charlottesville: University Press of Virginia.

Keizer, Arlene. 2004. *Black Subjects: Identity Formation in the Contemporary Narrative of Slavery*. Ithaca, N.Y.: Cornell University Press.

Koestenbaum, Wayne. 1993. *The Queen's Throat: Opera, Homosexuality and the Mystery of Desire*. New York: Penguin.

Kozain, Rustum. 1996. Miscast: Three Views on the Exhibition curated by Pippa Skotnes with Jos Thorne in the South African National Gallery (14 April–14 September 1996) by (1) Carmel Schrire (2) Rustum Kozain (3) Yvette Abrahams. *Southern African Review of Books* 44 (July/August 1996). Online. University of Ulm.

Kuspit, Donald. 2003. "Kara Walker's Cakewalk." *ArtNet*, 16 July–28 September. Online.

Landau, Paul S. 1996. "With Camera and Gun in Southern Africa: Inventing the Image of Bushmen, c. 1880 to 1935." *Miscast: Negotiating the Presence of the Bush-*

men, edited by Pippa Skotnes, 129–41. Cape Town, South Africa: University of Cape Town Press.

Lane, Christopher, ed. 1998. *The Psychoanalysis of Race*. New York: Columbia University Press.

Lauderdale Graham, Sandra. 1991. "Slavery's Impasse: Slave Prostitutes, Small-Time Mistresses and the Brazilian Law of 1871." *Comparative Studies in Society and History* 33 (4), 669–94.

Lewis, Desiree. 2005. "Bessie Head's Freedoms." Chimurenga website http://chimurenga.co.za/.

——. 1996. "The Cardinals and Bessie Head's Allegories of Self." *World Literature Today* 70 (1), 73–77.

Lindberg, Kathryne V. 2005. "Roots, Breaks, and the Performance of a Black Left Critique." *American Literary History* 17 (4), 831–55.

Lindfors, Bernth. 1985. "Courting the Hottentot Venus." *Africa* (Rome) 40, 133–48.

——. 1983. "The Hottentot Venus and Other African Attractions in Nineteenth-century England." *Australasian Drama Studies* 1 (2), 83–104.

Lionnet, Françoise. 1993. "Geographies of Pain: Captive Bodies and Violent Acts in the Fictions of Myriam Warner-Vieyra, Gayl Jones, and Bessie Head." *Callaloo* 16 (1), 132–52.

Loewen, James W. 1999. *Lies across America: What Our Historic Sites Got Wrong*. New York: Touchstone Books.

Lott, Eric. 1995. *Love and Theft: Blackface Minstrelsy and the American Working Class*. New York: Oxford University Press.

Lott, Tommy. 2000. "Kara Walker Speaks: A Public Conversation on Racism, Art, and Politics with Tommy Lott." *Black Renaissance/Renaissance Noire* 3 (1), 69–91.

Lowe, Lisa. 2006. "The Intimacies of Four Continents." *Haunted by Empire: Geographies of Intimacy in North American History*, edited by Ann Laura Stoler, 191–212. Durham, N.C.: Duke University Press.

Magowan, Kimberly. 1999. "Strange Bedfellows: Incest and Miscegenation in Thomas Dixon, William Faulkner, Ralph Ellison, and John Sayles." Ph.D. dissertation, University of California, Berkeley.

Magubane, Zine. 2001. "Which Bodies Matter? Feminism, Poststructuralism, Race, and the Curious Theoretical Odyssey of the 'Hottentot Venus.'" *Gender and Society* 15 (6), 816–34.

Manring, M. M. 1998. *Slave in a Box: The Strange Career of Aunt Jemima*. Charlottesville: University of Virginia Press.

Marquard, Jean. 1978–79. "Bessie Head: Exile and Community in Southern Africa." *London Magazine*, December–January, 48–61, 52–53.

Marriott, David. 2000. *On Black Men*. New York: Columbia University Press.

Mbeki, Thabo. 2002. "Letter from the President." African National Congress website, http//www.anc.org.za/.

Mbembe, Achille. 2003. "Necropolitics." *Public Culture* 15 (1), 11–40.

——. 2001a. *On the Postcolony*. Berkeley: University of California Press.

——. 2001b. "The Subject of the World." *Facing Up to the Past: Perspectives on the Commemoration of Slavery from Africa, the Americas and Europe*, edited by Gert Oostindie, 21–28. Kingston, Jamaica: Ian Randle.

McClintock, Anne. 1993. "Maid to Order: Commercial Fetishism and Gender Power." *Social Text* 37, 87–116.

McKible, Adam. 1994. " 'These Are the Facts of the Darky's History': Thinking History and Reading Names in Four African American Texts." *African American Review* 28 (2), 223–35.

McKittrick, Katherine. 2005. *Demonic Grounds: Black Women and the Cartographies of Struggle*. Minneapolis: University of Minnesota Press.

McKittrick, Katherine, and Clyde Woods. 2007. *Black Geographies and the Politics of Place*. Boston: South End Press.

McLaurin, Melton A. 1991. *Celia: A Slave*. Athens: University of Georgia Press.

Memmi, Albert. 1991. *The Colonizer and the Colonized*. 1957. Boston: Beacon Press.

Menand, Louis. 2002. *The Metaphysical Club: A Story of Ideas in America*. New York: Farrar, Straus, and Giroux.

Mercer, Kobena. 2003. "Diaspora Culture and the Dialogic Imagination." *Theorizing Diaspora*, edited by Jana Evans Braziel and Anita Mannur, 247–60. Cornwall, England: Blackwell.

——. 2001. "Avid Iconographies." *Isaac Julien*, edited by Kobena Mercer and Chris Darke, 7–21. London: Ellipsis.

——. 1997a. "Just Looking for Trouble: Robert Mapplethorpe and Fantasies of Race." *Dangerous Liaisons: Gender, Nation, and Postcolonial Perspectives*, edited by Anne McClintock, Aamir Mufti, and Ella Shohat, 240–55. Minnesota: University of Minnesota Press.

——. 1997b. "Witness at the Crossroads: An Artist's Journey in Post-colonial Space." *Relocating the Remains*, Keith Piper. Exhibition catalogue, 12–85. London: Institute of International Visual Arts.

——. 1996. "Decolonisation and Disappointment: Reading Fanon's Sexual Politics." *The Fact of Blackness: Frantz Fanon and Visual Representation*, edited by Alan Read, 114–31. Seattle: Bay Press.

——. 1995. "Busy in the Ruins of Wretched Phantasia." *Mirage: Enigmas of Race, Difference and Desire*, edited by David Bailey, 10–55. London: Institute of International Visual Arts.

——. 1994. *Welcome to the Jungle: New Positions in Black Cultural Studies*. New York: Routledge.

——. 1991. "Skin Head Sex Thing: Racial Difference and the Homoerotic Imaginary." *How Do I Look: Queer Film and Video*, edited by Bad Object-Choices, 169–210. Seattle: Bay Press.

Meyer, Richard. 2002. *Outlaw Representation: Censorship and Homosexuality in Twentieth-Century American Art*. New York: Oxford University Press.

——. 1991. "Imagining Sadomasochism: Robert Mapplethorpe and the Masquerade of Photography." 10 July. Available online at http://www.queerculturalcenter.org/.

Millin, Sarah Gertrude. 1924. *God's Stepchildren*. New York: Boni and Liveright.

Morgenstern, Naomi. 1996. "Mother's Milk and Sister's Blood: Trauma and the Neo-Slave Narrative." *Differences: A Journal of Feminist Critical Studies* 8 (2), 101–27.

Morley, David, and Kuan-Hsing Chen. 1996. *Stuart Hall: Critical Dialogues in Cultural Studies.* New York: Routledge.

Morrison, Paul. 2002. *The Explanation for Everything: Essays on Sexual Subjectivity.* New York: New York University Press.

Morrison, Toni. 1997. "Home." *The House That Race Built: Black Americans, U.S. Terrain,* edited by Wahneema Lubiano and Arnold Rampersad, 3–13. New York: Pantheon.

——. 1992. *Playing in the Dark: Whiteness and the Literary Imagination.* Cambridge, Mass.: Harvard University Press.

——. 1987. *Beloved.* New York: Plume Contemporary Fiction.

Moten, Fred. 2003. *In the Break: The Aesthetics of Black Radical Tradition.* Minneapolis: University of Minnesota Press.

——. 2002. "Black Mo'nin." *Loss: The Politics of Mourning,* edited by David L. Eng and David Kazanjian, 59–76. Berkeley: University of California Press.

——. 1999. Book review. *Drama Review* 43 (4), 169–75.

Motzafi-Haller, Pnina. 2002. *Fragmented Worlds, Coherent Lives: The Politics of Difference in Botswana.* Westport, Conn.: Greenwood.

——. 1994. "When the Bushman Are Known as Basarwa: Gender, Ethnicity, and Differentiation in Rural Botswana." *American Ethnologist* 21 (3), 539–63.

Mullen, Harryette. 1994. "Optic White: Blackness and the Production of Whiteness." *Diacritics* 24 (3–4), 71–89.

Muñoz, Jose. 1999. *Disidentifications: Queers of Color and the Performance of Politics.* Minneapolis: University of Minnesota Press.

Murray, Timothy. 1997. *Drama Trauma: Specters of Race and Sexuality in Performance Art.* New York: Routledge.

Nazareth, Peter. 2006. "Path of Thunder: Meeting Bessie Head." *Research in African Literatures* 37 (4), 211–29.

Nero, Charles. 2003. "Transvesting at Atlanta: Booker T. Washington as Queen Esther." Unpublished manuscript.

Ngwane, Zolani. 2001. " 'The Long Conversation': The Enduring Salience of Nineteenth-century Missionary/Colonial Encounters in Post-apartheid South Africa." *Interventions* 3 (1), 65–75.

Nixon, Rob. 1998. "Refugees and Homecomings: Bessie Head and the End of Exile." *Travellers' Tales: Narratives of Home and Displacement,* edited by George Robertson et al., 114–28. New York: Routledge.

Nkosi, Lewis. 1981. *Tasks and Masks: Themes and Styles of African Literature.* Harlow, Essex: Longman.

Norval, Aletta J. 2001. "Reconstructing National Identity and Renegotiating Memory: The Work of the TRC." *States of Imagination: Ethnographic Explorations of the Postcolonial State,* edited by Thomas Blom Hansen and Finn Stepputat, 182–203. Durham, N.C.: Duke University Press.

O'Brien, Anthony. 2001. *Against Normalization: Writing Radical Democracy in South Africa.* Durham, N.C.: Duke University Press.

Obrist, Hans-Ulrich. 1998–1999. "Everything Can Be Pictured in the Form of Shadows: Conversation with Kara Walker." Available online at Museum in Progress, www.mip.at.

Ogede, Ode. 1995. "Narrating History with a Vengeance: Interracial Marriage as Bessie Head's Doctrine for Racial Harmony in *Maru*." *International Fiction Review* 22, 25–30.

O'Grady, Lorraine. 2003. "Olympia's Maid: Reclaiming Black Female Sexuality." *The Feminism and Visual Culture Reader*, edited by Amelia Jones, 174–87. New York: Routledge.

Olaogun, Modupe. 2002. "Slavery and Etiological Discourse in the Writing of Ama Ata Aidoo, Bessie Head, and Buchi Emecheta." *Research in Africa–Literatures* 33 (2), 171–93.

———. 1994. "Irony and Schizophrenia in Bessie Head's *Maru*." *Research in African Literatures* 25 (4), 69–87.

Oliver, Kelly. 2001. *Witnessing: Beyond Recognition*. Minneapolis: University of Minnesota Press.

Orgeron, Devin. 2000. "Re-Membering History in Isaac Julien's 'The Attendant.'" *Film Quarterly* 53 (4), 32–40.

Pacteau, Francette. 1999. "Dark Continent." *With Other Eyes: Looking at Race and Gender in Visual Culture*, edited by Lisa Bloom, 88–104. Minneapolis: University of Minnesota Press.

Parker, Emma. 2001. "A New Hystery: History and Hysteria in Toni Morrison's *Beloved*." *Twentieth Century Literature* 47, 1–19.

Pendleton, David. 2001. "Out of the Ghetto: Queerness, Homosexual Desire and the Time-Image." *Strategies* 14 (1), 47–62.

Phelan, Peggy. 1993. *Unmarked: The Politics of Performance*. New York: Routledge.

Pindell, Howardeena. 2002. "Diaspora/Realities/Strategies." Paper presented at Trade Routes, History, Geography, Culture: Towards a Definition of Culture in the Late 20th Century, Johannesburg, South Africa, October 1997, updated with a new postscript, January 2002. Available at the UK Online website.

Pinder, Kymberly, ed. 2002. *Race-ing Art History: Critical Readings in Race and Art History*. New York: Routledge.

Qureshi, Sadiah. 2004. "Displaying Sara Baartman, the 'Hottentot Venus.'" *History of Science* 42 (1), 233–57.

Read, Alan, ed. 1996. *The Fact of Blackness: Frantz Fanon and Visual Representation*. Seattle: Bay Press.

Reinhardt, Mark. 2003. "The Art of Racial Profiling." *Kara Walker: Narratives of a Negress*, edited by Ian Berry, Darby English, Vivian Patterson, and Mark Reinhardt, 91–101. Cambridge, Mass.: MIT Press.

Roach, Joseph. 1996. *Cities of the Dead: Circum-Atlantic Performance*. New York: Columbia University Press.

Roberts, Diane. 1984. *The Myth of Aunt Jemima: Representations of Race and Region*. New York: Routledge.

Robins, Steven. 1998. "Silence in My Father's House: Memory, Nationalism, and

Narratives of the Body." *Negotiating the Past: The Making of Memory in South Africa*, edited by Sarah Nuttall and Carli Coetzee, 120–40. Cape Town, South Africa: Oxford University Press.

Rogin, Michael. 1996. *Blackface, White Noise: Jewish Immigrants in the Hollywood Melting Pot*. Berkeley: University of California Press.

Rogoff, Irit. 2001. " 'Without': A Conversation" (with Peggy Phelan). *Art Journal* 60 (3), 34–41.

Rooney, Caroline. 2000. *African Literature, Animism and Politics*. New York: Routledge.

——. 1992. " 'Dangerous Knowledge' and the Poetics of Survival: A Reading of *Our Sister Killjoy* and *A Question of Power*." *Motherlands: Black Women's Writing from Africa, the Caribbean and South Asia*, edited by Susheila Nasta, 99–126. New Brunswick, N.J.: Rutgers University Press.

Rose, Jacqueline. 2007. *The Last Resistance*. New York: Verso.

——. 2005. *The Question of Zion*. Princeton: Princeton University Press.

——. 2004. "The Body of Evil." *New Formations* 53 (1), 115–29.

——. 2003. *On Not Being Able to Sleep: Psychoanalysis and the Modern World*. Princeton: Princeton University Press.

——. 1996. *States of Fantasy: The Clarendon Lectures in English Literature 1994*. Oxford: Clarendon Press.

Rose, Phyllis. 1997. *The Year of Reading Proust: A Memoir in Real Time*. New York: Scribner.

Rowell, Charles H. 1982. "An Interview with Gayl Jones." *Callaloo* 16 (3), 32–53.

Rubin, Gayle S. 1993. "Thinking Sex: Notes for a Radical Theory of the Politics of Sexuality." *The Lesbian and Gay Studies Reader*. Edited by Henry Abelove, Michèle Aina Barale, and David M. Halperin, 3–44. New York: Routledge.

Rubin, Louis D., Jr. 1988. Foreword to *Secret and Sacred: The Diaries of James Henry Hammond, a Southern Slaveholder*. Edited by Carol Bleser, vii–xiv. New York: Oxford University Press.

Rushdy, Ashraf. 2001. *Remembering Generations: Race and Family in Contemporary African American Fiction*. Chapel Hill: University of North Carolina Press.

——. 2000. " 'Relate Sexual to Historical': Race, Resistance, and Desire in Gayl Jones's *Corregidora*." *African American Review* 34 (2), 273–97.

——. 1999. *Neo-Slave Narratives: Studies in the Social Logic of a Literary Form*. Oxford: Oxford University Press.

Saks, Eva. 2000. "Representing Miscegenation Law." *Interracialism: Black-White Intermarriage in American History, Literature, and Law*, edited by Werner Sollors, 61–81. Oxford: Oxford University Press.

Saltz, Jerry. 1996. "Kara Walker: Ill-Will and Desire." *Flash Art* 29, November–December, 82–86.

Sample, Maxine, ed. 2003. *Critical Essays on Bessie Head*. Westport, Conn.: Praeger.

Sanders, Mark. 2002. *Contingencies: The Intellectual and Apartheid*. Durham, N.C.: Duke University Press.

Schiebinger, Londa. 1993. *Nature's Body: Gender in the Making of Modern Science*. Boston: Beacon Press.

Scully, Pamela. "Malintzin, Pocahontas, and Krotoä: Indigenous Women and Myth Models of the Atlantic World." *Journal of Colonialism and Colonial History* 6, no. 3 (2005), e-journal.

Sedinger, Tracey. 2002. "Nation and Identification: Psychoanalysis, Race, and Sexual Difference." *Cultural Critique* 50 (1), 40–73.

Shange, Ntozake. 1992. "Fore/Play." *Erotique Noire/Black Erotica*, edited by Miriam Decosta-Willis, Reginald Martin, and Roseann P. Bell, xix-xx. New York: Anchor.

———. 1986. "Foreword." *Robert Mapplethorpe: Black Book*, n.p. New York: St. Martin's Press.

Sharpe, Christina. 2005. "Gayl Jones' 'Days That Were Pages of Hysteria.'" *Revisiting Slave Narratives / Les avatars contemporains des récits d'esclaves*, edited by Judith Misrahi-Barak, 159–76. Montpellier, France: Paul Valéry University.

———. 2000. "The Costs of Re-membering: What's at Stake in Gayl Jones's *Corregidora*." *African American Performance and Theatre History: A Critical Reader*, edited by David Krasner and Harry Elam, 306–27. New York: Oxford University Press.

———. 1999. Kara Walker, and Michael J. Charles. *Looking Forward, Looking Black*, exhibition catalogue, edited by Jo Anna Isaak, 40–44. Geneva, N.Y.: Hobart and William Smith Colleges Press.

Sharpley-Whiting, T. Denean. 1999. *Black Venus: Sexualized Savages, Primal Fears, and Primitive Narratives in French*. Durham, N.C.: Duke University Press.

Shaw, Gwendolyn DuBois. 2004. *Seeing the Unspeakable: The Art of Kara Walker*. Durham, N.C.: Duke University Press.

———. 2000. "Final Cut." *Parkett* 59, 128–37.

Sheets, Hilarie M. 2002. "Cut It Out! Kara Walker's Cutout Silhouettes of Antebellum Racial Stereotypes Are Lewd, Provocative—and Beautiful." *ArtNews* 101 (4), 26.

Silverman, Kaja. 1996. *The Threshold of the Visible World*. New York: Routledge.

Simon, Bruce. 1997. "Traumatic Repetition: Gayl Jones's *Corregidora*." *Race Consciousness: African-American Studies for the New Century*, edited by Judith Jackson Fossett and Jeffrey A. Tucker, 93–112. New York: New York University Press.

Skotnes, Pippa. 2001. "'Civilised off the Face of the Earth': Museum Display and the Silencing of the/Xam." *Poetics Today* 22 (2), 299–321.

———. 1996. *Miscast: Negotiating the Presence of the Bushman*. Exhibition catalogue. Cape Town, South Africa: University of Cape Town Press.

Sobieszek, Robert A. 2000. *Ghost in the Shell: Photography and the Human Soul, 1850–2000. Essays on Camera Portraiture*. Cambridge, Mass.: Los Angeles County Museum of Art and MIT Press.

Sollors, Werner. 1997. *Neither Black nor White yet Both: Thematic Explorations of Interracial Literature*. Cambridge, Mass.: Harvard University Press.

Solomon-Godeau, Abigail. 1995. "Representing Women: The Politics of Self-Representation." *Reframings: New American Feminist Photographies*, edited by Diane Neumaier, 296–310. Philadelphia: Temple University Press.

Spector, Nancy. 2000. "Kara Walker's 'Theater of Cruelty.'" *Safety Curtain: Kara Walker.* Museum in Progress, 36–39. Hanover, Germany: P and S Wein.

Spillers, Hortense. 2003a. "Changing the Letter: The Yokes, the Jokes of Discourse, or, Mrs. Stowe, Mr. Reed." *Black, White, and in Color: Essays on American Literature and Culture,* edited by Hortense Spillers, 176–203. Chicago: University of Chicago Press.

——. 2003b. "'The Little Man at Chehaw Station' Today." *Boundary 2* 30 (2), 6–19.

——. 2003c. "Mama's Baby, Papa's Maybe: An American Grammar Book." *Black, White, and in Color: Essays on American Literature and Culture,* edited by Hortense Spillers, 203–29. Chicago: University of Chicago Press.

——. 2003d. "All the Things You Could Be by Now, If Sigmund Freud's Wife Was Your Mother: Psychoanalysis and Race." *Black, White, and in Color: Essays on American Literature and Culture,* edited by Hortense Spillers, 376–427. Chicago: University of Chicago Press.

Steffen, Therese. 2002. "Between Transnationalism and globalization: Kara Walker's Cultural Hybridities." *Globalization.* SPELL: Swiss Papers in English Language and Literature. Edited by Frances Ilmberger and Alan Robinson, 89–112. Tübingen: Gunter Narr Verlag.

St. John, Maria. 2001. "'It Ain't Fittin': Cinematic and Fantasmatic Contours of Mammy in *Gone With the Wind* and Beyond." *Studies in Gender and Sexuality* 2 (2), 129–62.

——. 1999. "Cinematic and Fantasmatic Contours of Mammy: A Psychoanalytic Exploration of Race, Fantasy and Cultural Representation." *fort/da: The Journal of the Northern California Society for Psychoanalytic Psychology* 5 (2), 621.

Stoler, Ann Laura. 2006. "Tense and Tender Ties: The Politics of Comparison in North American History and (Post) Colonial Studies." *Haunted by Empire: Geographies of Intimacy in North American History,* edited by Ann Laura Stoler, 1–22. Durham, N.C.: Duke University Press.

——. 1995. *Race and the Education of Desire: Foucault's History of Sexuality and the Colonial Order of Things.* Durham, N.C.: Duke University Press.

Stowe, Harriet Beecher. 1982. *Uncle Tom's Cabin: Or Life among the Lowly.* 1852. New York: Bantam.

Strother, Z. S. 1999. "Display of the Body Hottentot." *Africans on Stage: Studies in Ethnological Show Business,* edited by Bernth Lindfors, 1–61. Bloomington: Indiana University Press.

Stychin, Carl F. 1996. "Promoting a Sexuality: Law and Lesbian and Gay Visual Culture in America." *Outlooks: Lesbian and Gay Sexualities and Visual Cultures,* edited by Peter Horn and Reina Lewis, 147–58. New York: Routledge.

Tate, Claudia C. 1979. "An Interview with Gayl Jones." *Black American Literature Forum* 13 (4), 142–48.

Taylor, Jane. 1996. "Arts of Resistance, Acts of Construction: Thoughts on the Contexts of South African Art, 1985–1995." *World Literature Today* 70 (1), 93–98.

Trouillot, Michel-Rolph. 1995. *Silencing the Past: Power and the Production of History.* Boston: Beacon Press.

Veneciano, Jorge Daniel. 1995. "Invisible Men: Race, Representation, and Exhibition(ism)." *Afterimage,* September–October, 11–15.

Vergés, Françoise. 1999a. "Colonizing Citizenship." *Radical Philosophy* 95, May–June, 3–7.

———. 1999b. *Monsters and Revolutionaries: Colonial Family Romance and Métissage.* Durham, N.C.: Duke University Press.

———. 1996. "Chains of Madness, Chains of Colonialism: Fanon and Freedom." *The Fact of Blackness: Frantz Fanon and Visual Representation,* edited by Alan Read, 46–75. Seattle: Bay Press.

Vigne, Randolph. 1991. *A Gesture of Belonging: Letters from Bessie Head 1965–1979.* New York: Heinemann.

Wagner, Anne M. 2003. "Kara Walker: The Black-White Relation." *Kara Walker: Narratives of a Negress,* edited by Ian Berry, Darby English, Vivian Patterson, and Mark Reinhardt, 91–101. Cambridge, Mass.: MIT Press.

Walker, Hamza. 1997. "Cut It Out." The Renaissance Society at the University of Chicago, newsletter, January, 3–18.

Walker, Kara. 2003a. "The Melodrama of *Gone with the Wind.*" Kara Walker. Art in the Twenty-First Century. Available online at pbs art:21 website.

———. 2003b. "Projecting Fictions: Insurrection! Our Tools Were Rudimentary, Yet We Pressed On." Kara Walker. Art in the Twenty-First Century. Available online at pbs art:21 website.

———. 2002a. "I Hate Being Lion Fodder: An Interview/Conversation via Email between Darius James and Kara Walker." db-art website.

———. 2002b. *Kara Walker.* Edited by Kara Walker, Stephan Berg, Silke Boerma, Eugenie Joo, and Robert Hobbs. Kunstverein Hannover.

———. 1999. "MOMA Conversations." Museum of Modern Art website.

———. 1998. *Kara Walker: The Renaissance Society at the University of Chicago,* 12 January–23 February, 1997. New York: Distributed Art Publications.

———. 1997. "The Big Black Mammy of the Antebellum South Is the Embodiment of History." *Kara Walker.* The Renaissance Society at the University of Chicago, newsletter, 12 January–23 February.

Wallace, Maurice O. 2002. *Constructing the Black Masculine: Identity and Ideality in African American Men's Literature and Culture, 1775–1995.* Durham, N.C.: Duke University Press.

Wallace, Michele. 2005. *Dark Designs and Visual Culture.* Durham, N.C.: Duke University Press.

———. 2003. "The Enigma of the Negress Kara Walker." *Kara Walker: Narratives of a Negress,* edited by Ian Berry, Darby English, Vivian Patterson, and Mark Reinhardt, 175–79. Cambridge, Mass.: MIT Press.

———. 2000. "*Uncle Tom's Cabin:* Before and after the Jim Crow Era." *Drama Review* 44 (1), 136–56.

Wallis, Brian. 1995. "Black Bodies, White Science: Louis Agassiz's Slave Daguerreotypes." *American Art* 9 (2), 189–219.

Ward, Jerry W., Jr. 1982. "Escape from Trublem: The Fiction of Gayl Jones." *Callaloo* 16 (3), 95–104.

Washington-Williams, Essie Mae, and William Stadiem. 2005. *Dear Senator: A Memoir by the Daughter of Strom Thurmond*. New York: Regan Books.

Weeks, Jeffrey. 1995. *Invented Moralities: Sexual Values in an Age of Uncertainty*. New York: Columbia University Press.

Weintraub, Linda. 2003. *In the Making: Creative Options for Contemporary Art*. New York: Distributed Art Publishers.

Western, John. 1997. *Outcast Cape Town*. Berkeley: University of California Press.

White, Louise. 1997. "The Traffic in Heads: Bodies, Borders, and the Articulation of Regional Histories." *Journal of Southern African Studies* 23 (2), 325–38.

Wicomb, Zoë. 2001. *David's Story*. New York: Feminist Press.

———. 1998. "Shame and Identity: The Case of the Coloured in South Africa." *Writing South Africa: Literature, Apartheid, and Democracy, 1970–1995*, edited by Derek Attridge and Rosemary Jolly, 91–107. Cambridge: Cambridge University Press.

———. 1996. "To Hear the Variety of Discourses." *South African Feminisms: Writing, Theory, and Criticism 1990–1994*, edited by M. J. Daymond, 45–55. 1990. New York: Garland.

———. 1993. Interviewed by Eva Hunter. *Between the Lines II: Interviews with Nadine Gordimer, Menán du Plessis, Zoë Wicomb, Lauretta Ngcobo*, edited by Eva Hunter and Craig MacKenzie, 79–96. Grahamstown, South Africa: National English Literary Museum.

Williams, Linda. 2002. *Playing the Race Card: Melodramas of Black and White from Uncle Tom to O. J. Simpson*. Princeton: Princeton University Press.

Williams, Patricia J. 2004. "Uncommon Ground: Diary of a Mad Law Professor." *The Nation*, 5 April.

———. 1996. "My Best White Friend: Cinderella Revisited." *The New Yorker* 72 (2), 94–97.

Wilson, Judith. 2003. "One Way or Another: Black Feminist Visual Theory." *The Feminism and Visual Culture Reader*, edited by Amelia Jones, 22–26. New York: Routledge.

Wiss, Rosemary. 1994. "Lipreading: Remembering Saartjie Baartman." *Australian Journal of Anthropology* 5 (1–2), 11–21.

Wood, Marcus. 2003. *Slavery, Empathy, and Pornography*. New York: Oxford University Press.

———. 2000. *Blind Memory: Visual Representations of Slavery in England and America 1780–1865*. New York: Routledge.

Wright, Richard. 1989. *Eight Men*. 1961. New York: Harper Perennial.

Wynter, Sylvia. 1992. "No Humans Involved: An Open Letter to My Colleagues." *Voices of the African Diaspora* 8 (2), 13–18.

Young, Hershini. 2005. *Haunting Capital: Memory, Text and the Black Diasporic Body (Re-Encounters with Colonialism)*. Hanover, N.H.: Dartmouth University Press.

Young, Jean. 1997. "The Re-objectification and Re-commodification of Saartjie Baartman in Suzan-Lori Parks's 'Venus.'" *African American Review* 31 (4), 699–709.

Zaeske, Susan. 2000. "Unveiling Esther as Pragmatic Radical Rhetoric." *Philosophy and Rhetoric* 33 (3), 193–220.

Žižek, Slavoj. 1997. *The Plague of Fantasies*. New York: Verso.

CHRISTINA SHARPE is an associate professor of English and the director of American Studies at Tufts University.

Library of Congress Cataloging-in-Publication Data

Sharpe, Christina Elizabeth
Monstrous intimacies : making post-slavery subjects / Christina Sharpe.
p. cm.—(Perverse modernities)
ISBN 978-0-8223-4591-6 (cloth : alk. paper)
ISBN 978-0-8223-4609-8 (pbk. : alk. paper)
1. African Americans in popular culture.
2. Women slaves—United States—Social conditions.
3. United States—Race relations—History.
I. Title. II. Series: Perverse modernities.
E185.625.S537 2010
305.896′073—dc22   2010011135